THE UNITED STATES CONSTITUTIC

THE UNITED STATES CONSTITUTION

200 Years of Anti-Federalist, Abolitionist, Feminist, Muckraking, Progressive, and Especially Socialist Criticism

Edited by Bertell Ollman
and Jonathan Birnbaum

NEW YORK UNIVERSITY PRESS
New York and London

Library of Congress Cataloging-in-Publication Data
The United States Constitution : 200 years of anti-federalist,
  abolitionist, feminist, muckraking, progressive, and especially
  socialist criticism / edited by Bertell Ollman and Jonathan
  Birnbaum.
       p.   cm.
   Includes bibliographical references.
   ISBN 0-8147-6169-0 (alk. paper) — ISBN 0-8147-6170-4
   (pbk. : alk. paper)
       1. United States—Constitutional history.   I. Ollman, Bertell.
   II. Birnbaum, Jonathan, 1956–
   KF4541.U54   1990
   342.73'029—dc20   90-5663
   [347.30229]   CIP

The American Constitution is the most wonderful work ever struck off at a given time by the brain and purpose of man.

William Gladstone

The people who own the country ought to govern it.

John Jay

[The Contras in Nicaragua] are the moral equal of our Founding Fathers.

Ronald Reagan

Contents

viii   CONTENTS

V. Appendices

THE UNITED STATES CONSTITUTION

Introduction

Bertell Ollman

When Moses set out ten fundamental laws for the Jewish people, he had God write them down on stone tablets. Lycurgus, too, represented the Constitution he drew up for ancient Sparta as a divine gift. According to Plato, whose book, *The Republic*, offers another version of the same practice, attributing the origins of a constitution to godly intervention is the most effective way of securing the kind of support needed for it to work. Otherwise, some people are likely to remain skeptical, others passive, and still others critical of whatever biases they perceive in these basic laws; and all would be less inclined to adhere to their mandates.

As learned men, the Framers of the American Constitution were well aware of the advantages to be gained by enveloping their achievement in religious mystery, but most of the people for whom they labored were religious Dissenters who favored a sharp separation between church and state, and, since they were mainly deists and atheists themselves, this particular tactic could not be used. So they did the next best thing, which was to keep the whole process of their work on the Constitution a closely guarded secret. Most Americans know that the Framers met for three months in closed session, but this is generally forgiven on the grounds that the then Congress of the United States had not commissioned them to write a new Constitution, and neither revolutionaries nor counterrevolutionaries can do all their work in the open. What few modern-day Americans realize, however, is that the Framers did their best to insure that we would never know the details of their deliberations. All the participants in the convention were sworn to lifelong secrecy, and when the debates were over, those who had taken notes were asked to hand them in to George Washington, whose final task as chairman of the convention was to get rid of the evidence. America's first president, it appears, was also its first shredder.

Fortunately, not all the participants kept their vows of silence or handed in all their notes. But it wasn't until 1840, a half century after the Constitution was put into effect, with the posthumous surfacing of James Madison's

1

extensive notes, that the American people could finally read in detail what had happened in those three crucial months in Philadelphia. What was revealed was neither divine nor diabolical, but simply human, an all-too human exercise in politics. Merchants, bankers, land speculators, ship owners, planters, and slave traders and owners, as well as the lawyers who made their money working for these groups, voiced their interests and fears in clear, uncluttered language; and, after settling a few, relatively minor disagreements, they drew up plans for a form of government that would serve these interests most effectively. But fifty years of silence had their desired myth-building result. The human actors were transformed into "Founding Fathers," their political savvy and common sense were now seen as all-surpassing wisdom, and their concern for their own class of property owners (and, to a lesser extent, for their section of the country and occupational group) had been elevated to universal altruism (in the liberal version) or self-sacrificing patriotism (in the preferred conservative view). Nor have we been completely spared the aura of religious mystery so favored by Plato. With the passage of years and the growing religiosity of our citizenry, it has become almost commonplace to hear that the Framers were also divinely inspired.

In 1987, the bicentennial of the writing of the Constitution, wherever one turned in the media, in schools and professional associations, in talks by politicians and other public figures, the same myths appeared. The Commission on the Bicentennial of the U.S. Constitution, which was set up under Chief Justice Burger to coordinate most of these efforts, demonstrated its own commitment to historical truth by initially taking as its slogan "200 Years of Peace, Prosperity, and Liberty."

Almost completely lost among all the patriotic nonsequitors was the underside of criticism and protest that has accompanied the Constitution from its very inception. Not everyone has been satisfied with treating the product of men as if it came from God. Even before the Constitution was officially adopted, many people, known to history as Anti-Federalists, questioned whether what was good for the property-owning factions that were so well represented in Philadelphia would be as good for those who owned little or no property. Then, as subsequently, the main questions raised dealt with the limited suffrage, the inadequate defense of individual rights and freedoms, the acceptance and even the strengthening of the institution of slavery, and the many benefits given to men of property.

Except for a few collections of Anti-Federalist essays, this tradition of criticism, which has continued right up to the present, has never been chronicled. Its arguments, most of which are as relevant and as important now as they ever were, are little known to the general public. Only Charles Beard's *Economic Interpretation of the Constitution* (1913) has received more than passing attention. The present volume is our modest attempt to redress this imbalance. In it we have gathered some of the most striking and insightful criticisms of the Constitution made during the last two hundred years. It is the other side of the story, the underside, the whispered side, often the side that had difficulty getting published, but also the popular side, representing the real majority, nonvoters as well as voters, women and blacks as well as white males. Not every school or group or period is equally represented here. The balance among them reflects our own view of what most needs to be heard at the present time. Still, the following selections offer a fair sampling of the views on the Constitution that have never made it into high school civics texts or media extravaganzas. If the words often sound like scratching on glass, remember that discussions of the Constitution were never meant to play like the national anthem.

Taken at face value, the Constitution is an attempt to fix the relations between state and federal governments, and among the three branches— legislative, executive, and judiciary—of the latter. Most accounts of this document have concentrated on the mechanical arrangements that make these balancing acts possible. In the process, the Constitution's basic assumptions and particularly its social and economic purposes have been grossly neglected. It is a little like learning in some detail how a car works before even knowing what kind of machine it is, what it is supposed to do, and why it was constructed in just this way. Learning the functioning of any system, whether mechanical or institutional, is not without value in determining its meaning and use, but we would do better to approach their symbiosis from the other side, to examine who needed what and how the specific structures created responded to these needs. What is really at stake in any political dispute, the real-life questions involved, and why different people take the positions they do, can never be adequately understood by focusing solely or even mainly on the legalistic forms in which the issues are presented and fought out.

In examining any political phenomena, it is always wise to ask, "Who benefits?" As regards the American constitutional system, the answer is given clearly, if somewhat crudely, by Senator Boies Penrose, a late nineteenth-century Republican from Pennsylvania, who told a business audience, "I believe in a division of labor. You send us to Congress; we pass the laws

under which you make money . . . and out of your profits you further
contribute to our campaign funds to send us back again to pass more laws to
enable you to make more money."[1] When a few years later Charles Beard
suggested that the same kind of considerations may have played a role in the
writing of the Constitution, he unleashed a political storm against his book
that has few if any parallels in our history. Then President Taft publicly
denounced this unseemly muckraking as besmirching the reputations of the
Founders. Not particularly noted for his indifference to economic gain when
he became president, Warren Harding, at that time a publisher, attacked
Beard's "filthy lies and rotten perversions" in an article entitled "Scavengers,
Hyena-Like, Desecrate the Graves of the Dead Patriots We Revere."[2] And
even as a growing number of professional historians came to accept Beard's
interpretation, the city of Seattle banned his book.

Obviously, Beard had touched a tender nerve, but it is also obvious that,
as Beard himself recognized, economic motivation is only part of the explanation for political phenomena. Other factors influence people's behavior,
and some people act often and even primarily out of other kinds of motives.
The problem is how to credit these necessary qualifications without unduly
compromising the important economic insight (albeit not that original, since
political theorists have known about the importance of economic motivation
since Plato).

In an attempt to redirect attention away from the mechanical and socially
uninformative details of checks and balances, criticisms of the Constitution
have proceeded on three distinct though closely related levels. The first, of
which Beard's work is an instance, concentrates on the people who wrote the
Constitution—on who they were and what they thought, feared, and wanted.
The second deals with the classes and subclasses to which they belonged and
which they more or less consciously represented—with the objective interests
of these classes and what was required to satisfy them. Here, the assumptions
and ways of thinking that correspond to membership in a particular class, or
the part of human understanding that comes from what we take for granted,
not so much because of who we are as of where we fit in society, are decisive.
Hence, for example, one might favor strong laws to protect private property
not because one wants to remain wealthy (though most wealthy people
probably do), but because one has been socialized as a member of a property-
owning class to take this requirement and its connection to life, liberty, and
the pursuit of happiness for granted. The third level introduces the nature of
the capitalist mode of production and tries to bring out how the Constitution,

together with other political institutions, functions as both cause and effect within the life process of a developing capitalist society.

From the start, most criticisms have been situated on the first and second of these levels, and this is reflected in the selections we have made for this book. However, given the necessary relations of all three levels, a fully adequate analysis of what our Constitution means would have to devote more attention to the larger context, capitalism, in which it was produced and which it helps in no small measure to reproduce. To be sure, capitalism doesn't exist apart from the social and economic classes whose struggle over opposing interests constitutes its central drama. Nor can these classes be completely understood apart from the lives of the real individuals who compose them. But the reverse is equally true; the actions of the individual Framers make little sense—except in various superficial interpretations—if viewed apart from the class interests they sought to further. Likewise, an understanding of the nature of these classes, their specific interests, and the conditions and means available to satisfy them requires a contextualization that could only come from an account of the enveloping capitalist system. It is early commercial capitalism in its free worker and slave variants that gave rise to the main property-owning classes represented in Philadelphia, that established the conditions for their alliance and made this alliance politically dominant, that led to the most pressing problems from which these classes suffered, and that provided both the possibilities and limits for the resolution of these problems.

Unfortunately, the book that treats the Constitution as a political extension of the capitalist mode of production and thus as an organic function of this historically developing whole, while not losing sight of how the Constitution is also a product of a particular class alliance *and* of the real individuals who gathered in Philadelphia, remains to be written. As a sign of the importance we attach to this still unfinished theoretical work, we have included a few pieces at the very end of our book that begin to address some of these questions.

For purposes of introduction, what still needs to be stressed—chiefly because most critics ignore it—is that on all three levels of analysis and throughout the entire two hundred years of its history, the Constitution has been a way of understanding reality as much as it has served to effect it. And it has succeeded in ordering society in part through how it has made people think about it, just as these practical achievements have secured widespread acceptance for the intellectual modes that they embody. In sum, an important part of the Constitution's work is ideological. As ideology, the Constitution provides us with a kind of bourgeois fairy tale where claims to equal rights and responsibilities are substituted for the harsh realities of class domination. Through the Constitution, the struggle over the legitimacy of any social act or relationship is removed from the plane of morality to that of law. Justice is no longer what is fair but what is legal, and politics itself is transformed into the technical wrangling of lawyers and courts. The Constitution organizes consent not least by its manner of organizing dissent. The fact that two-thirds of the world's lawyers practise in the United States is not, as they say, a coincidence.

Unlike political theory, the Constitution does not simply offer us a picture of reality, but through the state's monopoly on violence it forces citizens to act, or at least to speak, "as if." Acting as if the rule of law, equality of opportunity, freedom of the individual, and the neutrality of the state—all of which are inscribed in the Constitution—are more than formally true inhibits people's ability to recognize that they are all practically false and that the society set up with the help of the Constitution simply does not operate in these ways. It is not a matter of reality failing to live up to a set of commendable ideals, but of these ideals—misrepresenting as they do what is legal for what is actual, what is permissible in law for what is possible in society—serving to help mask this reality. When does an ideal become a barrier to the realization of what it putatively promotes? When people are encouraged to treat the ideal as a description, however imperfect, of the real, as in the claim "Our's is a society ruled by law," where what actually exists —and goes counter to this claim—is relegated to the role of a passing qualification. Viewed in this way, the dynamics of who is doing what to whom and why, together with the structural reforms needed to change things, can never be understood.

Finally, all such criticisms should not blind us to the many positive and progressive qualities of the Constitution, both for the time in which it was written and for the present day. By 1787 the Revolutionary War had been over for four years, but it was not clear that the English ruling class had accepted its result. What could be done to ensure the country's political independence? And how best to deal with the economic problems resulting from the disruption of trade and investment patterns that accompanied this independence? These problems were not very different than those confronting Third World nations that have gained their independence in our century, and in every case setting up a strong central government was, and remains, vital for their solution. Beyond this, and especially for the late eighteenth century, the Constitution deserves high marks for its attempt to limit the arbitrary power of government (providing some protection for its own critics) and for such measures as the elimination of all religious qualifications for voting and holding office.

As the years passed, the Constitution has also proved to be admirably suited for a society in transition from early to late capitalism—that is, from one dominated by merchant and financial capitalists and slave owners tied to capital through their production for a world market to one dominated by industrial and financial capitalists, both U.S. and multinational. By facilitating the accumulation of wealth on a scale never before realized in world history, the Constitution may also help to make possible a transition to socialism at a very high level of economic development. Few of these positive qualities come without their regressive aspects or side effects, but that should not keep us from recognizing their existence or importance or from making use of them when we can. Though these are not the same virtues that are trumpeted in most bicentennial celebrations of the Constitution, they are virtues; our criticisms do not lead us to the conclusion that the Constitution never should have existed. One studies the past neither to annul it nor to improve it, but to build upon it where that is possible. In learning how the Constitution works, for whom it works better and for whom it works worse, and how and why it acquired its character, we discover not only what the Constitution has meant but what it may yet mean in our future.

Can the Constitution serve a people bent on democratic socialist transformation of capitalist society? This is the question toward which the whole of our volume points without providing any clear and definite answer. The Constitution has done everything a document could possibly do to forestall such an eventuality, and as the central institutional prop of our capitalist society it continues to act in this way. And yet, despite its lopsided and deceptive form and the worst elitist intentions of its Framers, the changes it has undergone in the past two hundred years suggest that this possibility cannot be ruled out. Nothing, of course, came easy. Every amendment to the Constitution, just like every new interpretation by the Supreme Court (in some ways more important than new amendments), and each change of emphasis in its administration and enforcement came about as a result of popular struggle. Neither blacks, nor women, nor unpropertied males, for example, were simply handed the right to vote. It might be said that the expansion of democracy only occurred after it became clear that the influence of party machines, public education, newspapers, churches, mass spectator sports, patriotism, and especially the growth of the economic pie through capitalist development and American imperialistic adventures "abroad" (including Indian and Mexican lands west of the Mississippi) ensured that the newly enfranchised publics would not use their power for subversive ends.

But the most fundamental contradiction in the entire Constitution cannot be dismissed so easily. This is the contradiction between political democracy and economic servitude. The Framers did everything they could—consistent with winning acceptance for the document—to avoid placing the loaded gun of popular sovereignty in the hands of the people. They had no doubt as to what would happen to the grossly unequal distribution of property in our country (at present, 1 percent of the population owns 50 percent of all wealth) should this ever occur.[3] Well, this has occurred, and the mass of America's citizens have made little use of political democracy to obtain economic democracy. For some, therefore, the trial is over, and the verdict in. For us, the jury is still out. Capitalism *in extremis* has many catastrophes in store for all of us. And with the stakes so high, history can afford to take its time. Our hope is that this collection of criticisms of the one-sided, deceptive, and biased rules of the game by which we are all forced to play will hurry history along just that little bit and, in the process, encourage more thought on the role of the Constitution in the transition to a more just and equitable, that is socialist, society.

Our book is organized as follows: Part I outlines the main events and problems that led up to and contributed to the calling of the Constitutional Convention in 1787. Part II concentrates on what actually happened at the Convention. Part III deals with the two hundred–year history of interpretations and amendments that followed. Part IV offers a number of ideas that should prove helpful in constructing the adequate theory of the Constitution that still eludes us. Our contributors include the most important figures from the Anti-Federalist, Abolitionist, Feminist, Muckraking, Progressive, and Socialist traditions who have written on the Constitution from the beginning of the republic. Never before assembled in a single volume, their criticisms deserve to be much better known than they are, not so much for their sake as for ours.

Editors' note: The phrase "Second American Revolution" has three distinct meanings in this volume. For Gore Vidal (chapter 18) it refers to the prospects for revolution presaged by California's Proposition 13 tax revolt. For Eric Foner (chapter 20) and Herbert Aptheker (chapter 26) it describes the revolutionary changes embodied in the Constitution's Reconstruction-era amendments. And for I. F. Stone (chapter 21) it represents Charles Beard's sense of a post–Civil War transfer of class power from the southern planter aristocracy to an alliance of northern capitalists and western free-soil farmers.

Notes

1. Quoted in Mark Green, "Stamping Out Corruption," *New York Times*, 28 October 1986, A35.
2. Quoted by Forrest McDonald, New Introduction to Charles Beard's *An Economic Interpretation of the Constitution*. (New York: Free Press, 1986), xix.
3. Arthur L. Carter, "How About a Capital Accumulation Tax?" *New York Times*, 23 September 1986, A35.

I. PREHISTORY OF THE CONSTITUTION

1. Shays' Rebellion

Howard Zinn

Historian and playwright Howard Zinn is the author of *SNCC: The New Abolitionists* (1964), *Vietnam: The Logic of Withdrawal* (1967), *Disobedience and Democracy: Nine Fallacies on Law and Order* (1968), *The Politics of History* (1970), *Postwar America* (1973), and other works, and editor of *Justice in Everyday Life* (1974). His play, *Emma*, based on the life of the anarchist Emma Goldman, has been performed in Boston, New York, London, and Tokyo.

The following selection is excerpted from A *People's History of the United States* by Howard Zinn. Copyright © 1980 by Howard Zinn. Reprinted by permission of Harper and Row, Publishers, Inc.

The inferior position of blacks, the exclusion of Indians from the new society, the establishment of supremacy for the rich and powerful in the new nation —all this was already settled in the colonies by the time of the Revolution. With the English out of the way, it could now be put on paper, solidified, regularized, made legitimate, by the Constitution of the United States, drafted at a convention of Revolutionary leaders in Philadelphia.

. . . By 1787 there was not only a positive need for strong central government to protect the large economic interests, but also immediate fear of rebellion by discontented farmers. The chief event causing this fear was an uprising in the summer of 1786 in western Massachusetts, known as Shays' Rebellion.

In the western towns of Massachusetts there was resentment against the legislature in Boston. The new Constitution of 1780 had raised the property qualifications for voting. No one could hold state office without being quite wealthy. Furthermore, the legislature was refusing to issue paper money, as had been done in some other states, like Rhode Island, to make it easier for debt-ridden farmers to pay off their creditors.

Illegal conventions began to assemble in some of the western counties to organize opposition to the legislature. At one of these, a man named Plough Jogger spoke his mind:

> I have been greatly abused, have been obliged to do more than my part in the war; been loaded with class rates, town rates, province rates, Continental rates and all rates . . . been pulled and hauled by sheriffs, constables and collectors, and had my cattle sold for less than they were worth.
> . . . The great men are going to get all we have and I think it is time for us to rise and put a stop to it, and have no more courts, nor sheriffs, nor collectors nor lawyers.

The chairman of that meeting used his gavel to cut short the applause. He and others wanted to redress their grievances, but peacefully, by petition to the General Court (the legislature) in Boston.

However, before the scheduled meeting of the General Court, there were going to be court proceedings in Hampshire County, in the towns of Northampton and Springfield, to seize the cattle of farmers who hadn't paid their debts, to take away their land, now full of grain and ready for harvest. And so, veterans of the Continental army, also aggrieved because they had been treated poorly on discharge—given certificates for future redemption instead of immediate cash—began to organize the farmers into squads and companies. One of these veterans was Luke Day, who arrived the morning of court with a fife-and-drum corps, still angry with the memory of being locked up in debtors' prison in the heat of the previous summer.

The sheriff looked to the local militia to defend the court against these armed farmers. But most of the militia was with Luke Day. The sheriff did manage to gather five hundred men, and the judges put on their black silk robes, waiting for the sheriff to protect their trip to the courthouse. But there at the courthouse steps, Luke Day stood with a petition, asserting the people's constitutional right to protest the unconstitutional acts of the General Court, asking the judges to adjourn until the General Court could act on behalf of the farmers. Standing with Luke Day were fifteen hundred armed farmers. The judges adjourned.

Shortly after, at courthouses in Worcester and Athol, farmers with guns prevented the courts from meeting to take away their property, and the militia were too sympathetic to the farmers, or too outnumbered, to act. In Concord, a fifty-year-old veteran of two wars, Job Shattuck, led a caravan of carts, wagons, horses, and oxen onto the town green, while a message was sent to the judges:

The voice of the People of this county is such that the court shall not enter this courthouse until such time as the People shall have redress of the grievances they labor under at the present.

A county convention then suggested the judges adjourn, which they did.

At Great Barrington, a militia of a thousand faced a square crowded with armed men and boys. But the militia was split in its opinion. When the chief justice suggested the militia divide, those in favor of the court's sitting to go on the right side of the road, and those against on the left, two hundred of the militia went to the right, eight hundred to the left, and the judges adjourned. Then the crowd went to the home of the chief justice, who agreed to sign a pledge that the court would not sit until the Massachusetts General Court met. The crowd went back to the square, broke open the county jail, and set free the debtors. The chief justice, a country doctor, said: "I have never heard anybody point out a better way to have their grievances redressed than the people have taken."

The governor and the political leaders of Massachusetts became alarmed. Samuel Adams, once looked on as a radical leader in Boston, now insisted people act within the law. He said "British emissaries" were stirring up the farmers. People in the town of Greenwich responded: You in Boston have the money, and we don't. And didn't you act illegally yourselves in the Revolution? The insurgents were now being called Regulators. Their emblem was a sprig of hemlock.

The problem went beyond Massachusetts. In Rhode Island, the debtors had taken over the legislature and were issuing paper money. In New Hampshire, several hundred men, in September of 1786, surrounded the legislature in Exeter, asking that taxes be returned and paper money issued; they dispersed only when military action was threatened.

Daniel Shays entered the scene in western Massachusetts. A poor farm hand when the Revolution broke out, he joined the Continental army, fought at Lexington, Bunker Hill, and Saratoga and was wounded in action. In 1780, not being paid, he resigned from the army, went home, and soon found himself in court for nonpayment of debts. He also saw what was happening to others: a sick woman, unable to pay, had her bed taken from under her.

What brought Shays fully into the situation was that on September 19, the Supreme Judicial Court of Massachusetts met in Worcester and indicted eleven leaders of the rebellion, including three of his friends, as "disorderly, riotous and seditious persons" who "unlawfully and by force of arms" prevented "the execution of justice and the laws of the commonwealth." The Supreme Judicial Court planned to meet again in Springfield a week later, and there was talk of Luke Day's being indicted.

Shays organized seven hundred armed farmers, most of them veterans of the war, and led them to Springfield. There they found a general with nine hundred soldiers and a cannon. Shays asked the general for permission to parade, which the general granted, so Shays and his men moved through the square, drums banging and fifes blowing. As they marched, their ranks grew. Some of the militia joined, and reinforcements began coming in from the countryside. The judges postponed hearings for a day, then adjourned the court.

Now the General Court, meeting in Boston, was told by Governor James Bowdoin to "vindicate the insulted dignity of government." The recent rebels against England, secure in office, were calling for law and order. Sam Adams helped draw up a Riot Act, and a resolution suspending habeas corpus, to allow the authorities to keep people in jail without trial. A the same time, the legislature moved to make some concessions to the angry farmers, saying certain old taxes could now be paid in goods instead of money.

This didn't help. In Worcester, 160 insurgents appeared at the courthouse. The sheriff read the Riot Act. The insurgents said they would disperse only if the judges did. The sheriff shouted something about hanging. Someone came up behind him and put a sprig of hemlock in his hat. The judges left.

Confrontations between farmers and militia now multiplied. The winter snows began to interfere with the trips of farmers to the courthouses. When Shays began marching a thousand men into Boston, a blizzard forced them back, and one of his men froze to death.

An army came into the field, led by General Benjamin Lincoln, on money raised by Boston merchants. In an artillery duel, three rebels were killed. One soldier stepped in front of his own artillery piece and lost both arms. The winter grew worse. The rebels were outnumbered and on the run. Shays took refuge in Vermont, and his followers began to surrender. There were a few more deaths in battle, and then sporadic, disorganized, desperate acts of violence against authority: the burning of barns, the slaughter of a general's horses. One government soldier was killed in an eerie night-time collision of two sleighs.

Captured rebels were put on trial in Northampton and six were sentenced to death. A note was left at the door of the high sheriff of Pittsfield:

I understand that there is a number of my countrymen condemned to die because they fought for justice. I pray have a care that you assist not in the execution of so horrid a crime, for by all that is above, he that condemns and he that executes shall share alike. . . . Prepare for death with speed, for your life or mine is short. When the woods are covered with leaves, I shall return and pay you a short visit.

Thirty-three more rebels were put on trial and six more condemned to death. Arguments took place over whether the hangings should go forward. General Lincoln urged mercy and a Commission of Clemency, but Samuel Adams said: "In monarchy the crime of treason may admit of being pardoned or lightly punished, but the man who dares rebel against the laws of a republic ought to suffer death." Several hangings followed; some of the condemned were pardoned. Shays, in Vermont, was pardoned in 1788 and returned to Massachusetts, where he died, poor and obscure, in 1825.

It was Thomas Jefferson, in France as ambassador at the time of Shays' Rebellion, who spoke of such uprisings as healthy for society. In a letter to a friend he wrote: "I hold it that a little rebellion now and then is a good thing. . . . It is a medicine necessary for the sound health of government. . . . God forbid that we should ever be twenty years without such a rebellion. . . . The tree of liberty must be refreshed from time to time with the blood of patriots and tyrants. It is its natural manure."

But Jefferson was far from the scene. The political and economic elite of the country were not so tolerant. They worried that the example might spread. A veteran of Washington's army, General Henry Knox, founded an organization of army veterans, "The Order of the Cincinnati," presumably (as one historian put it) "for the purpose of cherishing the heroic memories of the struggle in which they had taken part," but also, it seemed, to watch out for radicalism in the new country. Knox wrote to Washington in late 1786 about Shays' Rebellion, and in doing so expressed the thoughts of many of the wealthy and powerful leaders of the country:

The people who are the insurgents have never paid any, or but very little taxes. But they see the weakness of government; they feel at once their own poverty, compared with the opulent, and their own force, and they are determined to make use of the latter, in order to remedy the former. Their creed is "That the property of the United States has been protected from the confiscations of Britain by the joint exertions of all, and therefore ought to be the common property of all. And he that attempts opposition to this creed is an enemy to equity and justice and ought to be swept from off the face of the earth."

2. The Articles of Confederation

Merrill Jensen

Merrill Jensen (1905–1980) was professor of history at the University of Wisconsin and the preeminent historian of the Confederation period, an era previously dismissed as "The Critical Period." His writings include *The New Nation: A History of the United States During the Confederation, 1781–1789* (1962), *The Making of the American Constitution* (1964), and *The Founding of a Nation* (1968).

The following selection is excerpted by permission from *The Articles of Confederation* (Madison: University of Wisconsin Press, 1940), 239–45.

The Articles of Confederation were the constitution of the United States from 1781 to 1789, when the Confederation Congress held its last session and turned over the government of the thirteen states to the new national government. The fact that the Articles of Confederation were supplanted by another constitution is no proof either of their success or of their failure. Any valid opinion as to the merits of the Articles must be based on a detailed and unbiased study of the Confederation period. Though no such comprehensive study has yet been made, it is possible to draw certain tentative conclusions by approaching the history of the period from the point of view of the American Revolution within the American states rather than from the point of view that the Constitution of 1787 was a necessity, the only alternative to chaos.

An analysis of the disputes over the Articles of Confederation makes it plain that they were not the result of either ignorance or inexperience. On the contrary, they were a natural outcome of the revolutionary movement within the American colonies. The radical leaders of the opposition to Great Britain after 1765 had consistently denied the authority of any government superior to the legislatures of the several colonies. From 1774 on, the radicals continued to deny the authority of a superior legislature whether located across the seas or within the American states. The reiteration of the idea of the supremacy of the local legislatures, coupled with the social and psychological forces which led men to look upon "state sovereignty" as necessary to the attainment of the goals of the internal revolution, militated against the creation of such a centralized government as the conservative elements in American society desired. It can be said that the constitution which the radicals created, the Articles of Confederation, was a constitutional expression of the philosophy of the Declaration of Independence.

Today "states' rights" and "decentralization" are the war cries of the conservative element, which is not wielding the influence in national affairs it once did and still longs to do. But in the eighteenth century decentralization and states' rights meant local self-government, and local self-government meant a form of agrarian democracy. The mass of the population was composed of small farmers, who in the long run could control the politics of their individual states. Since this was the belief of the fathers of the constitution of 1787, who were thus in substantial agreement with the radical leaders of 1776, the testimony might very well be regarded as conclusive.

The writing of the Articles of Confederation brought to the fore political issues that were to be of vast significance in the history of the United States. Many a debate in later years was merely a reiteration or an elaboration of arguments used in 1776 and 1777. Those ideas upon which it is necessary to place the inadequate but necessary label of "conservative" were as well expressed in 1776 as in 1787, and often by the same men: John Dickinson and James Wilson, for instance. The vital change which took place between 1776 and 1787 was not in ideas nor in attitudes but in the balance of political power. The radical organization which had brought about the Revolution disintegrated with success, for the radicals had won their real goal, local self-government. Radical leaders returned to their states to enjoy the results of their efforts unhampered by a central government of extensive power. The conservatives, on the other hand, made only occasional gains in the states, as in Massachusetts, where their rule was met by open rebellion in 1786. In other states the attack upon their position was a slow but sure process, as in Virginia. Some of them had realized in 1776 that centralization was their protection: a central government to suppress internal rebellions, to regulate trade, and to control the actions of the state governments as the British government had controlled the colonial governments.

The fight for centralization did not stop with the completion of the

Articles of Confederation. Discontent with the document was expressed in the private correspondence of such conservative leaders as Washington, Dickinson, Charles Carroll, Robert Morris, Gouverneur Morris, James Wilson, and Alexander Hamilton. Even before they were finally ratified Hamilton proposed a revolutionary convention to create the kind of government the conservatives wanted. Once the Articles had been ratified, many serious attempts were made to amend them in such a way as to strengthen the central organization. These attempts at amendment failed, as did efforts to "interpret" into the Articles certain "nationalistic" ideas foreign to both the purpose and character of the document. Even if such amendments had been adopted, the constitution would not have been satisfactory to the conservative element, for it was impossible to change its nature by mere amendment. From the conservative point of view it was the wrong *kind* of government. Even if Congress had been given a limited income, as was proposed in various amendments, the central government would still have been a federal government and therefore inadequate in conservative opinion. The alterations proposed during the Confederation period were not fundamental, for they did not touch the vital question of the distribution of power between the states and the central government. The vast field of undefined and unenumerated powers lay with the states. Congress could function only within an area of precisely delegated and carefully limited authority. It was the creature of the state governments and thus, ultimately, of the electorate of the states.

Centralized government with a legal veto on state laws, the power to enact general and uniform legislation, and the power to use arms to subdue rebellious social groups within the states, had disappeared with the Declaration of Independence. The Articles of Confederation were designed to prevent its reappearance, and for this reason were not, and never could be, adequate from the point of view of the conservatives, who wanted the essence of the British imperial system restored in the American states.

John Dickinson and his conservative committee had sought to lay the legal foundation of such a system in their first draft of articles of confederation. The document was involved and legalistic to the point of obscurity, but it was an obscurity which would lend itself readily to multiple interpretation. Legally, ultimate authority lay with the central government, for only one conditional guarantee was given to the states, and only one specific restraint was placed on Congress. The states were guaranteed the control of their "internal police" in matters where such control did not interfere with the Articles of Confederation. Congress was restrained only from levying taxes other than those for support of the post office. This was a great but not insurmountable obstacle in the way of centralization. The important point is that the vital area of undefined and unenumerated powers fell within the domain of the central government, as Thomas Burke demonstrated to Congress in 1777.

The final draft of the Articles of Confederation was, as James Wilson said in the convention of 1787, "how different." Certain powers and no others were delegated to Congress. No phrase in the document could be construed as making the central government supreme over the states. Nothing remotely resembling such phrases as "obligation of contract," "supremacy of the laws," "necessary and proper," or "general welfare" were to be found in it. The control of war and foreign affairs was expressly granted to Congress, as was the power to regulate the trade with Indians who were not members of any of the states, but Congress might not infringe upon the right of any state to legislate upon matters within its own limits. Congress was given the power to regulate the value of both its coinage and that of the states, but no control over the emission of paper money by the states. Congress was a court of last appeal, or rather a board of arbitration, in disputes between one state and another, and between private individuals claiming lands under different grants. Congress was given charge of the post office and the regulation of weights and measures. These were its "sole and exclusive" powers. In addition, it was given the authority to appoint a committee of the states to sit during the recesses of Congress and the power to control its own organization and sessions.

Eighteenth-century radicals looked upon the desire for office as a disease which fed upon office-holding. Hence they were careful to provide that Congress should never become an association of office-holders. No one could be a member of Congress for more than three out of any six years. No one could be president of Congress for more than one year out of any three; thus no individual would be likely to acquire much prestige as head of the central government. The delegates were subject to recall at any time by the state governments which had selected them, and hence were usually responsive to the will of their electorates as expressed in the state legislatures. This serves to explain why so many votes in Congress were often inconsistent with a given delegate's political and economic views.

The Articles of Confederation placed few restraints upon the states, and even these tended to be qualified out of existence. No state could receive or send embassies or enter into alliances or treaties without the consent of

Congress. No two or more states could enter into a confederation without the consent of Congress. No state could levy imports or duties which might interfere with stipulations in treaties made by Congress. No treaty made by Congress, on the other hand, could interfere with the right of a state to subject foreigners to the same imports and duties as were levied on its own citizens. The states were not to keep vessels of war in peacetime unless Congress deemed it to be necessary for purposes of defense. Neither could a state maintain troops unless Congress considered them necessary to garrison forts. States were forbidden to declare war without the consent of Congress except where sudden invasion would permit of no delay. Letters of marque and reprisal were to be granted only after a declaration of war by Congress and under conditions laid down by it. None of the restraints was a serious check upon the sovereignty of the states.

Between the states there was complete equality. Every state was required to have at least two representatives in Congress, and it might have as many as seven, though each delegation was to have only one vote. When more than two delegates from a state were present, the state's vote was decided by the majority of the delegation. If the vote was a tie, the state had no vote. Citizens of any state were allowed to emigrate freely to another. Extradition of criminals was provided for. The Articles declared that each state should give full faith to the judicial proceedings of every other state. Except in these things the states were not responsible to one another. The union that had been created was a federal union of equal states in which the central organization was carefully subordinated to the members of it.

The Articles of Confederation were designed to prevent the central government from infringing upon the rights of the states, whereas the Constitution of 1787 was designed as a check upon the power of the states and the democracy that found expression within their bounds. The character of the Articles of Confederation was the result of two realities: the reality of the psychological and legal independence of the states, and the reality of the belief that democracy was possible only within fairly small political units whose electorate had a direct check upon the officers of government. Such a check was impossible where the central government was far removed from the control of the people by distance and by law. The independence of the states was a product of colonial history. The distrust of centralization, of government spread over a great area, was the product of both political theory and practical experience. The rise of radicalism had been checked often enough to teach the radicals that central governments, however democratic in form, were fundamentally undemocratic in action.

This government, the product of the forces which brought about the American Revolution, failed not because it was inadequate but because the radicals failed to maintain the organization they had created to bring about the American Revolution. The radical movement was essentially a movement of parties within states, and their political and social aims were to a great extent local. To achieve their purpose, local independence, unity of all the states had been necessary. What the radicals failed to see was that they must continue their union if they were to maintain their local independence under the Articles of Confederation. Thomas Burke of North Carolina expressed the radical view admirably. Congress, he said, was a general council instituted for the purpose of opposing the usurpations of Great Britain and of conducting a war against her, of forming necessary foreign alliances, directing the army and navy, and making binding treaties. Since this was the nature of Congress and its powers, it eliminated "all pretence for continuance of a Congress after the war is concluded, or of assuming a power to any other purposes."

Thus when the radicals had won their war, most of them were well content to go home and continue with the program of action they had started long before the war began. The thwarting of that program by the local conservatives and the British government had been one of the major causes of the Revolution. Needless to say, the motives of the radicals were not always the highest or the most disinterested, but their program was essentially democratic in tendency, for it widened the bases of political power and it declared that men should be bound only by those laws to which they had given their consent. Above all, when that program was idealized, as in the Declaration of Independence, it declared that the purpose of government was the protection of the life, liberty, and happiness of the individual, and when it did not fulfill this ideal it should be overthrown. Such a revolution was a practical possibility in a state unchecked by an outside and superior authority. Such an authority was rendered impossible by the Articles of Confederation.

What the radicals did not see was that the conservative elements in American society had learned a bitter lesson at the hands of the radicals. They too could call conventions. They too could paint dark pictures of the times and blame the supposed woes of the country on the Articles of Confederation, as the radicals had blamed the British government before 1776.

They too could, and did, adopt the radical theory of the sovereignty of the people; in the name of the people they engineered a conservative counter-revolution and erected a nationalistic government whose purpose in part was to thwart the will of "the people" in whose name they acted. They too could use one name while pursuing a goal that was the opposite in fact. Thus, although the purpose of the conservatives was "nationalistic," they adopted the name "Federalist," for it served to disguise the extend of the changes they desired. True, the government they created had a good many "federal" features, but this was so because the conservatives were political realists and had to compromise with the political reality of actual state sovereignty.

What the conservatives in their turn failed to see was that the government they created might be captured by the radicals united on a national scale. Madison in *The Federalist* wrote that such a union was impossible, though he shortly helped to bring it about when faced with the workings of the government under the Constitution of 1787.

Wise old John Adams probably had the last word. Writing in 1808, he declared, "I have always called our Constitution a game at leapfrog."

3. The Establishment of a National Union

Louis M. Hacker

Economic historian Louis M. Hacker (1899–1987) wrote *Alexander Hamilton in the American Tradition* (1957), *The World of Andrew Carnegie* (1968), *The Course of American Economic Growth and Development* (1970), and other works. Hacker was a dean at Columbia University and a leading proponent of adult education. He was a professor of economics at Columbia from 1935 to 1967.

The following selection is excerpted from *The Triumph of American Capitalism*. Copyright © 1940, 1967 by Simon & Schuster, Inc. Reprinted by permission of Simon & Schuster, Inc.

"The Critical Period"

Despite their growing economic and political successes, men of large property continued to pretend—particularly after peace had been formally established in 1783—that their newly gained liberties were in danger. Peace did not bring in its wake economic chaos, as so frequently has been maintained; but it did threaten to slacken the advance that had been begun so signally during the years of the war's conduct.

Indeed, it may be argued plausibly, as Robert A. East does,[1] that the depression of 1785–86 was not due to a breakdown of the economic processes, but to the fact that merchants—particularly in the import trade— and land speculators—in western land deals—had overreached themselves. One might also make the point that the large-propertied interests took advantage of the revival of radical agitation in 1785–86 to insist that the failure of leveling government was at the heart of their distress; and, using temporary financial and business recession as a pretext and political uncertainty as a weapon, sought to entrench themselves once and for all in the seats of government through the establishment of a powerful national union.

Certainly, business was anything but languishing in the years immediately after the end of war. To quote Dr. East:

High rentals, building activity, and luxurious living actually impressed Franklin on his return to America in 1785. Stage coach routes and facilities were steadily being increased in various regions. The paper industry continued to grow, and important companies were organized for iron and woolen manufactures in 1786 and 1788. Above all, it is significant that capital was much sought after everywhere during "the critical" years. Interest rates were high in 1784. New York merchant capitalists were even invited to New Jersey and Connecticut, being promised liberal treatment. . . . And if it be argued that all this merely emphasized a great lack of capital, rather than a general demand for it, it can be pointed out in reply that there was no difficulty in securing subscriptions of specie value for large amounts of bank stock in 1784 in Philadelphia, Boston, and New York.

On every hand there were evidences of an expanding capitalist interest. Land companies for the exploitation of the new western territories were being organized and bands of pioneers were being sent out. Groups of capitalists were pooling their funds, seeking company charters, and establishing joint stocks. England had frowned on company organization during the colonial period and notably had refused to tolerate the formation of commercial banks. In fact, there were not more than five or six business charters granted during the whole period of imperial rule. But, once released from the confines of the Mercantile System, American capitalism rushed to organize. Eleven charters were requested and issued by state legislatures between 1781 and 1785; twenty-two between 1786 and 1790; and one hundred and fourteen between 1791 and 1795. The companies thus provided were to perform the characteristic functions of the mercantile capitalism of the period: build and maintain turnpikes, canals, bridges, and river-improvement projects; manufacture wrought iron, woolens, sailcloth, and glass; buy up and develop the wild lands; and establish commercial banks.

In this last field of activity, there was particular interest—and notable success. The Bank of North America was established at Philadelphia in 1781; the Bank of New York began to function in 1784; so did the Massachusetts Bank, at Boston, in the same year. Taking advantage of the high premium on English bills of exchange, these banks, through their discounting functions, were able to furnish invaluable assistance to merchants in the foreign trade—and of course, in the process, enriched their promoters. The banks also helped in the financing of company enterprise.

Nor was foreign trade stagnant. It is true there was a falling off in the export trade to England and the British West Indian islands, although in the latter case not nearly as much as has been generally assumed. Nevertheless, the years 1784 to 1788 saw a steady return to the volume of the prewar years. On the other hand, there were compensations from other quarters. The direct trade with France, started during the Revolution, continued to flourish so that Americans actually enjoyed a favorable balance during the 1780's. The commercial relations with Holland were particularly happy. The Dutch began to absorb more and more of those raw materials that, in the colonial period, could be moved, by the Acts of Trade and Navigation, to England alone. So, as Dr. East points out, the end of the so-called "critical period" saw the Dutch-American export trade fully half as great as the English-American trade; the balance of payments was in favor of the Americans; prices of commodities for foreign shipment were good, except for 1785 and 1786; and Dutch merchant bankers freely extended commercial credits to their American customers.

Further, the foreign West Indian trade was expanding. New direct commercial relations were being opened up with Scandinavia, Russia, and the Near East, and the great India and China trades were being tapped, thanks to the smashing of the English mercantilist restrictions. Certainly, in connection with this last, new chapters were being written in the history of American commerce.

The *Empress of China* sailed from New York in 1784 bound for the China Sea and Canton; the *Grand Turk* left Salem the next year for the same destination; in 1787 Boston merchants, operating on a joint-stock basis, fitted out a ship to tap the Northwest-China trade. Soon, American masters were as familiar with the ports of the Indian Ocean as they were with those of the Caribbean. American ships carried mixed cargoes to Europe; there they picked up consignments for Madagascar, Aden, Muscat, Madras, Calcutta, and the islands of the Eastern archipelagoes; and they traded in coffee, sugar, pepper, allspice, textiles, and chinaware. The Northwest-China trade was to become a rich source of profits for Yankee merchantmen. Otter and seal furs were acquired in the Northwest and carried to China and there exchanged for tea, fine textiles, and chinaware. Notably, Boston and New York merchants waxed rich on this traffic.

One cannot deny the commercial letdown of 1785–86. Prices for many staples at home—tobacco, lumber, flour—dropped; the merchants in the import trade, being largely concerned with domestic distribution, were therefore hard hit too. But this situation points to overexpansion of domestic production of raw materials and excess inventories rather than to a complete destruction of confidence at home and a drying up of markets at home and abroad. The fact is, the interstate barriers to trade, of which much has been made in justifying the thesis of collapse during this period, really played only a negligible role. After 1783, the restrictive state laws were really not functioning as far as domestic commerce was concerned, since products grown in the United States were being exempted from state import duties while American-owned vessels of sister states were often receiving preferential tonnage rates over those of foreign registry.

The point has been made: there must have been motives, other than the threat of complete business disorganization as a result of political decentralization, that prompted men of large property to agitate for a powerful national union from 1786 on. To quote Dr. East in conclusion:

> The Revolution was immediately followed by several years of confused readjustment; but some economic life was vigorous, at least until a sharp decline in prices for American produce took place in 1785; and even then it did not cease, though agriculture was particularly hard hit. Commerce had suffered even earlier, however, simply because the merchants had long been indulging in excessive importations at falling prices, and they thus helped to pave their own way to hard times. Their recovery led to the development of a new world-wide commerce which the Revolution had legalized, and this frequently promoted longer cooperatively financed voyages. The tendency of the hard times was to weed out the smaller business men to the eventual benefit of the larger, and to evolve more highly organized business communities; all of which cleared the way for greater business activity in the later years.[2]

Notes

1. R. A. East, *Business Enterprise in the American Revolutionary Era* (New York: Columbia University Press, 1938), 242.
2. Ibid., 261–62.

4. The United States in the World-Economy

John Agnew

John Agnew is professor of geography and director of the Social Science Program at the Maxwell Graduate School of Syracuse University. He is the author of *Place and Politics: The Geographical Mediation of State and Society* (1987) and coauthor of *Order and Skepticism: Human Geography and the Dialectic of Science* (1981) and *The City in Cultural Context* (1984).

The following selection is excerpted from *The United States in the World-Economy: A Regional Geography* (New York: Cambridge University Press, 1987), 14–15, 26, and 31–35. Reprinted by permission of Cambridge University Press.

The settlement along the Atlantic coast of North America that became the territorial-economic core of the United States was a product of European commercial-political expansion in the seventeenth and eighteenth centuries. American independence from Britain was the result of the breakdown of routinized trans-Atlantic relations brought on by the British revenue legislation of 1764[1] and, after Independence, America remained materially and ideologically tied to Europe.[2] So, altogether, the history of the United States cannot be separated from that of the world-economy.

However, it is important to stress that this does not involve us merely in some deductions from a universal history. Every place and state has its own particular and peculiar relationship to the evolution of the world-economy. . . . Furthermore, America was settled by Europeans as it was incorporated into the world-economy. It also became the first 'settler-state' after achieving its political independence from Britain. Within its original territory along the Atlantic coast it also contained contrasting, and ultimately incompatible, modes of socio-economic organization: a plantation agriculture based on slavery in the South and classic capitalist or 'free' enterprise in the North.

These and other particularities, for example the lack of foreign invasion and, until Vietnam, costly 'colonial' wars, have continued to interact with the 'shaping' of America by the world-economy since the late eighteenth century to create American history. American history, therefore, *is* different, but it is also critically dependent on America's interactions with the world-economy.

Colonial Trade

The life of the vast majority of the million and a half people in the British colonies at the mid-point of the eighteenth century was still dominated by the rhythms of agriculture. But now a sizable merchant class also thrived in half a dozen coastal cities, its trading operations bringing one of the sources of wealth that distinguished the eighteenth-century economy from that of the seventeenth. The great bulk of the accumulated wealth of America was derived either directly or indirectly from trade.[3] Though some manufacturing existed, its role in the accumulation of capital was not great. A merchant class of growing proportions was visible in Boston, New York, Philadelphia, Newport and Charleston by mid-century, its wealth based on trade. Even the rich planters of tidewater Virginia and the rice coast of South Carolina depended upon ships and the merchants who sold their tobacco and rice in the European markets. As colonial production rose and trade expanded, a business community emerged in the colonies, linking the provinces to one another and to the world-economy by lines of trade and identity of interest.[4]

But even on the eve of the American Revolution, nearly 90 percent of the population made at least part of their living from subsistence agriculture.[5] The economically most successful colonies were those which could produce commercial crops to meet demands from Europe.

Independence

It was remarked earlier that a notable characteristic of the thirteen British colonies was their large degree of political independence. The elective assemblies were frequently at odds with their governors and the other officials sent from London. It was also noted that Britain decisively defeated France in the French and Indian War and, by the Treaty of Paris in 1763, acquired France's colonies throughout North America. But once the threat from the French was removed a major incentive for the cooperation of colonists with the British was removed. Moreover, the British government decided, at what with hindsight appears to be a most inopportune moment, to tighten its imperial organization through a series of settlement restrictions and financial measures. The scene was now set for a major showdown between imperial authority and those with aspirations for colonial self-government. . . .

The steps leading to the American Revolution are well known and need not be related in detail. . . .

Once an American army was raised and in action, the decisive factor proved to be France's support for the rebels. France poured large amounts of war material into the colonies and provided an expeditionary force of 6,000 soldiers. In 1783 France's defeat of 1763 was avenged when their new allies, the Americans, achieved recognition of their independence from Britain under a new Treaty of Paris.

The origins of American Independence seem to lie in the breakdown of the routinized relations that bound together Britain and its American colonies before 1763. Until that time the various Navigation Acts governing trade served as a 'cement' for a commercial empire in which economic benefits and political loyalties were closely conjoined. With the new revenue legislation, however,

The former cement of favored trade relations that bound colonies and home country together had been dissolved. The new policy of taxation and exploitation of America in the interests of a political faction in England was a disintegrating force that destroyed loyalty. The degree of damage was different in different areas . . . The heavy taxation, the excessive fees, and the seizures were concentrated in a few trading colonies. These were the centers of the revolutionary movement.[6]

Most scholars agree that the restrictions on trade imposed by the Navigation Acts were regarded as unimportant rather than opposed by the colonists. It was not so much economic exploitation as the introduction of new rules to the 'game' after 1763 that precipitated the American Revolution.[7] This does not mean, of course, that there was no economic exploitation. Indeed there was, as numerous studies have shown.[8] But economic exploitation by itself cannot explain the growth of the colonists' desire for political independence.

Despite its seeming revolutionary character, however, the American revolt is noteworthy because it created no serious interruption to the 'flow' of American development. Both in intention and in fact the American Revolution conserved the past rather than rejected it. The radicals may have won the first round—they won the battle—but in the longer run they lost the war. Although there was some land confiscation and a large variety of political reforms, the American Revolution was remarkably conservative compared, say, to the later French and Russian Revolutions.[9] Most importantly, social institutions were left untouched: the class structure, the ideas of people concerning government, the distribution of wealth, the capitalistic economy.

Before 1776 the so-called radicals were actually of two persuasions in regard to their opposition to Britain. Though both factions of radicals opposed the British government's efforts at imperial centralization, their reasons for doing so were distinct. For one group *any* centralization threatened local control and hence colonial freedom. Its members supported the Articles of Confederation. For the other, centralization was objectionable only because British and not American officials undertook it. Its members supported the Constitution. After Independence these groups clashed repeatedly over the purpose of the Revolution, the direction the 'new nation' should move in, and the relative power that the various levels of government should enjoy.[10] This set the tone for American political debate down to the present day. On the one hand, there was a fear of strong government and, on the other hand, a view of government as a facilitator of 'private enterprise.'

But these two views, the former associated most clearly with the figure of Thomas Jefferson and the latter with the figure of Alexander Hamilton, were in practice conjoined—with predictable results. An American system was established in which government entered into partnership with enterprise.[11] From one direction the fear of a strong state led to the easy usurpation of public power by organized private interests. From another direction federalist activism directly encouraged public risk-taking in the interest of private profit-making. From the viewpoint of the world-economy perspective, therefore, the American Revolution is significant not because it created another independent state, however novel the circumstances, but because it created a new and *different* type of state that was later to transform the nature of the world-economy itself.

Notes

1. O. M. Dickerson, *The Navigation Acts and the American Revolution* (Philadelphia: University of Pennsylvania Press, 1951).
2. F. Gilbert, *The Beginnings of American Foreign Policy* (Princeton: Princeton University Press, 1961).
3. C. Rossiter, *Seedtime of the Republic* (New York: Random House, 1953).

4. G. O. Virtue, "Capitalistic Aspects of the Colonial Empire," in Virtue, ed., *Explorations in Economics* (New York: Harper, 1936).
5. G. M. Walton and J. F. Shepherd, *The Economic Rise of Early America* (Cambridge: Cambridge University Press, 1979).
6. Dickerson, *op. cit.*, p. 299.
7. L. A. Harper, "Mercantilism and the American Revolution," *American Historical Review*, vol. 23 (1942), pp. 1–15; and R. P. Thomas "British Imperial Policy and the Economic Interpretation of the American Revolution," *Journal of Economic History*, vol. 27 (1968), pp. 436–40.
8. G. M. Walton, "The New Economic History and the Burdens of the Navigation Acts," *Economic History Review*, 2nd ser., vol. 24 (1971), pp. 533–42.
9. Rossiter, *op. cit.*
10. O. Libby, "The Geographical Distribution of the Vote of the Thirteen States on the Federal Constitution, 1787–1788," *Bulletin of the University of Wisconsin*, vol. 1 (1894), pp. 7–116.
11. R. A. Lively, "The American System: A Review Article," *Business History Review*, vol. 29 (1955), pp. 81–96.

II. WHAT ACTUALLY HAPPENED IN PHILADELPHIA

5. The Spirit of the Constitution:
A Progressive Introduction

J. Allen Smith

J. Allen Smith (1860–1926) wrote the first Progressive critique of the Constitution, *The Spirit of American Government* (1907). Although his reputation for that work was later eclipsed by Charles Beard, his study preceded and influenced both Beard's *Economic Interpretation of the Constitution* (1913) and Vernon Louis Parrington's literary history, *Main Currents in American Thought* (1927–1930). Parrington dedicated his three-volume study to Smith and provided an introduction to Smith's last book, *The Growth and Decadence of Constitutional Government* (1930). A version of Smith's doctoral dissertation was published in 1896 as *The Multiple Money Standard*.

The following selection is excerpted from the preface to *The Spirit of American Government: Its Origins, Influence, and Relation to Democracy* (New York: Macmillan, 1907).

It is the purpose of this [work] to trace the influence of our constitutional system upon the political conditions which exist in this country to-day. This phase of our political problems has not received adequate recognition at the hands of writers on American politics. Very often indeed it has been entirely ignored, although in the short period which has elapsed since our Constitution was framed and adopted, the Western world has passed through a political as well as an industrial revolution.

In the eighteenth century the majority was outside of the pale of political rights. Government as a matter of course was the expression of the will of a minority. Even in the United States, where hereditary rule was overthrown by the Revolution, an effective and recognized minority control still survived through the property qualifications for the suffrage and for office-holding, which excluded a large proportion of the people from participation in political affairs. Under such conditions there could be but little of what is now known as democracy. Moreover, slavery continued to exist upon a large scale for nearly three-quarters of a century after the Constitution was adopted, and was finally abolished only within the memory of many now living.

It could hardly be expected that a political system set up for a community containing a large slave population and in which the suffrage was restricted, even among the free whites, should in any large measure embody the aims and ideas of present day democracy. In fact the American Constitution did not recognize the now more or less generally accepted principle of majority rule even as applying to the qualified voters. Moreover, it was not until several decades after the Constitution was adopted that the removal of property qualifications for voting allowed the people generally to have a voice in political affairs.

The extension of the suffrage was a concession to the growing belief in democracy, but it failed to give the masses an effective control over the general government, owing to the checks in the Constitution on majority rule. It had one important consequence, however, which should not be overlooked. Possession of the suffrage by the people generally led the undiscriminating to think that it made the opinion of the majority a controlling factor in national politics.

Our political writers have for the most part passed lightly over the undemocratic features of the Constitution and left the uncritical reader with the impression that universal suffrage under our system of government ensures the rule of the majority. It is this conservative approval of the Constitution under the guise of sympathy with majority rule, which has perhaps more than any thing else misled the people as to the real spirit and purpose of that instrument. It was by constantly representing it as the indispensable means of attaining the ends of democracy, that it came to be so generally regarded as the source of all that is democratic in our system of government. It is to call attention to the spirit of the Constitution, its inherent opposition to democracy, the obstacles which it has placed in the way of majority rule, that this [work] has been written.

The general recognition of the true character of the Constitution is necessary before we can fully understand the nature and origin of our political evils. It would also do much to strengthen and advance the cause of popular government by bringing us to a realization of the fact that the so-called evils of democracy are very largely the natural results of those constitutional checks on popular rule which we have inherited from the political system of the eighteenth century.

6. An Economic Interpretation of the Constitution

Charles A. Beard

Progressive historian Charles A. Beard (1874–1948) wrote *An Economic Interpretation of the Constitution of the United States* (1913), the influential study that continues to be the point of departure for any discussion or critique of the origin of the Constitution. He also wrote *The Supreme Court and the Constitution* (1912), *The Economic Basis of Politics* (1922), *Economic Origins of Jeffersonian Democracy* (1936), *Jefferson, Corporations and the Constitution* (1936), and numerous other works, and he coauthored, with Mary Beard, *The Rise of American Civilization* (1927; rev. ed., 1956).

The following selection is excerpted from *An Economic Interpretation of the Constitution of the United States* (New York: Macmillan, 1913), 19, 24, 26–35, 37, 40–42, 49–51, 63, 73, 149–53, 156–59, 164–66, 168–71, 173, 175–76, 178–80, 217–18, 237–38, 249–52, 290–91, and 324–25; footnotes are deleted.

A Survey of Economic Interests in 1787

The whole theory of the economic interpretation of history rests upon the concept that social progress in general is the result of contending interests in society—some favorable, others opposed, to change. On this hypothesis, we are required to discover at the very outset of the present study what classes and social groups existed in the United States just previous to the adoption of the Constitution and which of them, from the nature of their property, might have expected to benefit immediately and definitely by the overthrow of the old system and the establishment of the new. On the other hand, it must be discovered which of them might have expected more beneficial immediate results, on the whole, from the maintenance of the existing legal arrangements. . . .

The Disfranchised

In an examination of the structure of American society in 1787, we first encounter four groups whose economic status had a definite legal expression: the slaves, the indentured servants, the mass of men who could not qualify for voting under the property tests imposed by the state constitutions and laws, and women, disfranchised and subjected to the discriminations of the common law. These groups were, therefore, not represented in the Convention which drafted the Constitution, except under the theory that representation has no relation to voting. . . .

Passing beyond these groups which were politically nonexistent, except in so far as those who possessed the ballot and economic power were compelled to safeguard their rights against assaults from such quarters, we come to the social groupings within the politically enfranchised mass. Here we find no legal class distinctions. Social distinctions were very sharp, it is true, as every student of manners and customs well knows; but there were no outward legal signs of special class privileges.

Groups of Real Property Holders

Nevertheless, the possessors of property were susceptible of classification into several rather marked groups, though of course they shade off into one another by imperceptible gradations. Broadly speaking, there were the interests of real and personal property. Here, however, qualifications must be made. There was no such identity of interest between the large planters and the small inland farmers of the south as existed in England between the knights and yeomen. The real property holders may be classified into three general groups: the small farmers, particularly back from the sea-coast, scattered from New Hampshire to Georgia, the manorial lords, such as we find along the banks of the Hudson, and the slaveholding planters of the south.

1. The first of these groups, the small farmers, constituted a remarkably homogeneous class. The inland section was founded and recruited by mechanics, the poorer whites, and European (particularly Scotch-Irish) immigrants. It had peculiar social and political views arising from the crude nature of its environment, but its active political doctrines were derived from an antagonism to the seaboard groups. One source of conflict was connected with the possession of the land itself. Much of the western country had been

taken up by speculators and the settlers were either squatters or purchasers from large holders. . . .

In addition to being frequently in debt for their lands, the small farmers were dependent upon the towns for most of the capital to develop their resources. They were, in other words, a large debtor class, to which must be added, or course, the urban dwellers who were in a like unfortunate condition.

That this debtor class had developed a strong consciousness of identical interests in the several states is clearly evident in local politics and legislation. Shays' Rebellion in Massachusetts, the disturbances in Rhode Island, New Hampshire, and other northern states, the activities of the paper-money advocates in state legislatures, the innumerable schemes for the relief of debtors, such as the abolition of imprisonment, paper money, laws delaying the collection of debts, propositions requiring debtors to accept land in lieu of specie at a valuation fixed by a board of arbitration—these and many other schemes testify eloquently to the fact that the debtors were conscious of their status and actively engaged in establishing their interest in the form of legal provisions. Their philosophy was reflected in the writings of Luther Martin, delegate to the Convention from Maryland, who disapproved of the Constitution, partly on the ground that it would put a stop to agrarian legislation.

2. The second group of landed proprietors, the manorial lords of the Hudson valley region, constituted a peculiar aristocracy in itself and was the dominant class in the politics of New York during the period between the Revolution and the adoption of the Constitution, as it had been before the War. It was unable or unwilling to block the emission of paper money, because the burden of that operation fell on the capitalists rather than itself. It also took advantage of its predominance to shift the burden of taxation from the land to imports, and this fact contributed powerfully to its opposition to the Constitution, because it implied a transference of the weight of taxation for state purposes to the soil. Its spokesmen indulged in much high talk of state's rights, in which Federalist leaders refused to see more than a hollow sham made to cover the rural gentry's economic supremacy.

3. The third group of landed proprietors were the slaveholders of the south. It seems curious at the first glance that the representatives of the southern states which sold raw materials and wanted competition in shipping were willing to join in a union that subjected them to commercial regulations

devised immediately in behalf of northern interests. An examination of the records shows that they were aware of this apparent incongruity, but that there were overbalancing compensations to be secured in a strong federal government.

Money-lending and the holding of public securities were not confined to the north by any means; although, perhaps, as Calhoun long afterward remarked, the south was devoid of some of the artifices of commerce which characterized New England. Neither were attempts at relieving debtors by legislative enactment restricted to Massachusetts and Rhode Island. The south had many men who were rich in personalty, other than slaves, and it was this type, rather than the slaveholding planter as such, which was represented in the Convention that framed the Constitution. The majority of the southern delegates at Philadelphia in 1787 were from the towns or combined a wide range of personalty operations with their planting. On this account there was more identity of interest among Langdon of Portsmouth, Gerry of Boston, Hamilton of New York, Dayton of New Jersey, Robert Morris of Philadelphia, McHenry of Baltimore, Washington on the Potomac, Williamson of North Carolina, the Pinckneys of Charleston, and Pierce of Savannah than between these several men and their debt-burdened neighbors at the back door. Thus nationalism was created by a welding of economic interests that cut through state boundaries.

The southern planter was also as much concerned in maintaining order against slave revolts as the creditor in Massachusetts was concerned in putting down Shays' "desperate debtors." And the possibilities of such servile insurrections were by no means remote. Every slave owner must have felt more secure in 1789 when he knew that the governor of his state could call in the strong arm of the federal administration in case a domestic disturbance got beyond the local police and militia. . . .

Groups of Personal Property Interests

A second broad group of interests was that of personal property as contrasted with real property. This embraced, particularly, money loaned, state and continental securities, stocks of goods, manufacturing plants, soldiers' scrip, and shipping. The relative proportion of personalty to realty in 1787 has not been determined and it is questionable whether adequate data are available for settling such an important matter.

Personalty in Money. . . . Money capital was suffering in two ways under the Articles of Confederation. It was handicapped in seeking profitable outlets by the absence of protection for manufactures, the lack of security in investments in western lands, and discriminations against American shipping by foreign countries. It was also being positively attacked by the makers of paper money, stay laws, pine barren acts, and other devices for depreciating the currency or delaying the collection of debts. In addition there was a widespread derangement of the monetary system and the coinage due to the absence of uniformity and stability in the standards. . . .

Personalty in Public Securities. Even more immediately concerned in the establishment of a stable national government were the holders of state and continental securities. The government under the Articles of Confederation was not paying the interest on its debt and its paper had depreciated until it was selling at from one-sixth to one-twentieth of its par value. . . .

The enormous total of the national debt after state and national securities were funded is shown by Hamilton's report of January 16, 1795:

Foreign Debt	$13,745,379.35
Funded domestic debt	60,789,914.18
Unsubscribed debt	1,561,175.14
Total unredeemed debt	$76,096,468.67

. . . If we leave out of account the foreign debt, it appears that some $60,000,000 worth of potential paper lay in the hands of American citizens in the spring of 1787. This paper was changing hands all of the time at varying prices. The common selling price in good markets before the movement for the Constitution got under way ranged from one-sixth to one-tenth its face value; and some of it sold as low as twenty to one. In fact, many holders regarded continental paper as worthless, as it might have been had the formation of the Constitution been indefinitely delayed. It seems safe to hazard a guess, therefore, that at least $40,000,000 gain came to the holders of securities through the adoption of the Constitution and the sound financial system which it made possible. This leaves out of account the large fortunes won by the manipulation of stocks after the government was established and particularly after the founding of the New York Stock Exchange in 1792.

. . . The amount gained by public security holders through the adoption of the new system was roughly equivalent to the value of all the lands as listed for taxation in Connecticut. It was but little less than the value of the lands in New Hampshire, Vermont, and Rhode Island. It was about equivalent to one-half the value of the lands in New York and to two-thirds the value of the lands in Massachusetts. It amounted to at least ten dollars for every man, woman, and child in the whole United States from New Hampshire to Georgia. . . .

Personalty in Manufacturing and Shipping. The third group of personalty interests embraced the manufacturing population, which was not inconsiderable even at that time. A large amount of capital had been invested in the several branches of industry and a superficial study of the extensive natural resources at hand revealed the immense possibilities of capitalistic enterprise.

The supporters of the Constitution were so earnest and so persistent in their assertion that commerce was languishing and manufactures perishing for the lack of protection that there must have been some justification for their claims, although it is impossible to say how widespread the havoc really was. . . .

That innumerable manufacturing, shipping, trading, and commercial interests did, however, look upon the adoption of the Constitution as the sure guarantee that protection could be procured against foreign competition, is fully evidenced in the memorials laid before Congress in April, May, and June, 1789, asking for the immediate enactment of discriminatory tariff laws. . . .

Capital Invested in Western Lands. Although companies had been formed to deal in western lands on a large scale before the Revolution, it was not until the close of the War that effective steps were taken toward settlement.

The situation was this: Congress under the Articles of Confederation adopted a policy of accepting certificates in part payment for lands; and it was hoped by some that the entire national debt might be extinguished in this way. However, the weakness of the Confederation, the lack of proper military forces, the uncertainty as to the frontiers kept the values of the large sections held for appreciation at an abnormally low price. . . .

The weight of the several species of property in politics is not determined by the amount, but rather by the opportunities offered to each variety for gain and by the degree of necessity for defence against hostile legislation designed to depreciate values or close opportunities for increments. When viewed in this light the reason for the special pressure of personalty in politics in 1787 is apparent. It was receiving attacks on all hands from the depreciators and it found the way to profitable operations closed by governmental action or neglect. If we may judge from the politics of the Congress under the Articles of Confederation, two related groups were most active: those working for the establishment of a revenue sufficient to discharge the interest and principal of the public debt, and those working for commercial regulations advantageous to personalty operations in shipping and manufacturing and in western land speculations.

It should be remembered also that personalty is usually more active than real property. It is centralized in the towns and can draw together for defence or aggression with greater facility. The expectation of profits from its manipulation was much larger in 1787 than from real property. It had a considerable portion of the professional classes attached to it; its influence over the press was tremendous, not only through ownership, but also through advertising and other patronage. It was, in short, the dynamic element in the movement for the new Constitution.

The Movement for the Constitution

Certain tentative conclusions emerge at this point.

Large and important groups of economic interests were adversely affected by the system of government under the Articles of Confederation, namely, those of public securities, shipping and manufacturing, money at interest; in short, capital as opposed to land.

The representatives of these important interests attempted through the regular legal channels to secure amendments to the Articles of Confederation which would safeguard their rights in the future, particularly those of the public creditors.

Having failed to realize their great purposes through the regular means, the leaders in the movement set to work to secure by a circuitous route the assemblying of a Convention to "revise" the Articles of Confederation with the hope of obtaining, outside of the existing legal framework, the adoption of a revolutionary programme.

Ostensibly, however, the formal plan of approval by Congress and the state legislatures was to be preserved. . . .

The Economic Interests of the Members of the Convention

Having shown that four groups of property rights were adversely affected by the government under the Articles of Confederation, and that economic motives were behind the movement for a reconstruction of the system, it is now necessary to inquire whether the members of the Convention which drafted the Constitution represented in their own property affiliations any or all of these groups. In other words, did the men who formulated the fundamental law of the land possess the kinds of property which were immediately and directly increased in value or made more secure by the results of their labors at Philadelphia? Did they have money at interest? Did they own public securities? Did they hold western lands for appreciation? Were they interested in shipping and manufactures?

The purpose of such an inquiry is not, of course, to show that the Constitution was made for the personal benefit of the members of the Convention. Far from it. Neither is it of any moment to discover how many hundred thousand dollars accrued to them as a result of the foundation of the new government. The only point here considered is: Did they represent distinct groups whose economic interests they understood and felt in concrete, definite form through their own personal experience with identical property rights, or were they working merely under the guidance of abstract principles of political science? . . .

A survey of the economic interests of the members of the convention presents certain conclusions:

A majority of the members were lawyers by profession.

Most of the members came from towns, on or near the coast, that is, from the regions in which personalty was largely concentrated.

Not one member represented in his immediate personal economic interests the small farming or mechanic classes.

The overwhelming majority of members, at least five-sixths, were immediately, directly, and personally interested in the outcome of their labors at Philadelphia, and were to a greater or less extent economic beneficiaries from the adoption of the Constitution.

1. Public security interests were extensively represented in the Convention. Of the fifty-five members who attended no less than forty appear on the Records of the Treasury Department for sums varying from a few dollars up to more than one hundred thousand dollars. Among the minor holders were Bassett, Blount, Brearley, Broom, Butler, Carroll, Few, Hamilton, L. Martin, Mason, Mercer, Mifflin, Read, Spaight, Wilson, and Wythe. Among the larger holders (taking the sum of about $5000 as the criterion) were Baldwin, Blair, Clymer, Dayton, Ellsworth, Fitzsimons, Gilman, Gerry, Gorham, Jenifer, Johnson, King, Langdon, Lansing, Livingston, McClurg,

R. Morris, C. C. Pinckney, C. Pinckney, Randolph, Sherman, Strong, Washington, and Williamson.

It is interesting to note that, with the exception of New York, and possibly Delaware, each state had one or more prominent representatives in the Convention who held more than a negligible amount of securities, and who could therefore speak with feeling and authority on the question of providing in the new Constitution for the full discharge of the public debt:

Langdon and Gilman, of New Hampshire.

Gerry, Strong, and King, of Massachusetts.

Ellsworth, Sherman, and Johnson, of Connecticut.

Hamilton, of New York. Although he held no large amount personally, he was the special pleader for the holders of public securities and the maintenance of public faith.

Dayton, of New Jersey.

Robert Morris, Clymer, and Fitzsimons, of Pennsylvania.

Mercer and Carroll, of Maryland.

Blair, McClurg, and Randolph, of Virginia.

Williamson, of North Carolina.

The two Pinckneys, of South Carolina.

Few and Baldwin, of Georgia.

2. Personalty invested in lands for speculation was represented by at least fourteen members: Blount, Dayton, Few, Fitzsimons, Franklin, Gilman, Gerry, Gorham, Hamilton, Mason, R. Morris, Washington, Williamson, and Wilson.

3. Personalty in the form of money loaned at interest was represented by at least twenty-four members: Bassett, Broom, Butler, Carroll, Clymer, Davie, Dickinson, Ellsworth, Few, Fitzsimons, Franklin, Gilman, Ingersoll, Johnson, King, Langdon, Mason, McHenry, C. C. Pinckney, C. Pinckney, Randolph, Read, Washington, and Williamson.

4. Personalty in mercantile, manufacturing, and shipping lines was represented by at least eleven members: Broom, Clymer, Ellsworth, Fitzsimons, Gerry, King, Langdon, McHenry, Mifflin, G. Morris, and R. Morris.

5. Personalty in slaves was represented by at least fifteen members: Butler, Davie, Jenifer, A. Martin, L. Martin, Mason, Mercer, C. C. Pinckney, C. Pinckney, Randolph, Read, Rutledge, Spaight, Washington, and Wythe.

It cannot be said, therefore, that the members of the Convention were "disinterested." On the contrary, we are forced to accept the profoundly significant conclusion that they knew through their personal experiences in economic affairs the precise results which the new government that they were setting up was designed to attain. As a group of doctrinaires, like the Frankfort assembly of 1848, they would have failed miserably; but as practical men they were able to build the new government upon the only foundations which could be stable: fundamental economic interests.

The Constitution as an Economic Document

It is difficult for the superficial student of the Constitution, who has read only the commentaries of the legists, to conceive of that instrument as an economic document. It places no property qualifications on voters or officers; it gives no outward recognition of any economic groups in society; it mentions no special privileges to be conferred upon any class. It betrays no feeling, such as vibrates through the French constitution of 1791; its language is cold, formal, and severe. . . .

The Federalist, on the other hand, presents in a relatively brief and systematic form an economic interpretation of the Constitution by the men best fitted, through an intimate knowledge of the ideals of the framers, to expound the political science of the new government. This wonderful piece of argumentation by Hamilton, Madison, and Jay is in fact the finest study in the economic interpretation of politics which exists in any language; and whoever would understand the Constitution as an economic document need hardly go beyond it. . . .

The Underlying Political Science of the Constitution

Before taking up the economic implications of the structure of the federal government, it is important to ascertain what, in the opinion of *The Federalist*, is the basis of all government. The most philosophical examination of the foundations of political science is made by Madison in the tenth number. Here he lays down, in no uncertain language, the principle that the first and elemental concern of every government is economic.

1. "The first object of government," he declares, is the protection of "the diversity in the faculties of men, from which the rights of property originate." The chief business of government, from which, perforce, its essential nature must be derived, consists in the control and adjustment of conflicting economic interests. After enumerating the various forms of propertied interests

which spring up inevitably in modern society, he adds: "The regulation of these various and interfering interests forms the principal task of modern legislation, and involves the spirit of party and faction in the ordinary operation of the government."

2. What are the chief causes of these conflicting political forces with which the government must concern itself? Madison answers. Of course fanciful and frivolous distinctions have sometimes been the cause of violent conflicts; "but the most common and durable sources of factions has been the various and unequal distribution of property. Those who hold and those who are without property have ever formed distinct interests in society. Those who are creditors, and those who are debtors, fall under a like discrimination. A landed interest, a manufacturing interest, a mercantile interest, a moneyed interest, with many lesser interests grow up of necessity in civilized nations, and divide them into different classes actuated by different sentiments and views."

3. The theories of government which men entertain are emotional reactions to their property interests. "From the protection of different and unequal faculties of acquiring property, the possession of different degrees and kinds of property immediately results; *and from the influence of these on the sentiments and views of the respective proprietors, ensues a division of society into different interests and parties.*"

Legislatures reflect these interests. "What," he asks, "are the different classes of legislators but advocates and parties to the causes which they determine." There is no help for it. "The causes of faction cannot be removed," and "we well know that neither moral nor religious motives can be relied on as an adequate control."

4. Unequal distribution of property is inevitable, and from it contending factions will rise in the state. The government will reflect them, for they will have their separate principles and "sentiments"; but the supreme danger will arise from the fusion of certain interests into an overbearing majority, which Madison, in another place, prophesied would be the landless proletariat— an overbearing majority which will make its "rights" paramount, and sacrifice the "rights" of the minority. "To secure the public good," he declares, "and private rights against the danger of such a faction and at the same time preserve the spirit and the form of popular government is then the great object to which our inquiries are directed."

5. How is this to be done? Since the contending classes cannot be eliminated and their interests are bound to be reflected in politics, the only

way out lies in making it difficult for enough contending interests to fuse into a majority, and in balancing one over against another. The machinery for doing this is created by the new Constitution and by the Union. *(a)* Public views are to be refined and enlarged "by passing them through the medium of a chosen body of citizens." *(b)* The very size of the Union will enable the inclusion of more interests so that the danger of an overbearing majority is not so great. "The smaller the society, the fewer probably will be the distinct parties and interests composing it; the fewer the distinct parties and interests, the more frequently will a majority be found of the same party. . . . Extend the sphere, and you take in a greater variety of parties and interests; you make it less probable that a majority of the whole will have a common motive to invade the rights of other citizens; or if such a common motive exists, it will be more difficult for all who feel it to discover their strength and to act in unison with each other."

Q. E. D., "in the extent and proper structure of the Union, therefore, we behold a republican remedy for the diseases most incident to republican government."

The Structure of Government or the Balance of Powers

The fundamental theory of political economy thus stated by Madison was the basis of the original American conception of the balance of powers which is formulated at length in four numbers of *The Federalist*. . . .

Nevertheless, it may be asked why, if the protection of property rights lay at the basis of the new system, there is in the Constitution no provision for property qualifications for voters or for elected officials and representatives. This is, indeed, peculiar when it is recalled that the constitutional history of England is in a large part a record of conflict over the weight in the government to be enjoyed by definite economic groups, and over the removal of the property qualifications early imposed on members of the House of Commons and on the voters at large. But the explanation of the absence of property qualifications from the constitution is not difficult. . . .

Propositions to establish property restrictions were defeated, not because they were believed to be inherently opposed to the genius of American government, but for economic reasons—strange as it may seem. These economic reasons were clearly set forth by Madison in the debate over landed qualifications for legislators in July, when he showed, first, that slight property qualifications would not keep out the small farmers whose paper money schemes had been so disastrous to personalty; and, secondly, that landed property qualifications would exclude from Congress the representatives of "those classes of citizens who were not landholders," *i.e.* the personalty interests. This was true, he thought, because the mercantile and manufacturing classes would hardly be willing to turn their personalty into sufficient quantities of landed property to make them eligible for a seat in Congress.

The other members also knew that they had most to fear from the very electors who would be enfranchised under a slight freehold restriction, for the paper money party was everywhere bottomed on the small farming class. As Gorham remarked, the elections at Philadelphia, New York, and Boston, "where the merchants and mechanics vote, are at least as good as those made by freeholders only." The fact emerges, therefore, that the personalty interests reflected in the Convention could, in truth, see no safeguard at all in a freehold qualification against the assaults on vested personalty rights which had been made by the agrarians in every state. And it was obviously impossible to establish a personalty test, had they so desired, for there would have been no chance of securing a ratification of the Constitution at the hands of legislatures chosen by freeholders, or at the hands of conventions selected by them. . . .

Indeed, there was little risk to personalty in thus allowing the Constitution to go to the states for approval without any property qualifications on voters other than those which the state might see fit to impose. Only one branch of new government, the House of Representatives, was required to be elected by popular vote; and, in case popular choice of presidential electors might be established, a safeguard was secured by the indirect process. Two controlling bodies, the Senate and Supreme Court, were removed altogether from the possibility of popular election except by constitutional amendment. Finally, the conservative members of the Convention were doubly fortified in the fact that nearly all of the state constitutions then in force provided real or personal property qualifications for voters anyway, and radical democratic changes did not seem perilously near.

The Powers Conferred upon the Federal Government

1. The powers for positive action conferred upon the new government were few, but they were adequate to the purposes of the framers. . . .

The taxing power was the basis of all other positive powers, and it afforded the revenues that were to discharge the public debt in full. Provision was made for this discharge in Article VI to the effect that "All debts contracted and engagements entered into before the adoption of this Constitution shall be valid against the United States under this Constitution as under the Confederation." . . .

2. Congress was given, in the second place, plenary power to raise and support military and naval forces, for the defence of the country against foreign and domestic foes. These forces were to be at the disposal of the President in the execution of national laws; and to guard the states against renewed attempts of "desperate debtors" like Shays, the United States guaranteed to every commonwealth a republican form of government and promised to aid in quelling internal disorder on call of the proper authorities.

The army and navy are considered by the authors of *The Federalist* as genuine economic instrumentalities. . . .

The army and navy are to be not only instruments of defence in protecting the United States against the commercial and territorial ambitions of other countries; but they may be used also in forcing open foreign markets. What discriminatory tariffs and navigation laws may not accomplish the sword may achieve. . . .

3. In addition to the power to lay and collect taxes and raise and maintain armed forces on land and sea, the Constitution vests in Congress plenary control over foreign and interstate commerce, and thus authorizes it to institute protective and discriminatory laws in favor of American interests, and to create a wide sweep for free trade throughout the whole American empire. . . .

4. Another great economic antagonism found its expression in the clause conferring upon Congress the power to dispose of the territories and make rules and regulations for their government and admission to the Union. In this contest, the interests of the states which held territories came prominently to the front; and the ambiguity of the language used in the Constitution on this point may be attributed to the inability of the contestants to reach precise conclusions. The leaders were willing to risk the proper management of the land problem after the new government was safely launched; and they were correct in their estimate of their future political prowess.

These are the great powers conferred on the new government: taxation, war, commercial control, and disposition of western lands. Through them public creditors may be paid in full, domestic peace maintained, advantages obtained in dealing with foreign nations, manufactures protected, and the development of the territories go forward with full swing. The remaining powers are minor and need not be examined here. What implied powers lay in the minds of the framers likewise need not be inquired into; they have long been the subject of juridical speculation.

None of the powers conferred by the Constitution on Congress permits a direct attack on property. The federal government is given no general authority to define property. It may tax, but indirect taxes must be uniform, and these are to fall upon consumers. Direct taxes may be laid, but resort to this form of taxation is rendered practically impossible, save on extraordinary occasions, by the provision that they must be apportioned according to population—so that numbers cannot transfer the burden to accumulated wealth. The salve trade may be destroyed, it is true, after the lapse of a few years; but slavery as a domestic institution is better safeguarded than before. . . .

Restrictions Laid upon State Legislatures

Equally important to personalty as the positive powers conferred upon Congress to tax, support armies, and regulate commerce were the restrictions imposed on the states. Indeed, we have the high authority of Madison for the statement that of the forces which created the Constitution, those property interests seeking protection against omnipotent legislatures were the most active. . . .

Two small clauses embody the chief demands of personalty against agrarianism: the emission of paper money is prohibited and the states are forbidden to impair the obligation of contract. The first of these means a return to a specie basis—when coupled with the requirement that the gold and silver coin of the United States shall be the legal tender. The Shays and their paper money legions, who assaulted the vested rights of personalty by the process of legislative depreciation, are now subdued forever, and money lenders and security holders may be sure of their operations. Contracts are to be safe, and whoever engages in a financial operation, public or private, may know that state legislatures cannot destroy overnight the rules by which the game is played.

A principle of deep significance is written in these two brief sentences. The economic history of the states between the Revolution and the adoption of the Constitution is compressed in them. They appealed to every money lender, to every holder of public paper, to every man who had any personalty at stake. The intensity of the economic interests reflected in these two prohibitions can only be felt by one who has spent months in the study of American agrarianism after the Revolution. In them personalty won a significant battle in the conflict of 1787–1788. . . .

Hamilton on several occasions laid great stress on the contract clause as one of the features of the Constitution which had warmly commended it to its supporters. . . .

The Process of Ratification

On the 17th day of September, 1787, the Convention at Philadelphia finished its work and transmitted the new Constitution to Congress, with the suggestion that "it should afterwards be submitted to a convention of delegates chosen in each state by the people thereof, under the recommendation of its legislature for their assent and ratification; and that each convention assenting to and ratifying the same should give notice thereof to the United States in Congress assembled." The Philadelphia Convention further proposed that when nine states had ratified the new instrument, it should go into effect as between the states ratifying the same. Eleven days later, on September 28, the Congress, then sitting in New York, resolved to accept the advice of the Convention, and sent the Constitution to the state legislatures to be transmitted by them to conventions chosen by the voters of the respective commonwealths.

This whole process was a departure from the provision of the then fundamental law of the land—the Articles of Confederation—which provided that all alterations and amendments should be made by Congress and receive the approval of the legislature of every state. If to-day the Congress of the United States should call a national convention to "revise" the Constitution, and such a convention should throw away the existing instrument of government entirely and submit a new frame of government to a popular referendum, disregarding altogether the process of amendment now provided, we should have something analogous to the great political transformation of 1787–89. The revolutionary nature of the work of the Philadelphia Convention is correctly characterized by Professor John W. Burgess when he states that had such acts been performed by Julius or Napoleon, they would have been pronounced *coups d'etat*. . . .

A survey of the facts . . . yields several important generalizations:

Two states, Rhode Island and North Carolina refused to ratify the Constitution until after the establishment of the new government which set in train powerful economic forces against them in their isolation.

In three states, New Hampshire, New York, and Massachusetts, the popular vote as measured by the election of delegates to the conventions was adverse to the Constitution; and ratification was secured by the conversion of opponents and often the repudiation of their tacit (and in some cases express) instructions.

In Virginia the popular vote was doubtful.

In the four states which ratified the constitution with facility, Connecticut, New Jersey, Georgia, and Delaware, only four or five weeks were allowed to elapse before the legislatures acted, and four or five weeks more before the elections to the conventions were called; and about an equal period between the elections and the meeting of the conventions. This facility of action may have been due to the general sentiment in favor of the Constitution; or the rapidity of action may account for the slight development of the opposition.

In two commonwealths, Maryland and South Carolina, deliberation and delays in the election and the assembling of the conventions resulted in an undoubted majority in favor of the new instrument; but for the latter state the popular vote has never been figured out.

In one of the states, Pennsylvania, the proceedings connected with the ratification of the Constitution were conducted with unseemly haste.

The Popular Vote on the Constitution

While one hesitates to generalize about the vote cast in favor of the Constitution on the basis of the fragmentary evidence available, it seems worth while, nevertheless, to put together several related facts bearing on the matter.

In addition to the conclusion, brought out by Dr. Jameson, that about 5 per cent of the population voted in Massachusetts in the period under consideration, we have other valuable data. Dr. Paullin has shown that the electoral vote in the presidential election of 1788 in New Hampshire was 2.8 per cent of the free population; that the vote in Madison's electoral district in Virginia in the same election was 2.7 per cent of the white population; that the vote in the first congressional election in Maryland was 3.6 per cent of the white population and that the vote in the same congressional election in Massachusetts was 3 per cent. Speaking of the exercise of the franchise as a whole in the period, Dr. Paullin says, "The voting was done chiefly by a small minority of interested property holders, a disproportionate share of whom in the northern states resided in the towns, and the wealthier and more talented of whom like a closed corporation controlled politics."

In view of these figures, in view of the data given above on the election of delegates (to the ratifying conventions) in the cities of Boston, Philadelphia, and Baltimore, in view of the fact that the percentage participating in the country was smaller than in the towns, and in view of the fact that only 3 per cent of the population resided in cities of over 8000, it seems a safe guess to say that not more than 5 per cent of the population in general, or in round numbers, 160,000 voters, expressed an opinion one way or another on the Constitution. In other words, it is highly probable that not more than one-fourth or one-fifth of the adult white males took part in the election of delegates to the state conventions. If anything, this estimate is high.

Now in four of the states, New Hampshire, Massachusetts, New York, and Virginia, the conventions at the time of their election were either opposed to the ratification of the Constitution or so closely divided that it was hard to tell which way the final vote would go. These four states, with Rhode Island and North Carolina, which were at first against ratification, possessed about three-fifths of the population—in round numbers 1,900,000 out of 3,200,000 free persons. Of the 1,900,000 population in these states we may, with justice it seems, set off at least 900,000 that is, 45,000 voters as representing the opposition. Add to these the voters in Pennsylvania who opposed the ratification of the Constitution, approximately 6000, and we have 51,000 dissenting voters, against ratification. Adding the dissenters in Maryland, South Carolina, and Connecticut, and taking the other states as unanimous, we may reasonably conjecture that of the estimated 160,000 who voted in the election of delegates, not more than 100,000 men favored the adoption of the Constitution at the time it was put into effect—about one in six of the adult males.

Admitting that these figures are rough guesses, it appears, nevertheless, that the Constitution was not "an expression of the clear and deliberate will of the whole people," nor of a majority of the adult males, nor at the outside of one-fifth of them.

Indeed, it may very very well be that a majority of those who voted were against the adoption of the Constitution as it then stood. Such a conjecture can be based on the frank statement of no less an authority than the great Chief Justice Marshall who took a prominent part in the movement which led to the formation and ratification of the new instrument of government.

At all events, the disfranchisement of the masses through property qualifications and ignorance and apathy contributed largely to the facility with
which the personalty-interest representatives carried the day. The latter were
alert everywhere, for they knew, not as a matter of theory, but as a practical
matter of dollars and cents, the value of the new Constitution. They were
well informed. They were conscious of the identity of their interests. They
were well organized. They knew for weeks in advance, even before the
Constitution was sent to the states for ratification, what the real nature of the
contest was. They resided for the most part in the towns, or the more thickly
populated areas, and they could marshall their forces quickly and effectively.
They had also the advantage of appealing to all discontented persons who
exist in large numbers in every society and are ever anxious for betterment
through some change in political machinery.

Talent, wealth, and professional abilities were, generally speaking, on the
side of the Constitutionalists. The money to be spent in the campaign of
education was on their side also; and it was spent in considerable sums for
pamphleteering, organizing parades and demonstrations, and engaging the
interest of the press. A small percentage of the enormous gain to come
through the appreciation of securities alone would have financed no mean
campaign for those days.

The opposition on the other hand suffered from the difficulties connected
with getting a backwoods vote out to the town and county elections. This
involved sometimes long journeys in bad weather, for it will be remembered
that the elections were held in the late fall and winter. There were no such
immediate personal gains to be made by the security holders on the other
side. It was true the debtors knew that they would probably have to settle
their accounts in full and the small farmers were aware that taxes would have
to be paid to discharge the national debt if the Constitution was adopted; and
the debtors everywhere waged war against the Constitution—of this there is
plenty of evidence. But they had no money to carry on their campaign; they
were poor and uninfluential—the strongest battalions were not on their side.
The wonder is that they came so near defeating the Constitution at the polls.

Economics of the Vote on the Constitution

Inasmuch as the movement for the ratification of the Constitution centred
particularly in the regions in which mercantile, manufacturing, security, and
personalty interests generally had their greatest strength, it is impossible to

escape the conclusion that holders of personalty saw in the new government a strength and defence to their advantage.

Inasmuch as so many leaders in the movement for ratification were large security holders, and inasmuch as securities constituted such a large proportion of personalty, this economic interest must have formed a very considerable dynamic element, if not the preponderating element, in bringing about the adoption of the new system.

The state conventions do not seem to have been more "disinterested" than the Philadelphia convention; but in fact the leading champions of the new government appear to have been, for the most part, men of the same practical type, with actual economic advantages at stake.

The opposition to the Constitution almost uniformly came from the agricultural regions, and from the areas in which debtors had been formulating paper money and other depreciatory schemes.

Conclusions

At the close of this long and arid survey—partaking of the nature of catalogue —it seems worth while to bring together the important conclusions for political science which the data presented appear to warrant.

The movement for the Constitution of the United States was originated and carried through principally by four groups of personalty interests which had been adversely affected under the Articles of Confederation: money, public securities, manufactures, and trade and shipping.

The first firm steps toward the formation of the Constitution were taken by a small and active group of men immediately interested through their personal possessions in the outcome of their labors.

No popular vote was taken directly or indirectly on the proposition to call the Convention which drafted the Constitution.

A large propertyless mass was, under the prevailing suffrage qualifications, excluded at the outset from participation (through representatives) in the work of framing the Constitution.

The members of the Philadelphia convention which drafted the Constitution were, with a few exceptions, immediately, directly, and personally interested in, and derived economic advantages from, the establishment of the new system.

The Constitution was essentially an economic document based upon the concept that the fundamental private rights of property are anterior to government and morally beyond the reach of popular majorities.

The major portion of the members of the Convention are on record as recognizing the claim of property to a special and defensive position in the Constitution.

In the ratification of the Constitution, about three-fourths of the adult males failed to vote on the question, having abstained from the elections at which delegates to the state conventions were chosen, either on account of their indifference or their disfranchisement by property qualifications.

The Constitution was ratified by a vote of probably not more than one-sixth of the adult males.

It is questionable whether a majority of the voters participating in the elections for the state conventions in New York, Massachusetts, New Hampshire, Virginia, and South Carolina, actually approved the ratification of the Constitution.

The leaders who supported the Constitution in the ratifying conventions represented the same economic groups as the members of the Philadelphia Convention; and in a large number of instances they were also directly and personally interested in the outcome of their efforts.

In the ratification, it became manifest that the line of cleavage for and against the Constitution was between substantial personalty interests on the one hand and the small farming and debtor interests on the other.

The Constitution was not created by "the whole people" as the jurists have said; neither was it created by "the states" as Southern nullifiers long contended; but it was the work of a consolidated group whose interests knew no state boundaries and were truly national in their scope.

7. The Antifederalists

Jackson Turner Main

Jackson Turner Main, professor of history at the University of Colorado, is the author of "Charles A. Beard and the Constitution," *William and Mary Quarterly* (1960), *The Social Structure of Revolutionary America* (1965), *The Upper House in Revolutionary America* (1967), *Political Parties Before the Constitution* (1973), and *Society and Economy in Colonial Connecticut* (1985).

The following selection is reprinted from *The Antifederalists: Critics of the Constitution, 1781–1788*, by Jackson Turner Main. © 1962 The University of North Carolina Press. Published for the Institute of Early American History and Culture, Williamsburg, Va. Reprinted by permission.

If urban classes were not divided, was there not a class division implicit in a sectional alignment over the Constitution? This thesis, which was most fully developed by Libby, set east versus west, or, to be more accurate, seacoast versus backcountry. Libby's protagonists were the debtor areas of the interior and the creditor, mercantile centers near the coast. Emphasizing the issues which separated the two general regions, he stressed the correlation between Antifederalism and paper money as a proof of his hypothesis.[1]

This interpretation has much truth. There had most certainly been just such a division all during the colonial period, and it continued to be of great importance for many decades. There is an abundance of evidence to support this explanation; as a matter of fact, the contrast between seacoast and interior was in some cases even more marked than Libby believed. The strength of Antifederalism was greater in upstate New York and backcountry South Carolina than he appreciated, and he did not fully exploit the possibilities of Rhode Island or of Maine. It is also true, as he contended, that paper money was a factor in the contest. In Massachusetts, towns opposing paper were

Federal by about four to one, while pro-paper money towns were Antifederal by an even wider margin.[2] The hard (or less soft) money towns in New Hampshire were Federal; most of the Antifederal strength in Connecticut was found in paper money districts; and the case of Rhode Island is sufficiently familiar. In New York it was the Clinton party which favored bills of credit in 1784, 1785, and 1786. Delegates from the Federal counties of New York, Kings, and Richmond, had voted against such issues; and when Suffolk and Queens counties finally changed sides and voted for ratification, they joined long-time allies on the paper money question. The same was true of the individuals involved: New York's Federalists had opposed paper money, whereas Antifederal members of the convention had voted for it, twenty-one to eleven; of the eleven Antifederalists who had opposed paper money, no less than seven were among those who ultimately changed sides on the Constitution or refrained from voting. Thus the advocates of hard money drew together in support of the Constitution. In Maryland and in Virginia the paper money forces opposed ratification. This was also the case in North Carolina, while in South Carolina, Antifederal strength lay in the backcountry, which had favored inflation.

All of the foregoing, however, does not prove an exact correlation between Antifederalism and the advocacy of paper money. There are a large number of exceptions, and of course there is a limit to the number which may be admitted without invalidating a rule. Leaving aside the fact that many Antifederalists, especially the leaders, specifically denounced state currency emissions, we have to consider the following exceptions: (1) in South Carolina, a large number of planters, most of whom became Federalists, supported the state's paper emission; (2) most Antifederalists in Virginia (including the planters) were opposed to paper money; (3) in Maryland, according to Crowl, attitudes toward paper money are not the key to the situation, and indeed the correlation with opinions on the Constitution is certainly not high; (4) New Jersey endorsed both paper money and the Constitution; (5) in Pennsylvania, although it is probable that a majority of the people were Federal, a majority favored paper money; (6) in Connecticut, paper money sentiment was far stronger than Antifederalism. Other exceptions could be cited.

That paper money sentiment was in some degree a factor in the existence of Antifederalism is scarcely to be doubted—the Antifederalists drew more heavily by far than their opponents from the ranks of paper money advocates; however the correlation is by no means complete. A different approach is necessary if all, or even most, of the facts are to be explained, and the real causes for the alignment understood. It will be necessary first to examine the positions taken by the different social or economic groups.

Among the groups into which the population might conceivably be divided, there were some whose members did not take a consistent stand on the Constitution. It has already been observed that religious and racial groups insofar as they voted together seldom did so for reasons connected with religion or race. Speculators in western lands varied in their attitude toward the Constitution; their votes were determined by local factors or personal interest.[3] Members of the "intelligentsia," if such a thing existed then—the writers, teachers, artists, and the like—were divided almost equally; doctors showed a slight but indecisive tendency toward Federalism.

Merchants, on the other hand, were virtually unanimous in endorsing the Constitution. It would not be quite accurate to say that every one of them supported ratification, but at least 80 per cent of them were Federal. It did not matter where they were located—in Boston or in Savannah, Pittsburgh, or Alexandria—nor what their economic status was, they were Federal almost to a man. In addition all, or very nearly all, of those who were immediately dependent upon commercial activities held similar views. This was the "Mercantile Interest" which, as John Adams once defined it, included "Merchants, Mechanicks, Labourers."[4] Understood in this way, the word takes in important segments of the population, including shipowners, seamen and other persons in maritime industries, the "mechanics and artisans," the apprentices and other hired employees in almost every town, and all those who depended upon any of the above.[5] But the commercial interest was not just urban. The commercial centers were supported by nearby rural areas which depended upon the towns as markets and as agencies through which their produce was exported overseas. That is to say, the commercial interest also embraced large numbers of farmers, and the influence of each town radiated, perhaps in a degree relative to its size or commercial significance. The same influence permeated the rich river valleys and bound the great planters and other large landowners in the commercial nexus. Just as in physics each point along a beam of light itself acts as a point source of light, so also the major channels of commerce, rivers or roads, influenced the country through which they passed. The mercantile interest, understood in this broad sense, is the key to the political history of the period. Its counterpart is the non-commercial interest of the subsistence farmer. This is a socioeconomic division based on a geographical location and sustains a class as well as a sectional interpretation of the struggle over the Constitution.[6]

A brief review of the evidence will make clear the importance of this generalization. In Maine, the seacoast towns, dependent on the export of fish or lumber, favored ratification by a margin of over two to one, while the largely self-sufficient towns of the interior were Antifederal. The towns along the Connecticut River favored ratification. This was true in Connecticut, Massachusetts (with a few exceptions in the northern part of the state), New Hampshire, and possibly Vermont, where the southeastern counties became Federalist strongholds. The situation in Rhode Island is also striking. At first Federal strength was probably limited to four towns, all on the coast, including the only important commercial centers. Three other towns which may have been Federal in 1788 were also coastal. In 1790 all of the towns which supported the Constitution were with two exceptions on the coast. From Narragansett Bay, the center of commercial activity, Federalist strength gradually reached out into the adjacent hinterland. In New England, then, the major division was between the areas, or people, who depended on commerce, and those who were largely self-sufficient. That the distinction was recognized at the time is shown by the observations of the residents of Spencer (Worcester County) who referred to their town as one of those whose "Distent Situation, from the metropolis . . . Renders the profits, of . . . farmes, Very Inconsiderable, to Those, of an equal Bigness, and Quality, near, the Maritime And, market Towns."[7]

In New York and in the remaining states the data cannot be quite so precise because the political unit was the county rather than the town, and it is therefore more difficult to distinguish the commercial from the non-commercial interest. The Federalism of the towns, however, is obvious and has been sufficiently discussed. The Federalism of the countryside surrounding New York City is also to be noted; so too is the remark of Thomas Tredwell that the contest was "between navigating and non-navigating individuals."[8] Spaulding notes the opposition of merchants and non-merchants and observes that "the Clintonians were scarcely interested in commerce,"[9] while Cochran defines the Antifederalists as farmers "who had no direct interest in trade or commerce."[10]

The vote in Pennsylvania is also significant. Counties which had immediate access to the Delaware (Philadelphia, Bucks, Northampton) or which were but a score of miles distant (Montgomery and Chester) together with the counties adjoining the lower Susquehanna (Lancaster and York) cast thirty-seven votes for and only one against the Constitution, whereas the remainder of the state cast twenty-two votes against and nine for ratification.

George Bryan believed that an important feature of the division was the fact that men of trade and their supporters were Federal; he contrasted the counties near to and remote from "the navigation" and observed of the mechanics, "such as depend on commerce and navigation, in favor." John Armstrong found that Antifederalism was dominant among the "country people."[11] New Jersey and Delaware do not quite fit this, or any other pattern, although it might be noted that both were favorably situated for supplying domestic and foreign markets. In Maryland the only Antifederal support came from the country; the location of the state between the Chesapeake and the Potomac may be compared with that of the Northern Neck between the Potomac and the Rappahannock.

In assessing the situation in Virginia, it is illuminating to consider the vote in 1785 granting commercial powers to Congress. Although it is not quite a straightforward test of the commercial and non-commercial interests, yet the correlation between the alignment on this issue and that on the Constitution is striking. The Federalist counties (including the "Alleghany" region) favored the measure by a margin of over two to one, while Antifederal counties rejected it by nearly three to one.[12] It is true that there were few merchants or commercial towns in the state, but the great planters were essentially commercial farmers who recognized that their future depended on trade, and it is no accident that Virginians took the lead in the effort to bestow the commerce power on Congress. On the other hand large parts of the state were further from the trade routes, so that many people either had nothing directly to do with commerce or did not recognize any identity of interest with the mercantile community. It has already been noted that the division within the state was fundamentally that of the river valleys versus the non-valley areas. The vast majority of counties which bordered the major streams were Federal, whereas Antifederal strength lay principally in the regions more distant from such waterways, notably in the Southside.

The fact that North Carolina contained a large proportion of subsistence farmers certainly was instrumental in shaping its Antifederalism. Evidence has already been adduced which indicates that the planters in the southeastern portion of the state, in spite of their greater wealth, had on several issues been opposed to the merchants, whereas the northeastern planters had voted on the other side. It is significant that the Constitution's sole support came from the Albermarle Sound counties and from the towns.

Still farther south, the foreign trade of South Carolina had always been of fundamental importance, symbolized by the interrelationship of planter and merchant in Charleston; all along the coast the producers of rice, indigo, and forest products voted with the city. On the southern border, the Savannah River drew inhabitants of both banks into the Federal camp, for not only did South Carolinians dwell under its influence but nearly the entire state of Georgia was at this time contained within the single river valley.

In all parts of the country, therefore, the commercial interest with its ramifications, including those who depended primarily and directly upon commerce, were Federal, and the "non-navigating" folk were Antifederal.

The mercantile interest drew many groups into its orbit. Manufacturers were with few exceptions comprehended within the term "artisans and mechanics." They were skilled workers with a small shop or master craftsmen with a few apprentices. Such men either depended directly upon overseas trade, producing goods for export (coopers, sailmakers, and dozens of others) or sold their products to those who were merchants or closely associated with merchants. In addition it is well known that they hoped for protection against British competition. They are therefore to be included as part of the commercial interest, and their very livelihood seemed to them to depend upon the adoption of the Constitution. Few of these men were chosen to the ratifying conventions, but many voted, or expressed their opinion in less formal ways (as in Boston), and their attitude is clear. In addition there were some, though not yet many, who owned fairly large establishments. A number of these men—upwards of a dozen—did attend the conventions and were Federalists with but one or two exceptions. Other businessmen were also dependent upon commerce. The majority—indeed nearly 70 percent—of the lawyers and judges favored ratification. When they lived in non-commercial areas, such as in parts of Virginia, they were Antifederal, or where peculiar circumstances existed the usual condition might be changed: in North Carolina the lawyers (Federal) and judges (Antifederal) had been previously opposed,[13] while in New York the Clintonian party contained its share of both. Judgeship or a law practice in itself did not determine political belief, but it did predispose the individual to act in concert with those of equal status or similar economic interest.

With regard to the creditors of the federal government the situation is somewhat different. The whole question of the debt is a very complex one, but some tentative observations may be made. It is almost certainly true that most of the debt was held by Federalists, for the certificates were concentrated in the more wealthy and the urban areas. It does not require more than a superficial examination of the records to secure the evidence of this.[14] Three different groups may be distinguished. First, there were those holding public securities who lived in states which were paying the interest in a fairly satisfactory manner. These men, in their capacity as security holders, would not be vitally affected by the Constitution unless they feared a local change of policy. Second, there were those owning certificates who lived in states which were not paying the interest in a satisfactory manner. These men would gain heavily by the ratification. Third, there were those who held no securities. The last two need further discussion.

The mere fact that a person held securities did not mean that he favored ratification. Most of the creditors owned too small amounts to constitute a vital interest. In Virginia, although about a third of the members of the ratifying convention subscribed to the loan of 1790, only a handful had $1,000 in securities. Fully 85 per cent of the delegates either had no securities or their holdings were too small to have constituted a motivating factor. Six of the large holders, moreover, were Antifederal. Presumably these men can be exempted from the imputation of economic motive, and in the case of certain other known creditors it is evident that other considerations governed their decision: Isaac Vanmeter, a West Virginian; Archibald Stuart of the Shenandoah Valley; John Marshall; and Edmund Randolph. When all the facts are considered, it becomes evident that the personal holdings of the delegates were not an important factor in shaping their political convictions. Similarly, in Pennsylvania only nine members of the convention held large amounts; four of them were Antifederal. In New York security holders were at first more numerous among Antifederal than Federal delegates to the convention, but it is instructive to note that about half of the Antifederal security holders were among those who changed sides on the final vote. Only seven of those who had securities held large amounts; four of these were chosen as Antifederalists, and three of the four changed sides.

It seems clear that of the approximately three hundred members of the conventions in these three important states, not over 10 per cent could have been persuaded to favor ratification because of the public securities they held. It is true that outside of the conventions there were large security holders, and that a great deal of money was at stake, but it is evident that the public creditors comprised only one of many interests.

In regard to those who did not own public securities the situation is quite complex. It would be to their interest to keep the tax burden as low as possible, but in some cases the Constitution might actually be advantageous. McCormick argues convincingly that New Jersey favored ratification because the taxes for payment of the debt would be lowered.[15] In other cases ratification would make little difference if taxes were already being levied for the purpose. In still other states the non-holders did stand to lose, and there were objections to the Constitution on that ground. The division certainly was not simply one of holder versus non-holder. A majority of the former favored ratification and a majority of the latter opposed it, but in neither case was the distribution of the debt at all decisive; probably, with some exceptions, it was not even very important compared with the influence of commercial factors.

The influence of private debts was undoubtedly very great. In the absence of extensive data concerning who owed whom, it is necessary to proceed by inference; this, however, may be done with some confidence. There were two major types of debtors: those who had fallen into debt because they were poor (typified by the small farmer), and those who had borrowed although they had considerable property (typified by Southern planters). Just as there is no strict dividing line between farmer and planter, so also one variety of debtor merges into the other; nevertheless a broad distinction exists. The different classes of debtors behaved differently. George Bryan remarked that in Pennsylvania debtors as a group did not agree on ratification, for, as he pointed out, "debtors are often creditors in their turn." Those who were engaged in business had to pay their debts promptly if they were to receive the further credits which were essential to them, and such men therefore held creditor views about "sound money" and "honesty in business." This category included most characteristically the merchants, but many, if not most, of the large landowners as well. In general, it seems that the class of what might be termed well-to-do debtors were divided in their attitude toward the Constitution, but that a majority of them were Federal. In South Carolina, measures benefiting debtors had found much support in the Federal eastern parishes; many Virginia planters who were in debt to British or American merchants were Federal; in Pennsylvania some prominent Republicans supported a paper money bill. In New York the Federalist Henry Remsen and other merchants petitioned for relief from debts due to British merchants.[16] The Shenandoah Valley delegates were Federal, though at least six of them were well-to-do debtors.[17] Another student has found that those owing money to British merchants were divided politically.[18] It may be concluded that although some large property holders opposed the Constitution because of their debts, the majority were Federalists regardless.[19]

The other type of debtor, typified by the small farmer, was numerically more important. The testimony of contemporaries, the number of court suits, and the passage of various laws demonstrate the prevalence of debtors in every state. The decided majority were in the Antifederal column. We have seen that advocates of paper money were apt to be Antifederalists; so also were those who favored other measures aiding debtors. In South Carolina, for example, a valuation law, an instalment law, and a "Pine Barrens" law were supported by the western counties; the votes on such matters previously discussed reveal an alignment very similar to that on the Constitution, even including the uncertain stand of those parishes which changed sides.[20] Benjamin Rush and Charles Pinckney both emphasized the importance of these issues.[21] In Virginia the votes on bills concerning the British treaty are especially significant, as are those postponing taxes in 1783 and 1784.[22] Similar correlations existed elsewhere: in North Carolina, New York, and all of the New England states. In general, then, creditors were usually to be found on the Federalist side; debtors, with many exceptions especially among the more well-to-do, were Antifederal. This fact confirms the generalizations that have been previously made concerning the alignment on ratification.

When a question so complex as the ratification of the Constitution is examined, it is to be expected that any generalization will be surrounded by exceptions. If too much attention is devoted to these exceptions, the generalization may become obscured or disguised, if not entirely hidden, so that one may even be mistaken for the other. On the other hand, if the over-all view is to be successfully maintained, and the generalization proved valid, the exceptions must be accounted for. In the case we are considering, it would be too much to contend that the division between commercial and non-commercial elements entirely accounts for the alignment over the Constitution, and even when it is added that a division along class lines is also evident, much remains unexplained.

Along the great arc of the frontier, for example, were two areas which were Federal because of their peculiar circumstances. These are, first, back-country Georgia, which wanted protection from the Indians, and second, a region including West Virginia, the Shenandoah Valley, and western Pennsylvania, which hoped that a strong central government could drive out the British and Indians. In these areas, military and diplomatic considerations, rather than socio-economic factors, determined a preference for the Constitution. There were also several instances in which the influence of prominent local leaders brought Federalism to unlikely spots. Such was probably the case in northern New Hampshire, Huntingdon and Luzerne counties in

Pennsylvania, and parts of Berkshire County in Massachusetts. Another exceptional instance is the strength of Federalism in the interior of Connecticut, which is especially surprising when contrasted with the Antifederalism of Rhode Island; the reasons are to be found in the quite different economic, political, and perhaps even cultural backgrounds of the two areas.[23]

The magnitude of the Antifederalists' victory in New York and their quick defeat in Pennsylvania are equally puzzling; the Hudson was a great commercial highway which should have recruited strength for Federalism in the interior, whereas much of the Quaker state was backcountry and should have adhered to Antifederalism. Here the major explanation lies in contrasting political trends in the two states. In Pennsylvania, the conservative Republicans were increasing in strength, whereas in New York the Clintonian party had governed so successfully that it had never lost control. Special circumstances, like those we have already noted, governed the situation in other states, such as New Jersey, Delaware, and Maryland.

But after all of these facts have been taken into account, we can return to the major generalization: that the struggle over the ratification of the Constitution was primarily a contest between the commercial and the non-commercial elements in the population. This is the most significant fact, to which all else is elaboration, amplification, or exception. The Federalists included the merchants and the other town dwellers, farmers depending on the major cities, and those who produced a surplus for export. The Antifederalists were primarily those who were not so concerned with, or who did not recognize a dependence upon, the mercantile community and foreign markets. Such people were often isolated from the major paths of commerce and usually were less well-to-do because they produced only enough for their own purposes. Because of this basic situation, a majority of the large property holders were Federal, but this division along class lines did not exist in the towns and not everywhere in the country. It was real enough however to find reflections in the political ideas of both sides. Because the Federalists dominated the towns and the rich valleys, they included most of the public and private creditors, great landowners, lawyers and judges, manufacturers and shipowners, higher ranking civil and military officials, and college graduates. Although the Antifederalists derived their leadership from such men, the rank and file were men of moderate means, with little social prestige, farmers often in debt, obscure men for the most part.

Antifederal thought was shaped by the composition and objectives of the party, but was modified by the social and political attitudes of the articulate leaders through whom it was expressed. Only a few of these leaders came from the small farmers or truly represented them. They frequently defended views somewhat less democratic than those of their constituents, and they were often out of sympathy with the economic demands of the rank and file, especially in the case of paper money and debtor relief legislation. As a result, Antifederalism as formulated by its most prominent spokesmen sometimes lacks the democratic overtones we have attributed to it.

But the democratic implication existed. As a body of political thought, Antifederalism had a background in English and American political theory long before the Constitution was drafted. Its principles were embodied in the Articles of Confederation; later they were elaborated in the controversy over the impost. Always the emphasis was on local rule and the retention of power by the people, which were democratic tenets in that age. Such a body of thought could of course by used by special interest groups; its bare political doctrine was put forth in opposition to the impost by the merchants of Rhode Island and Massachusetts. But it was always more congenial to the many than the few. Throughout the 1780's, whenever the question of sovereignty arose, the same men representing the same interests rehearsed the arguments they were to employ in debating the Constitution. Although the Antifederalist position was employed to mask special interests, it was fundamentally anti-aristocratic; whoever used its arguments had to speak in terms which implied, if they did not clearly define, a democratic content. It was therefore peculiarly congenial to those who were tending toward democracy, most of whom were soon to rally around Jefferson. The Antifederalists, who lost their only major battle, are forgotten while the victors are remembered, but it is not so certain which is the more memorable.

Notes

1. [Orin G. Libby, *The Geographical Distribution of the Vote of the Thirteen States on the Federal Constitution* (Madison, 1894).—EDS.]
2. Based on scattered sources. Pro-paper money towns cast only 3 votes for and 22 votes against ratification; anti-paper money towns favored ratification 29 to 7.
3. Hugh Williamson wrote to Madison, "For myself I conceive that my opinions are not biased by private Interest, but having claims to a considerable Quantity of Land in the Western Country I am fully persuaded that the Value of those Lands must be increased by an efficient federal Govt." June 2, 1788, *North Carolina Historical Review*, 14 (1937), 161. But most leading citizens of Ken-

tucky and Tennessee were of a different opinion. Most land speculators in the North were Federalists.

4. To James Warren, Oct. 20, 1774, Edmund C. Burnett, ed., *Letters of Members of the Continental Congress*, I (Washington, 1921), 240.

5. It is beyond the scope of this work to examine in any detail why individuals or groups become Federalist but it is evident that the mechanics and artisans, among other things, hoped for protection against British competition.

6. The division was to continue, at least into the next decade. Manning Dauer, in his study, *The Adams Federalists* (Baltimore, 1953), 7, contrasts the political behavior of "the more self-sufficient farming sections" with that of "the exporting agricultural sections." The resemblance between his conclusions and my interpretation is very striking.

7. Quoted in Oscar and Mary Flug Handlin, *Commonwealth; A Study of the Role of Government in the American Economy: Massachusetts, 1774–1861* (New York, 1947), 32. Spencer opposed the supplementary fund, opposed the impost, favored paper money, was active in Shays' Rebellion, opposed sending troops into the Shaysite country, and favored Hancock over Bowdoin, in the election of 1787, by 87 to 7. James Draper, *History of Spencer, Massachusetts, from its Earliest Settlement to the Year 1860: including a Brief Sketch of Leicester, to the Year 1753* (Worcester, n. d.), 61–67. It was of course Antifederal.

8. Jonathan Elliot, ed., *The Debates in the Several State Conventions, on the Adoption of the Federal Constitution*, II (Washington, 1854), 396.

9. Ernest Spaulding, *New York in the Critical Period, 1783–1789* (New York, 1932), 7, 28.

10. Thomas C. Cochran, *New York in the Confederation: An Economic Study* (Philadelphia, 1932), 168.

11. To General William Irvine, Carlisle, Jan. 9, 1788, Irvine Papers, IX, Hist. Soc. Pa.

12. That is, when adjustments are made to allow for the votes of several men who were for a grant of commercial powers but opposed the particular measure in question.

13. The judges had been chosen by the legislature and had taken the popular side throughout the decade. For example the lawyers were defending the property rights of loyalists whereas the judges upheld state laws unfavorable to the tories. A. Maclaine to Iredell, Mar. 6, 1786, Griffith John McCree, ed., *Life and Correspondence of James Iredell*, II (New York, 1858),137–38, 183; *Daily Advertiser* (Charleston), Jan. 1, 1788; Louise Irby Trenholme, *Ratification in North Carolina*, (New York, 1932), 153.

14. I have studied the records for New York, Massachusetts, Pennsylvania, and Virginia, but again rely heavily on the work of E. James Ferguson. See his "State Assumption of the Federal Debt during the Confederation," *Miss. Valley Hist. Rev.*, 38 (1951–1952), 403–24. His book, *The Power of the Purse*, read in manuscript, makes it clear that the importance of the debt was greater than indicated in the text. Until a detailed study is made of the political views of the larger holders it is impossible to be certain.

15. [Richard P. McCormick, *Experiment in Independence* (New Brunswick, 1950).— EDS.]

16. Spaulding, *New York in the Critical Period*, 26, see also pp. 8, 71n.

17. Freeman H. Hart, *Valley of Virginia in the American Revolution* (Chapel Hill, 1942), 123, 132.

18. Ben R. Baldwin, The Debts Owed by Americans to British Creditors, 1763–1902 (unpubl. Ph. D. diss., Indiana Univ., 1932).

19. See for instance the list of those owing debts to British firms as given in Isaac Samuel Harrell, *Loyalism in Virginia* (Philadelphia, 1926), 27–28, 171; most of them were Federalists.

20. For example, on a vote to change the depreciation table, Federal parishes voted 56–10 in the negative (of the ten, four came from the west), while Antifederal parishes and counties voted affirmatively, 40–8, and those divided or shifting on ratification voted 11–10 in the negative. *State Gazette of S.-C.* (Charleston), Mar. 12, 1787.

21. Rush to Ramsay, in Brunhouse, "Ramsay," *Journal of So. Hist.*, 9 (1943), 554; Pinckney in Elliot, ed., *Debates*, IV, 334.

22. In the last year cited, Federal counties east of the Blue Ridge opposed postponement 27–7, Antifederal counties favored it 24–13.

23. Connecticut and Rhode Island did not share quite the same cultural background: orthodox Congregationalism and Episcopalianism in Connecticut exerted a different influence than the more heterodox faiths of Rhode Island. Economically, the farmers of Connecticut seem to have been more prosperous than those of Rhode Island. In Rhode Island, the great anti-impost feeling stimulated by the merchants had predisposed opinion against the Constitution. The merchants, who were changing their minds about centralization, secured political power in 1786, but passed some unpopular measures and were promptly repudiated with resultant loss of prestige. In Connecticut, on the other hand, the future Federalists managed to retain the respect of the majority. In Rhode Island the commercial towns were therefore left isolated, whereas they had much backcountry support in Connecticut.

8. Selections from Anti-Federalist Critics

Between 1787 and 1789 the Anti-Federalists campaigned against adoption of the Constitution. Four examples of their efforts are included.

Patrick Henry (1736–1799), renowned orator, member of the Continental Congress, and later Governor of Virginia, spoke in opposition at the Virginia State Ratifying Convention in June 1788. The text is excerpted from speeches delivered on 4 and 5 June.

"Observations on the New Constitution and on the Federal and State Conventions by a Columbian Patriot," a pamphlet distributed in New York and probably elsewhere in 1788, is now attributed to the playwright, poet, and historian Mercy Otis Warren (1728–1814). Her plays lampooning the British, written before and during the Revolutionary War, helped undermine Loyalist sentiment. John Adams, displeased with Warren's portrayal of him in her *History of the Rise, Progress and Termination of the American Revolution* (1805), infamously responded, "History is not the province of the ladies."

Essays by Brutus were published between October 1787 and April 1788. Although some have attributed them to Robert Yates, their precise authorship is unknown. "Essay #3" originally ran in the *New York Journal* on 15 November 1787, and was frequently reprinted.

"Essay by None of the Well-Born Conspirators" originally appeared in the (Philadelphia) *Freeman's Journal* on 23 April 1788. Its author is unknown.

The fullest compilation of Anti-Federalist arguments is *The Complete Anti-Federalist*, edited with commentary and notes by Herbert J. Storing with the assistance of Murray Dry, 7 vols. (Chicago: University of Chicago Press, 1981). For the full texts of this chapter's excerpts see vol. 2, 377–83, for Brutus; vol. 3, 194–95, for "None of the Well-Born Conspirators"; vol. 4, 270–87, for "A Columbian Patriot" (Mercy Otis Warren), and vol. 5, 207–54, for Patrick Henry.

Speeches of Patrick Henry in the Virginia State Ratifying Convention

Mr. Chairman. —The public mind, as well as my own, is extremely uneasy at the proposed change of Government. Give me leave to form one of that number of those who wish to be thoroughly acquainted with the reasons of this perilous and uneasy situation—and why we are brought hither to decide on this great national question. I consider myself as the servant of the people of this Commonwealth, as a centinel over their rights, liberty, and happiness. I represent their feelings when I say, that they are exceedingly uneasy, being brought from the state of full security, which they enjoyed, to the present delusive appearance of things. A year ago the minds of our citizens were at perfect repose. Before the meeting of the late Federal Convention at Philadelphia, a general peace, and an universal tranquility prevailed in this country;—but since that period they are exceedingly uneasy and disquieted. When I wished for an appointment to this Convention, my mind was extremely agitated for the situation of public affairs. I conceive the republic to be in extreme danger. . . . And for what? I expected to have heard the reasons of an event so unexpected to my mind, and many others. Was our civil polity, or public justice, endangered or sapped? Was the real existence of the country threatened—or was this preceded by a mournful progression of events?

This proposal of altering our Federal Government is of a most alarming nature: . . . you ought to be extremely cautious, watchful, jealous of your liberty; for instead of securing your rights you may lose them forever. If a wrong step be now made, the Republic may be lost forever. If this new Government will not come up to the expectation of the people, and they should be disappointed—their liberty will be lost, and tyranny must and will arise. I repeat it again, and I beg Gentlemen to consider, that a wrong step made now will plunge us in misery, and our Republic will be lost. It will be necessary for this Convention to have a faithful historical detail of the facts, that preceded the session of the Federal Convention, and the reasons that actuated its members in proposing an entire alteration of Government—and demonstrate the dangers that awaited us: If they were of such awful magnitude, as to warrant a proposal so extremely perilous as this, I must assert, that this Convention has an absolute right to a thorough discovery of every circumstance relative to this great event. And here I would make this enquiry of those worthy characters who composed a part of the late Federal Convention. I am sure they were fully impressed with the necessity of forming a great consolidated Government, instead of a confederation. That this is a consolidated Government is demonstrably clear, and the danger of such a Government, is, to my mind, very striking. I have the highest veneration of those Gentlemen,—but, Sir, give me leave to demand, what right had they to say, *We, the People.* My political curiosity, exclusive of my anxious solicitude for the public welfare, leads me to ask who authorised them to speak the language of, *We, the People,* instead of *We, the States?* . . . That they exceeded their power is perfectly clear. It is not mere curiosity that actuates me—I wish to hear the real actual existing danger, which should lead us to take those steps so dangerous in my conception. Disorders have arisen in other parts of America, but here, Sir, no dangers, no insurrection or tumult, has happened—every thing has been calm and tranquil. . . . The Federal Convention ought to have amended the old system—for this purpose they were solely delegated: The object of their mission extended to no other consideration. You must therefore forgive the solicitation of one unworthy member, to know what danger could have arisen under the present confederation, and what are the causes of this proposal to change our Government.

. . . Here is a revolution as radical as that which separated us from Great Britain. It is as radical, if in this transition our rights and privileges are endangered, and the sovereignty of the States be relinquished: And cannot we plainly see, that this is actually the case? . . . You are not to inquire how your trade may be increased, nor how you are to become a great and powerful people, but how your liberties can be secured; for liberty ought to be the direct end of your Government. . . .

Is it necessary for your liberty, that you should abandon those great rights by the adoption of this system? Is the relinquishment of the trial by jury, and the liberty of the press, necessary for your liberty? Will the abandonment of your most sacred rights tend to the security of your liberty? Liberty [is] the greatest of all earthly blessings—give us that precious jewel, and you may take every thing else. . . .

I acknowledge that licentiousness is dangerous, and that it ought to be provided against: I acknowledge also the new form of Government may effectually prevent it: Yet, there is another thing it will as effectually do: it will oppress and ruin the people. There are sufficient guards placed against sedition and licentiousness: For when power is given to this Government to suppress these, or, for any other purpose, the language it assumes is clear, express, and unequivocal, but when this Constitution speaks of privileges, there is an ambiguity, Sir, a fatal ambiguity;—an ambiguity which is very astonishing: . . .

In some parts of the plan before you, the great rights of freemen are endangered, in other parts absolutely taken away. How does your trial by jury stand? In civil cases gone—not sufficiently secured in criminal—this best privilege is gone: But we are told that we need not fear, because those in power being our Representatives, will not abuse the powers we put in their hands: I am not well versed in history, but I will submit to your recollection, whether liberty has been destroyed most often by the licentiousness of the people, or by the tyranny of rulers? I imagine, Sir, you will find the balance on the side of tyranny: Happy will you be if you miss the fate of those nations, who, omitting to resist their oppressors, or negligently suffering their liberty to be wrested from them, have groaned under intolerable despotism. Most of the human race are now in this deplorable condition: And those nations who have gone in search of grandeur, power and splendor, have also fallen a sacrifice, and been the victims of their own folly: While they acquired those visionary blessings, they lost their freedom. My great objection to this Government is, that it does not leave us the means of defending our rights; or, of waging war against tyrants: It is urged by some Gentlemen, that this new plan will bring us an acquisition of strength, an army, and the militia of the States: This is an idea extremely ridiculous: Gentlemen cannot be in earnest. This acquisition will trample on your fallen liberty: Let my beloved Americans guard against that fatal lethargy that has pervaded the universe: Have we the means of resisting disciplined armies, when our only defence, the militia is put into the hands of Congress? The Honorable Gentleman said, that great danger would ensue if the Convention rose without adopting this system: I ask, where is that danger? I see none: Other Gentlemen have told us within these walls, that the Union is gone—or, that the Union will be gone: Is not this trifling with the judgment of their fellow-citizens? Till they tell us the ground of their fears, I will consider them as imaginary: I rose to make enquiry where those dangers were; they could make no answer: I believe I never shall have that answer: Is there a disposition in the people of this country to revolt against the dominion of laws? Has there been a single tumult in Virginia?

   . . . Let not Gentlemen be told, that it is not safe to reject this Government. Wherefore is it not safe? We are told there are dangers; but those dangers are ideal; they cannot be demonstrated: To encourage us to adopt it, they tell us, that there is a plain easy way of getting amendments: When I come to contemplate this part, I suppose that I am mad, or, that my countrymen are so: The way to amendment, is, in my conception, shut. . . . For four of the smallest States, that do not collectively contain one-tenth part of the population of the United States, may obstruct the most salutary and necessary amendments: Nay, in these four States, six-tenths of the people may reject these amendments; and suppose, that amendments shall be opposed to amendments (which is highly probable) is it possible, that three-fourths can ever agree to the same amendments? A bare majority in these four small States may hinder the adoption of amendments; so that we may fairly and justly conclude, that one-twentieth part of the American people, may prevent the removal of the most grievous inconveniences and oppression, by refusing to accede to amendments. A trifling minority may reject the most salutary amendments. Is this an easy mode of securing the public liberty? It is, Sir, a most fearful situation, when the most contemptible minority can prevent the alteration of the most oppressive Government; for it may in many respects prove to be such: Is this the spirit of republicanism? What, Sir, is the genius of democracy? Let me read that clause of the Bill of Rights of Virginia, which relates to this: 3d cl. "That Government is or ought to be instituted for the common benefit, protection, and security of the people, nation, or community: Of all the various modes and forms of Government, that is best which is capable of producing the greatest degree of happiness and safety, and is most effectually secured against the danger of mal-administration, and *that whenever any Government shall be found inadequate, or contrary to these purposes, a majority of the community hath, an undubitable, unalienable and indefeasible right to reform, alter, or abolish it, in such manner as shall be judged most conducive to the public weal.*" This, Sir, is the language of democracy; that a majority of the community have a right to alter their Government when found to be oppressive: But how different is the genius of your new Constitution from this? . . .

. . . An opinion has gone forth, we find, that we are a contemptible people: The time has been when we were thought otherwise: Under this same despised Government, we commanded the respect of all Europe: Wherefore are we now reckoned otherwise? The American spirit has fled from hence: It has gone to regions, where it has never been expected: It has gone to the people of France in search of a splendid Government—a strong energetic Government. Shall we imitate the example of those nations who have gone from a simple to a splendid Government? Are those nations more worthy of our imitation? What can make an adequate satisfaction to them for the loss they suffered in attaining such a Government for the loss of their liberty? If we admit this Consolidated Government it will be because we like a great splendid one. Some way or other we must be a great and mighty empire; we must have an army, and a navy, and a number of things: When the American spirit was in its youth, the language of America was different: Liberty, Sir, was then the primary object. We are descended from a people whose Government was founded on liberty: Our glorious forefathers of Great-Britain, made liberty the foundation of every thing. That country is become a great, mighty, and splendid nation; not because their Government is strong and energetic; but, sir, because liberty is its direct end and foundation: We drew the spirit of liberty from our British ancestors; by that spirit we have triumphed over every difficulty: But now, Sir, the American spirit, assisted by the ropes and chains of consolidation, is about to convert this country to a powerful and mighty empire: If you make the citizens of this country agree to become the subjects of one great consolidated empire of America, your Government will not have sufficient energy to keep them together: Such a Government is incompatible with the genius of republicanism: There will be no checks, no real balances, in this Government: What can avail your specious imaginary balances, your rope-dancing, chain-rattling, ridiculous ideal checks and contrivances? But, Sir, we are not feared by foreigners: we do not make nations tremble: Would this, Sir, constitute happiness, or secure liberty? I trust, Sir, our political hemisphere will ever direct their operations to the security of those objects. . . .

This Constitution is said to have beautiful features; but when I come to examine these features, Sir, they appear to me horridly frightful: Among other deformities, it has an awful squinting; it squints towards monarchy: And does not this raise indignation in the breast of every American? Your President may easily become King: Your Senate is so imperfectly constructed that your dearest rights may be sacrificed by what may be a small minority; and a very small minority may continue forever unchangeably this Government, although horridly defective: Where are your checks in this Government? . . .

Where is the responsibility—that leading principle in the British government? In that government a punishment, certain and inevitable, is provided: But in this, there is no real actual punishment for the grossest maladministration. They may go without punishment, though they commit the most outrageous violation on our immunities. That paper may tell me they will be punished. I ask, by what law? They must make the law—for there is no existing law to do it. What—will they make a law to punish themselves? This, Sir, is my great objection to the Constitution, that there is no true responsibility—and that the preservation of our liberty depends on the single

change of men being virtuous enough to make laws to punish themselves. . . .

The history of Switzerland clearly proves, we might be in amicable
alliance with those States without adopting this Constitution. Switzerland is
a Confederacy, consisting of dissimilar Governments. This is an example
which proves that Governments of dissimilar structure may be Confederated;
that Confederate Republic has stood upwards of 400 years; and although
several of the individual republics are democratic, and the rest aristocratic,
no evil has resulted from this dissimilarity, for they have braved all the power
of France and Germany during that long period.

Observations on the New Constitution, and on the Federal and State Conventions by a Columbian Patriot (Mercy Otis Warren)

Sic transit gloria Americana.

. . . On these shores freedom has planted her standard, diped in the
purple tide that flowed from the veins of her martyred heroes; and here every
uncorrupted American yet hopes to see it supported by the vigour, the
justice, the wisdom and unanimity of the people, in spite of the deep-laid
plots, the secret intrigues, or the bold effrontery of those interested and
avaricious adventurers for place, who intoxicated with the ideas of distinction
and preferment, have prostrated every worthy principle beneath the shrine of
ambition. Yet these are the men who tell us republicanism is dwindled into
theory—that we are incapable of enjoying our liberties—and that we must
have a master.—Let us retrospect the days of our adversity, and recollect
who were then our friends; do we find them among the sticklers for aristo-
cratick authority? No, they were generally the same men who now wish to
save us from the distractions of anarchy on the one hand, and the jaws of
tyranny on the other; where then were the class who now come forth
importunately urging that our political salvation depends on the adoption of
a system at which freedom spurns?—Were not some of them hidden in the
corners of obscurity, and others wrapping themselves in the bosom of our
enemies for safety? Some of them were in the arms of infancy; and others

speculating for fortune, by sporting with public money; while a few, a very few of them were magnanimously defending their country, and raising a character, which I pray heaven may never be sullied by aiding measures derogatory to their former exertions. But the revolutions in principle which time produces among mankind, frequently exhibits the most mortifying instances of human weakness; and this alone can account for the extraordinary appearance of a few names, once distinguished in the honourable walks of patriotism, but now found on the list of the Massachusetts assent to the ratification of a Constitution, which, by the undefined meaning of some parts, and the ambiguities of expression in others, is dangerously adapted to the purposes of an immediate *aristocratic tyranny*; that from the difficulty, if not impracticability of its operation, must soon terminate in the most *uncontrouled despotism*.

All writers on government agree, and the feelings of the human mind witness the truth of these political axioms, that man is born free and possessed of certain unalienable rights—that government is instituted for the protection, safety, and happiness of the people, and not for the profit, honour, or private interest of any man, family, or class of men—That the origin of all power is in the people, and that they have an incontestible right to check the creatures of their own creation, vested with certain powers to guard the life, liberty and property of the community . . . But there are certain seasons in the course of human affairs, when Genius, Virtue, and Patriotism, seems to nod over the vices of the times; and perhaps never more remarkably, than at the present period; or we should not see such a passive disposition prevail in some, who we must candidly suppose, have liberal and enlarged sentiments; while a supple multitude are paying a blind and idolatrous homage to the opinions of those who by the most precipitate steps are treading down their dear bought privileges . . .

. . .[I] will particularize some of the most weighty objections to its passing . . .

[1.] [A]nnual election is the basis of responsibility.—Man is not immediately corrupted, but power without limitation, or amenability, may endanger the brightest virtue—whereas a frequent return to the bar of their Constituents is the strongest check against the corruptions to which men are liable, either from the intrigues of others of more subtle genius, or the propensities of their own hearts . . . nor has any one ever defended Biennial, Triennial, or Septennial, Elections, either in the British House of Commons, or in the debates of Provincial assemblies, on general and free principles: but it is unnecessary to dwell long on this article, as the best political writers have supported the principles of annual elections with a precision, that cannot be confuted, though they may be darkned, by the sophistical arguments that have been thrown out with design, to undermine all the barriers of freedom.

2. There is no security in the profered system, either for the rights of conscience, or the liberty of the Press . . .

3. There are no well defined limits of the Judiciary Powers, they seem to be left as a boundless ocean . . .

4. The Executive and the Legislative are so dangerously blended as to give just cause of alarm, and every thing relative thereto, is couched in such ambiguous terms—in such vague and indefinite expression, as is a sufficient ground without any other objection, for the reprobation of a system, that the authors dare not hazard to a clear investigation.

5. The abolition of trial by jury in civil causes.—This mode of trial the learned Judge Blackstone observes, "has been coeval with the first rudiments of civil government, that property, liberty and life, depend on maintaining in its legal force the constitutional trial by jury." . . . Even the party who have been disposed to swallow, without examination, the proposals of the *secret conclave*, have started on a discovery that this essential right was curtailed; and shall a privilege, the origin of which may be traced to our Saxon ancestors—that has been a part of the law of nations, even in the fewdatory systems of France, Germany and Italy—and from the earliest records has been held so sacred, both in ancient and modern Britain, that it could never be shaken by the introduction of Norman customs, or any other conquests or change of government—shall this inestimable privilege be relinquished in America. . . ?

6. Though it has been said by Mr. *Wilson* and many others, that a Standing-Army is necessary for the dignity and safety of America, yet freedom revolts at the idea, when the Divan, or the Despot, may draw out his dragoons to suppress the murmurs of a few, who may yet cherish those sublime principles which call forth the exertions, and lead to the best improvement of the human mind. It is hoped this country may yet be governed by milder methods than are usually displayed beneath the bannerets of military law.—Standing armies have been the nursery of vice and the bane of liberty from the Roman legions, to the establishment of the artful Ximenes, and from the ruin of the Cortes of Spain, to the planting the British cohorts in the capitals of America:—By the edicts of authority vested in the sovereign power by the proposed constitution, the militia of the country, the bulwark

of defence, and the security of national liberty is no longer under the controul of civil authority; but at the rescript of the Monarch, or the aristocracy, they may either be employed to extort the enormous sums that will be necessary to support the civil list—to maintain the regalia of power—and the splendour of the most useless part of the community, or they may be sent into foreign countries for the fulfilment of treaties, stipulated by the President and two thirds of the Senate.

7. Notwithstanding the delusory promise to guarantee a Republican form of government to every State in the Union—If the most discerning eye could discover any meaning at all in the engagement, there are no resources left for the support of internal government, or the liquidation of the debts of the State. Every source of revenue is in the monopoly of Congress, and if the several legislatures in their enfebled state, should against their own feelings be necessitated to attempt a dry tax for the payment of their debts, and the support of internal police, even this may be required for the purposes of the general government.

8. As the new Congress are empowered to determine their own salaries, the requisitions for this purpose may not be very moderate, and the drain for public moneys will probably rise past all calculation . . .

9. There is no provision for a rotation, nor any thing to prevent the perpetuity of office in the same hands for life; which by a little well timed bribery, will probably be done, to the exclusion of men of the best abilities from their share in the offices of government. . . .

10. The inhabitants of the United States, are liable to be draged from the vicinity of their own county, or state, to answer to the litigious or unjust suit of an adversary, on the most distant borders of the Continent: in short the appelate jurisdiction of the Supreme Federal Court, includes an unwarrantable stretch of power over the the liberty, life, and property of the subject, through the wide Continent of America.

11. One Representative to thirty thousand inhabitants is a very inadequate representation: and every man who is not lost to all sense of freedom to his country, must reprobate the idea of Congress altering by law, or on any pretence whatever, interfering with any regulations for the time, places, and manner of choosing our own Representatives.

12. If the sovereignty of America is designed to be elective, the circumscribing the votes to only ten electors in this State, and the same proportion in all the others, is nearly tantamount to the exclusion of the voice of the

people in the choice of their first magistrate. It is vesting the choice solely in an aristocratic junto . . .

13. A Senate chosen for six years will, in most instances, be an appointment for life, as the influence of such a body over the minds of the people will be coequal to the extensive powers with which they are vested, and they will not only forget, but be forgotten by their constituents—a branch of the Supreme Legislature thus set beyond all responsibility is totally repugnant to every principle of a free government.

14. There is no provision by a bill of rights to guard against the dangerous encroachments of power in too many instances to be named: but I cannot pass over in silence the insecurity in which we are left with regard to warrants unsupported by evidence—the daring experiment of granting *writs of assistance* in a former arbitrary administration is not yet forgotten in the Massachusetts; nor can we be so ungrateful to the memory of the patriots who counteracted their operation, as so soon after their manly exertions to save us from such a detestable instrument of arbitrary power, to subject ourselves to the insolence of any petty revenue officer to enter our houses, search, insult, and seize at pleasure. . . .

15. The difficulty, if not impracticability, of exercising the equal and equitable powers of government by a single legislature over an extent of territory that reaches from the Mississippi to the Western lakes, and from them to the Atlantic ocean, is an insuperable objection to the adoption of the new system. . . .

16. It is an indisputed fact, that not one legislature in the United States had the most distant idea when they first appointed members for a convention, entirely commercial, or when they afterwards authorised them to consider on some amendments of the Federal union, that they would without any warrant from their constituents, presume on so bold and daring a stride, as ultimately to destroy the state governments, and offer a *consolidated system*, irreversible but on conditions that the smallest degree of penetration must discover to be impracticable.

17. The first appearance of the article which declares the ratification of nine states sufficient for the establishment of the new system, wears the face of dissention, is a subversion of the union of the Confederated States, and tends to the introduction of anarchy and civil convulsions, and may be a means of involving the whole country in blood.

18. The mode in which this constitution is recommended to the people

to judge without either the advice of Congress, or the legislatures of the several states, is very reprehensible—it is an attempt to force it upon them before it could be thoroughly understood, and may leave us in that situation, that in the first moments of slavery the minds of the people agitated by the remembrance of their lost liberties, will be like the sea in a tempest, that sweeps down every mound of security.

. . . [I]t is to be feared we shall soon see this country rushing into the extremes of confusion and violence, in consequence of the proceedings of a set of gentlemen, who disregarding the purposes of their appointment, have assumed powers unauthorised by any commission, have unnecessarily rejected the confederation of the United States, and annihilated the sovereignty and independence of the individual governments.

. . . It has been observed by a zealous advocate for the new system, that most governments are the result of fraud or violence, and this with design to recommend its acceptance—but has not almost every step towards its fabrication been fraudulent in the extreme? Did not the prohibition strictly enjoined by the general Convention, that no member should make any communication to his Constituents, or to gentlemen of consideration and abilities in the other States, bear evident marks of fraudulent designs?—This circumstance is regretted in strong terms by Mr. Martin, a member from Maryland, who acknowledges "He had no idea that all the wisdom, integrity, and virtue of the States was contained in that Convention, and that he wished to have corresponded with gentlemen of eminent political characters abroad, and to give their sentiments due weight"—he adds, "so extremely solicitous were they, that their proceedings should not transpire, that the members were prohibited from taking copies of their resolutions, or extracts from the Journals, without express permission, by vote." —And the hurry with which it has been urged to the acceptance of the people, without giving time, by adjournments, for better information, and more unanimity has a deceptive appearance. . . .

But it is a republican principle that the majority should rule. . . . [I]f after all, on a dispassionate and fair discussion, the people generally give their voice for a voluntary dereliction of their privileges, let every individual who chooses the active scenes of life, strive to support the peace and unanimity of his country, though every other blessing may expire—And while the statesman is plodding for power, and the courtier practising the arts of dissimulation without check—while the rapacious are growing rich by oppression, and fortune throwing her gifts into the lap of fools, let the sublimer characters, the philosophic lovers of freedom who have wept over her exit, retire to the calm shades of contemplation, there they may look down with pity on the inconsistency of human nature, the revolutions of states, the rise of kingdoms, and the fall of empires.

Essay #3 by Brutus

. . . The first important object that presents itself in the organization of this government, is the legislature. This is to be composed of two branches: the first to be called the general assembly, and is to be chosen by the people of the respective states, in proportion to the number of their inhabitants, and is to consist of sixty-five members, with powers in the legislature to encrease the number, not to exceed one for every thirty thousand inhabitants. The second branch is to be called the senate, and is to consist of twenty-six members, two of which are to be chosen by the legislatures of each of the states.

In the former of these there is an appearance of justice, in the appointment of its members—but if the clause, which provides for this branch, be stripped of its ambiguity, it will be found that there is really no equality of representation, even in this house.

The words are "representatives and direct taxes, shall be apportioned among the several states, which may be included in this union, according to their respective numbers, which shall be determined by adding to the whole number of free persons, including those bound to service for a term of years, and excluding Indians not taxed, three fifths of all other persons." —What a strange and unnecessary accumulation of words are here used to conceal from the public eye, what might have been expressed in the following concise manner. Representatives are to be proportioned among the states respectively, according to the number of freemen and slaves inhabiting them, counting five slaves for three free men.

"In a free state," says the celebrated Montesquieu, "every man, who is supposed to be a free agent, ought to be concerned in his own government, therefore the legislature should reside in the whole body of the people, or their representatives." But it has never been alledged that those who are not free agents, can, upon any rational principle, have any thing to do in government, either by themselves or others. If they have no share in government, why is the number of members in the assembly, to be increased on their account? Is it because in some of the states, a considerable part of the property of the inhabitants consists in a number of their fellow men, who are held in bondage, in defiance of every idea of benevolence, justice, and religion, and contrary to all the principles of liberty, which have been publickly avowed in the late glorious revolution? If this be a just ground for representation, the horses in some of the states, and the oxen in others, ought to be represented—for a great share of property in some of them, consists in these animals; and they have as much controul over their own actions, as these poor unhappy creatures, who are intended to be described in the above recited clause, by the words, "all other persons." By this mode of apportionment, the representatives of the different parts of the union, will be extremely unequal: in some of the southern states, the slaves are nearly equal in number to the free men; and for all these slaves, they will be entitled to a proportionate share in the legislature—this will give them an unreasonable weight in the government, which can derive no additional strength, protection, nor defence from the slaves, but the contrary. Why then should they be represented? What adds to the evil is, that these states are to be permitted to continue the inhuman traffic of importing slaves, until the year 1808—and for every cargo of these unhappy people, which unfeeling, unprincipled, barbarous, and avaricious wretches, may tear from their country, friends and tender connections, and bring into those states, they are to be rewarded by having an increase of members in the general assembly.

There appears at the first view a manifest inconsistency, in the apportionment of representatives in the senate, upon the plan of a consolidated government. On every principle of equity, and propriety, representation in a government should be in exact proportion to the numbers, or the aid afforded by the persons represented. How unreasonable, and unjust then is it, that Delaware should have a representation in the senate, equal to Massachusetts, or Virginia? The latter of which contains ten times her numbers and is to contribute to the aid of the general government in that proportion? This article of the constitution will appear the more objectionable, if it is considered, that the powers vested in this branch of the legislature are very extensive, and greatly surpass those lodged in the assembly, not only general purposes, but, in many instances, for the internal police of the states. The other branch of the legislature, in which, if in either, a f[a]int spark of democracy is to be found, should have been properly organized and established—but upon examination you will find, that this branch does not possess the qualities of a just representation, and that there is no kind of security, imperfect as it is, for its remaining in the hands of the people.

It has been observed, that the happiness of society is the end of government—that every free government is founded in compact: and that, because it is impracticable for the whole community to assemble, or when assembled, to deliberate with wisdom, and decide with dispatch, the mode of legislating by representation was devised.

The very term, representative, implies, that the person or body chosen for this purpose, should resemble those who appoint them—a representation of the people of America, if it be a true one, must be like the people. It ought to be so constituted, that a person, who is a stranger to the country, might be able to form a just idea of their character, by knowing that of their representatives. They are the sign—the people are the thing signified. It is absurd to speak of one thing being the representative of another, upon any other principle. The ground and reason of representation, in a free government, implies the same thing. Society instituted government to promote the happiness of the whole, and this is the great end always in view in the delegation of powers. It must then have been intended, that those who are placed instead of the people, should possess their sentiments and feelings, and be governed by their interests, or, in other words, should bear the strongest resemblance of those in whose room they are substituted. It is obvious, that for an assembly to be a true likeness of the people of any country, they must be considerably numerous. —One man, or a few men, cannot possibly represent the feelings, opinions, and characters of a great multitude. In this respect, the new constitution is radically defective. —The house of assembly, which is intended as a representation of the people of America, will not, nor cannot, in the nature of things, be a proper one—sixty-five men cannot be found in the United States, who hold the sentiments, possess the feelings, or are acqainted with the wants and interests of this vast country. This extensive continent is made up of a number of different classes of people: and to have a proper representation of them, each class ought to have an opportunity of choosing their best informed men for the purpose; but this cannot possibly be the case in so small a number. The state of New-York, on the present apportionment, will send six members to the assembly: I will venture to affirm, that number cannot be found in the state, who will bear a just resemblance to the several classes of people who compose it. In this assembly, the farmer, merchant, mecanick, and other various orders of people, ought to be represented according to their respective weight and numbers; and the representatives ought to be intimately acquainted with the wants, understand the interests of the several orders in the society, and feel a proper sense and becoming zeal to promote their prosperity. I cannot conceive that any six men in this state can be found properly qualified in these respects to discharge such important duties: but supposing it possible to find them, is there the least degree of probability that the choice of the people will fall upon such men? According to the common course of human affairs, the natural aristocracy of the country will be elected. Wealth always creates influence, and this is generally much increased by large family connections: this class in society will for ever have a great number of dependents; besides, they will always favour each other—it is their interest to combine—they will therefore constantly unite their efforts to procure men of their own rank to be elected—they will concenter all their force in every part of the state into one point, and by acting together, will most generally carry their election. It is probable, that but few of the merchants, and those the most opulent and ambitious, will have a representation from their body—few of them are characters sufficiently conspicuous to attract the notice of the electors of the state in so limited a representation. The great body of the yeomen of the country cannot expect any of their order in this assembly— the station will be too elevated for them to aspire to—the distance between the people and their representatives, will be so very great, that there is no probability that a farmer, however respectable, will be chosen—the mechanicks of every branch, must expect to be excluded from a seat in this Body— It will and must be esteemed a station too high and exalted to be filled by any but the first men in the state, in point of fortune; so that in reality there will be no part of the people represented, but the rich, even in that branch of the legislature, which is called the democratic. —The well born, and highest orders in life, as they term themselves, will be ignorant of the sentiments of the midling class of citizens, strangers to their ability, wants, and difficulties, and void of sympathy, and fellow feeling. This branch of the legislature will not only be an imperfect representation, but there will be no security in so small a body, against bribery, and corruption—It will consist at first, of sixty-five, and can never exceed one for every thirty thousand inhabitants; a majority of these, that is, thirty-three are a quorum, and a majority of which, or seventeen, may pass any law—so that twenty-five men, will have the power to give away all the property of the citizens of these states—what security therefore can there be for the people, where their liberties and property are at the disposal of so few men? It will literally be a government in the hands of the few to oppress and plunder the many. You may conclude with a great degree of certainty, that it, like all others of a similar nature, will be managed by influence and corruption, and that the period is not far distant, when this will be the case, if it should be adopted; for even now there are some among us, whose characters stand high in the public estimation, and who have had a principal agency in framing this constitution, who do not scruple to say, that this is the only practicable mode of governing a people, who think with that degree of freedom which the Americans do — this government will have in their gift a vast number of offices of great honor and emolument. The members of the legislature are not excluded from appointments; and twenty-five of them, as the case may be, being secured, any measure may be carried.

The rules of this country must be composed of very different materials from those of any other, of which history gives us any account, if the majority of the legislature are not, before many years, entirely at the devotion of the executive—and these states will soon be under the absolute domination of one, or a few, with the fallacious appearance of being governed by men of their own election.

The more I reflect on this subject, the more firmly am I persuaded, that the representation is merely nominal—a mere burlesque; and that no security is provided against corruption and undue influence. No free people on earth, who have elected persons to legislate for them, ever reposed that confidence in so small a number . . .

Essay by None of the Well-Born Conspirators

In public disquisitions, especially political controversies, one of the parties generally adopt some *cant word or phrase*, whereby they may be distinguished from their opponents; and what renders the circumstance remarkably curious, the *word or phrase* is nineteen times out of twenty wrong applied. Thus in the party politics of Britain, under one administration *candor* was their *shibboleth*, when the most *abusive, uncandid*, and *dirty-mouthed* scoundrels in the kingdom were the favorites of *court*; under another, *economy*, was the watch-word, yet *profuseness* and *produgality* in public concerns, was then at their *no plus ultra*; again *national honor*, was bazed about, when not a fragment of *honor, principle*, or even *national courage* could be traced at court; this was in Lord North's ever memorable administration. Now in an exact agreement with this plan, one of our American political parties, are incessantly bellowing out, *federalism, federal measures, federal gentlemen,* etc. etc.

If the words, Federal, Federalism, etc. are to be taken in their general and common acceptations, as derived from Foedas, a league, or covenant, entered into for the mutual advantage of all; there cannot be found a greater abuse of words than in this instance; for our modern federalists, namely, the advocates of the new constitution, evidently aim at nothing but the elevation and aggrandizement of a few over the many. The *liberty, property* and every social comfort in life of the yeomanry in America, are to be sacrificed at the *altar* of tyranny. *Federalism* then taken in this sense must imply something very remote from its original natural import; it must, (and truly there is no help for saying it) signify a league entered into against the sacred liberties of the people; that is in plain terms a conspiracy; and this is the fifth signification of the word Foedas, given by Ainsworth in his excellent Latin dictionary. Perhaps the consciences of the conspirators in the *dark conclave* urged them to assume a name which might be in some measure a key to disclose their perfidy. Conscience is a stern arbiter, and often compels us to witness against ourselves. Accompanied by such a faithful monitor the abettors of despotism adopted an epithet that should, when perfectly understood, be the true index to their base intentions. Take the word Federalism directly or indirectly, and it amounts neither to more nor less in its modern acceptation than a conspiracy of the *Well-born few,* against the sacred rights and privileges of their fellow citizens.

9. The Constitution and Slavery

Frederick Douglass

Frederick Douglass (c. 1817–1895) escaped from slavery in 1838. He published the story of his life as a slave, *Narrative of the Life of Frederick Douglass*, in 1845, and he edited an abolitionist weekly, the *North Star* (Rochester, New York), from 1847 to 1864.

The following selection is excerpted from "The Constitution and Slavery," *North Star*, 16 March 1849.

The Constitutionality of Slavery

The Constitution of the United States.—What is it? Who made it? For whom and for what was it made? Is it from heaven or from men? How, and in what light are we to understand it? If it be divine, divine light must be our means of understanding it; if human, humanity, with all its vices and crimes, as well as its virtues, must help us to a proper understanding of it. All attempts to explain it in the light of heaven must fail. It is human, and must be explained in the light of those maxims and principles which human beings have laid down as guides to the understanding of all written instruments, covenants, contracts and agreements, emanating from human beings, and to which human beings are parties, both on the first and the second part. It is in such a light that we propose to examine the Constitution; and in this light we hold it to be a most cunningly-devised and wicked compact, demanding the most constant and earnest efforts of the friends of righteous freedom for its complete overthrow. It was "conceived in sin, and shapen in iniquity." But this will be called mere declamation, and assertion—mere "heat without light"—sound and fury signify nothing.—Have it so. Let us then argue the question with all the coolness and clearness of which an unlearned fugitive slave, smarting under the wrongs inflicted by this unholy Union, is capable. We cannot talk "lawyer like" about law—about its emanating from the bosom of God!—about government, and of its seat in the great heart of the Almighty!—nor can we, in connection with such an ugly matter-of-fact looking thing as the United States Constitution, bring ourselves to split hairs about the alleged legal rule of interpretation, which declares that an "act of the Legislature may be set aside when it contravenes natural justice." We have to do with facts, rather than theory. The Constitution is not an abstraction. It is a living, breathing fact, exerting a mighty power over the nation of which it is the bond of Union.

Had the Constitution dropped down from the blue overhanging sky, upon a land uncursed by slavery, and without an interpreter, although some difficulty might have occurred in applying its manifold provisions, yet so cunningly is it framed, that no one would have imagined that it recognized or sanctioned slavery. But having a terrestrial, and not a celestial origin, we find no difficulty in ascertaining its meaning in all the parts which we allege to relate to slavery. Slavery existed before the Constitution, in the very States by whom it was made and adopted.—Slaveholders took a large share in making it. It was made in view of the existence of slavery, and in a manner well calculated to aid and strengthen that heaven-daring crime.

Take, for instance, article Ist, section 2d, to wit: "Representatives and direct taxes shall be apportioned among the several States which may be included within this Union, according to their respective numbers, which shall be determined by adding to the whole number of *free* persons, including those bound to service for a term of years, and including Indians not taxed, *three-fifths of all other persons.*"

A diversity of persons are here described—*persons* bound to service for a *term of years*, Indians not taxed, and three fifths of *all other persons*. Now, we ask, in the name of common sense, can there be an honest doubt that, in States where there are slaves, that they are included in this basis of representation? To us, it is as plain as the sun in the heavens that this clause does, and was intended to mean, that the slave States should enjoy a representation of their human chattels under this Constitution. Beside, the term free, which is generally, though not always, used as the correlative of slave, "all other persons," settles the question forever that slaves are here included.

It is contended on this point by Lysander Spooner and others, that the words, "all other persons," used in this article of the Constitution, relates *only* to aliens. We deny that the words will bear any such construction. Are we to presume that the Constitution, which so carefully points out a class of persons for exclusion, such as "Indians not taxed," would be silent with respect to another class which it was meant equally to exclude? We have never studied logic, but it does seem to us that such a presumption would be very much like an absurdity. And the absurdity is all the more glaring, when it is remembered that the language used immediately after the words "excluding Indians not taxed," (having done with exclusion) it includes *all other persons.*" It is as easy to suppose that the Constitution contemplates *including* Indians, (against its express declaration to the contrary,) as it is to suppose that it should be construed to mean the exclusion of slaves from the basis of representation, against the express language, "including all other persons." Where all are included, none remain to be excluded. The reasonings of those who take the opposite view of this clause, appears very much like quibbling, to use no harsher word. One thing is certain about this clause of the Constitution. It is this—that under it, the slave system has enjoyed a large and domineering representation in Congress, which has given laws to the whole Union in regard to slavery, ever since the formation of the government.

Satisfied that the view we have given of this clause of the Constitution is the only sound interpretation of it, we throw at once all those parts and particulars of the instrument which refer to slavery, and constitute what we conceive to be the slaveholding compromises of the Constitution, before the reader, and beg that he will look with candor upon the comments which we propose to make upon them.

"Art. 5th, Sec. 8th. —Congress shall have power to suppress insurrections."

"Art. 1st, Sec. 9th. —The migration or importation of any such persons as any of the States now existing shall think proper to admit, shall not be prohibited by Congress prior to the year one thousand eight hundred and eight; but a tax or a duty may be imposed, not exceeding ten dollars for each person."

"Art. 4th, Sec. 2d. —No person held to service or labor in one State, escaping into another, shall in consequence of any law or regulation therein, be discharged from such service or labor, but shall be delivered up on claim of the party to whom such service or labor may be due."

"Art. 4th, Sec. 4th. —The United States shall guarantee to every State in this Union a Republican form of Government; and shall protect each of them against invasion; and on application of the Legislature, or of the Executive, (when the Legislature cannot be convened,) against domestic violence."

The first article and ninth section is a full, complete and broad sanction of the slavetrade for twenty years. In this compromise of the Constitution, the parties to it pledged the national arm to protect that infernal trade for twenty years. While all other subjects of commerce were left under the control of Congress, this species of commerce alone was Constitutionally exempted. And why was this the case? Simply because South Carolina and Georgia declared, through their delegates that framed the Constitution, that they would not come into the Union if this traffic in human flesh should be prohibited. Mr. Rutledge, of South Carolina, (a distinguished member of the Convention that framed the Constitution,) said, "if the Convention thinks that North Carolina, South Carolina, and Georgia, will ever agree to the plan, *unless their right to import slaves be untouched,* the expectation is vain." Mr. Pinckney said, South Carolina could never receive the plan, "*if it prohibits the slavetrade.*" In consequence of the determination of these States to stand out of the Union in case the traffic in human flesh should be prohibited, and from one general desire to establish a Union, this ninth section of the first article was adopted, as *a compromise;* and shameful as it is, it is by no means more shameful than others which preceded and succeeded it. The slaveholding South, by that unyielding tenacity and consistency with which they usually contend for their measures, triumphed, and the doughface North was brought to the disgraceful terms in question, just as they have been ever since on all questions touching the subject of slavery.

As a compensation for their base treachery to human freedom and justice, the North were permitted to impose a tax of ten dollars for each person imported, with which to swell the coffers of the national treasury, thus baptising the infant Republic with blood-stained gold.

Art. 4, Sec. 2—This article was adopted with a view to restoring fugitive slaves to their masters—ambiguous, to be sure, but sufficiently explicit to answer the end sought to be attained. Under it, and in accordance with it, the Congress enacted the atrocious "law of '93," making it penal in a high degree to harbor or shelter the flying fugitive. The whole nation that adopted it, consented to become kidnappers, and the whole land converted into slave-hunting ground.

Art. 4, Sec. 4—Pledges the national arm to protect the slaveholder from *domestic violence,* and is the safeguard of the Southern tyrant against the vengeance of the outraged and plundered slave. Under it, the nation is bound to do the bidding of the slaveholder, to bring out the whole naval and military power of the country, to crush the refractory slaves into obedience to their cruel masters. Thus has the North, under the Constitution, not only consented to form bulwarks around the system of slavery, with all its bloody enormities, to prevent the slave from escape, but has planted its uncounted feet and tremendous weight on the heaving hearts of American bondmen, to prevent them from rising to gain their freedom. Could Pandemonium devise a Union more inhuman, unjust, and affronting to God and man, than this? Yet such is the Union consummated under the Constitution of the United States. It is truly a compact demanding immediate disannulment, and one which, with our view of its wicked requirements, we can never enter.

10. A Compact With Hell

William Lloyd Garrison
and the Massachusetts Anti-Slavery Society

William Lloyd Garrison (1805–1879) founded and edited the abolitionist weekly the *Liberator* (1831–1865). At an 1854 Independence Day gathering in Framingham, Massachusetts, he burned a copy of the Constitution and said: "So perish all compromises with tyranny!"

Resolved, That the Compact which exists between the North and the South is a 'covenant with death, and an agreement with hell,' —involving both parties in atrocious criminality, —and should be immediately annulled.

January 1843 resolution of the Massachusetts Anti-Slavery Society, introduced by William Lloyd Garrison, and subsequently also adopted for the editorial masthead of Garrison's abolitionist weekly, the Liberator

11. Slavery and the Founding Fathers

W. E. B. Du Bois

W. E. B. Du Bois (1868–1963) was a founder of Pan-Africanism, the Niagra Movement and the National Association for the Advancement of Colored People (NAACP). He edited the NAACP's journal, the *Crisis*, from 1910 to 1932. His voluminous writings as scholar, novelist, and political activist include *The Suppression of the African Slave Trade* (1896), *The Philadelphia Negro* (1899), *The Souls of Black Folk* (1903), *Black Reconstruction in America* (1935), *Dusk of Dawn* (1940), and *The World and Africa* (1947).

The following selection is excerpted from the published version of Du Bois' Harvard dissertation, *The Suppression of the African Slave Trade to the United States of America, 1638–1870* (New York: Longmans, Green, 1896), 54–62.

32. The First Proposition. Slavery occupied no prominent place in the Convention called to remedy the glaring defects of the Confederation, for the obvious reason that few of the delegates thought it expedient to touch a delicate subject which, if let alone, bade fair to settle itself in a manner satisfactory to all. Consequently, neither slavery nor the slave-trade is specifically mentioned in the delegates' credentials of any of the States, nor in Randolph's, Pinckney's, or Hamilton's plans, nor in Paterson's propositions. Indeed, the debate from May 14 to June 19, when the Committee of the Whole reported, touched the subject only in the matter of the ratio of representation of slaves. With this same exception, the report of the Committee of the Whole contained no reference to slavery or the slave-trade, and the twenty-three resolutions of the Convention referred to the Committee of Detail, July 23, and 26, maintain the same silence.

The latter committee, consisting of Rutledge, Randolph, Gorham, Ellsworth, and Wilson, reported a draft of the Constitution August 6, 1787.

The committee had, in its deliberations, probably made use of a draft of a national Constitution made by Edmund Randolph.[1] One clause of this provided that "no State shall lay a duty on imports;" and, also, "1. No duty on exports. 2. No prohibition on such inhabitants as the United States think proper to admit. 3. No duties by way of such prohibition." It does not appear that any reference to Negroes was here intended. In the extant copy, however, notes in Edward Rutledge's handwriting change the second clause to "No prohibition on such inhabitants or people as the several States think proper to admit."[2] In the report, August 6, these clauses take the following form: —

"Article VII. Section 4. No tax or duty shall be laid by the legislature on articles exported from any state; nor on the migration or importation of such persons as the several states shall think proper to admit; nor shall such migration or importation be prohibited."[3]

33. The General Debate. This, of course, referred both to immigrants ("migration") and to slaves ("importation").[4] Debate on this section began Tuesday, August 22, and lasted two days. Luther Martin of Maryland precipitated the discussion by a proposition to alter the section so as to allow a prohibition or tax on the importation of slaves. The debate immediately became general, being carried on principally by Rutledge, the Pinckneys, and Williamson from the Carolinas; Baldwin of Georgia; Mason, Madison, and Randolph of Virginia; Wilson and Gouverneur Morris of Pennsylvania; Dickinson of Delaware; and Ellsworth, Sherman, Gerry, King, and Langdon of New England.[5]

In this debate the moral arguments were prominent. Colonel George Mason of Virginia denounced the traffic in slaves as "infernal;" Luther Martin of Maryland regarded it as "inconsistent with the principles of the revolution, and dishonorable to the American character." "Every principle of honor and safety," declared John Dickinson of Delaware, "demands the exclusion of slaves." Indeed, Mason solemnly averred that the crime of slavery might yet bring the judgment of God on the nation. On the other side, Rutledge of South Carolina bluntly declared that religion and humanity had nothing to do with the question, that it was a matter of "interest" alone. Gerry of Massachusetts wished merely to refrain from giving direct sanction to the trade, while others contented themselves with pointing out the inconsistency of condemning the slave-trade and defending slavery.

The difficulty of the whole argument, from the moral standpoint, lay in the fact that it was completely checkmated by the obstinate attitude of South Carolina and Georgia. Their delegates—Baldwin, the Pinckneys, Rutledge, and others—asserted flatly, not less than a half-dozen times during the debate, that these States "can never receive the plan if it prohibits the slave-trade;" that "if the Convention thought" that these States would consent to a stoppage of the slave-trade, "the expectation is vain."[6] By this stand all argument from the moral standpoint was virtually silenced, for the Convention evidently agreed with Roger Sherman of Connecticut that "it was better to let the Southern States import slaves than to part with those States."

In such a dilemma the Convention listened not unwillingly to the *non possumus* arguments of the States' Rights advocates. The "morality and wisdom" of slavery, declared Ellsworth of Connecticut, "are considerations belonging to the States themselves;" let every State "import what it pleases;" the Confederation has not "meddled" with the question, why should the Union? It is a dangerous symptom of centralization, cried Baldwin of Georgia; the "central States" wish to be the "vortex for everything," even matters of "a local nature." The national government, said Gerry of Massachusetts, had nothing to do with slavery in the States; it had only to refrain from giving direct sanction to the system. Others opposed this whole argument, declaring, with Langdon of New Hampshire, that Congress ought to have this power, since, as Dickinson tartly remarked, "The true question was, whether the national happiness would be promoted or impeded by the importation; and this question ought to be left to the national government, not to the states particularly interested."

Beside these arguments as to the right of the trade and the proper seat of authority over it, many arguments of general expediency were introduced. From an economic standpoint, for instance, General C. C. Pinckney of South Carolina "contended, that the importation of slaves would be for the interest of the whole Union. The more slaves, the more produce." Rutledge of the same State declared: "If the Northern States consult their interest, they will not oppose the increase of slaves, which will increase the commodities of which they will become the carriers." This sentiment found a more or less conscious echo in the words of Ellsworth of Connecticut, "What enriches a part enriches the whole." It was, moreover, broadly hinted that the zeal of Maryland and Virginia against the trade had an economic rather than a humanitarian motive, since they had slaves enough and to spare, and wished to sell them at a high price to South Carolina and Georgia, who needed more. In such case restrictions would unjustly discriminate against the latter

States. The argument from history was barely touched upon. Only once was there an allusion to "the example of all the world" "in all ages" to justify slavery,[7] and once came the counter declaration that "Greece and Rome were made unhappy by their slaves."[8] On the other hand, the military weakness of slavery in the late war led to many arguments on that score. Luther Martin and George Mason dwelt on the danger of a servile class in war and insurrection; while Rutledge hotly replied that he "would readily exempt the other states from the obligation to protect the Southern against them;" and Ellsworth thought that the very danger would "become a motive to kind treatment." The desirability of keeping slavery out of the West was once mentioned as an argument against the trade: to this all seemed tacitly to agree.[9]

Throughout the debate it is manifest that the Convention had no desire really to enter upon a general slavery argument. The broader and more theoretic aspects of the question were but lightly touched upon here and there. Undoubtedly, most of the members would have much preferred not to raise the question at all; but, as it was raised, the differences of opinion were too manifest to be ignored, and the Convention, after its first perplexity, gradually and perhaps too willingly set itself to work to find some "middle ground" on which all parties could stand. The way to this compromise was pointed out by the South. The most radical pro-slavery arguments always ended with the opinion that "if the Southern States were let alone, they will probably of themselves stop importations."[10] To be sure, General Pinckney admitted that, "candidly, he did not think South Carolina would stop her importations of slaves in any short time;" nevertheless, the Convention "observed," with Roger Sherman, "that the abolition of slavery seemed to be going on in the United States, and that the good sense of the several states would probably by degrees complete it." Economic forces were evoked to eke out moral motives: when the South had its full quota of slaves, like Virginia it too would abolish the trade; free labor was bound finally to drive out slave labor. Thus the chorus of "*laissez-faire*" increased; and compromise seemed at least in sight, when Connecticut cried, "Let the trade alone!" and Georgia denounced it as an "evil." Some few discordant notes were heard, as, for instance, when Wilson of Pennsylvania made the uncomforting remark, "If South Carolina and Georgia were themselves disposed to get rid of the importation of slaves in a short time, as had been suggested, they would never refuse to unite because the importation might be prohibited."

With the spirit of compromise in the air, it was not long before the general terms were clear. The slavery side was strongly intrenched, and had a clear and definite demand. The forces of freedom were, on the contrary, divided by important conflicts of interest, and animated by no very strong and decided anti-slavery spirit with settled aims. Under such circumstances, it was easy for the Convention to miss the opportunity for a really great compromise, and to descend to a scheme that savored unpleasantly of "log-rolling." The student of the situation will always have good cause to believe that a more sturdy and definite anti-slavery stand at this point might have changed history for the better.

34. The Special Committee and the "Bargain." Since the debate had, in the first place, arisen from a proposition to tax the importation of slaves, the yielding of this point by the South was the first move toward compromise. To all but the doctrinaires, who shrank from taxing men as property, the argument that the failure to tax slaves was equivalent to a bounty, was conclusive. With this point settled, Randolph voiced the general sentiment, when he declared that he "was for committing, in order that some middle ground might, if possible, be found." Finally, Gouverneur Morris discovered the "middle ground," in his suggestion that the whole subject by committed, "including the clauses relating to taxes on exports and to a navigation act. These things," said he, "may form a bargain among the Northern and Southern States." This was quickly assented to; and sections four and five, on slave-trade and capitation tax, were committed by a vote of 7 to 3, [11] and section six, on navigation acts, by a vote of 9 to 2. [12] All three clauses were referred to the following committee: Langdon of New Hampshire, King of Massachusetts, Johnson of Connecticut, Livingston of New Jersey, Clymer of Pennsylvania, Dickinson of Delaware, Martin of Maryland, Madison of Virginia, Williamson of North Carolina, General Pinckney of South Carolina, and Baldwin of Georgia.

The fullest account of the proceedings of this committee is given in Luther Martin's letter to his constituents, and is confirmed in its main particulars by similar reports of other delegates. Martin writes: "A committee of *one* member from each state was chosen by ballot, to take this part of the system under their consideration, and to endeavor to agree upon some report which should reconcile those states [i.e., South Carolina and Georgia]. To this committee also was referred the following proposition, which had been reported by the committee of detail, viz.: 'No navigation act shall be passed without the assent of two thirds of the members present in each house' — a proposition which the staple and commercial states were solicitous to retain, lest their commerce should be placed too much under the power of the Eastern States, but which these last States were as anxious to reject. This committee — of which also I had the honor to be a member — met, and took under their consideration the subjects committed to them. I found the *Eastern* States, notwithstanding their *aversion to slavery*, were very willing to indulge the Southern States at least with a temporary liberty to prosecute the slave trade, provided the Southern States would, in their turn, gratify *them*, by laying no restriction on navigation acts; and after a very little time, the committee, by a great majority, agreed on a report, by which the general government was to be prohibited from preventing the importation of slaves for a limited time, and the restrictive clause relative to navigation acts was to be omitted." [13]

That the "bargain" was soon made is proven by the fact that the committee reported the very next day, Friday, August 24, and that on Saturday the report was taken up. It was as follows: "Strike out so much of the fourth section as was referred to the committee, and insert 'The migration or importation of such persons as the several states, now existing, shall think proper to admit, shall not be prohibited by the legislature prior to the year 1800; but a tax or duty may be imposed on such migration or importation, at a rate not exceeding the average of the duties laid on imports.' The fifth section to remain as in the report. The sixth section to be stricken out." [14]

35. The Appeal to the Convention. The ensuing debate, [15] which lasted only a part of the day, was evidently a sort of appeal to the House on the decisions of the committee. It throws light on the points of disagreement. General Pinckney first proposed to extend the slave-trading limit to 1808, and Gorham of Massachusetts seconded the motion. This brought a spirited protest from Madison: "Twenty years will produce all the mischief that can be apprehended from the liberty to import slaves. So long a term will be more dishonorable to the American character than to say nothing about it in the Constitution." [16] There was, however, evidently another "bargain" here; for, without farther debate, the South and the East voted the extension, 7 to 4, only New Jersey, Pennsylvania, Delaware, and Virginia objecting. The ambiguous phraseology of the whole slave-trade section as reported did not pass without comment; Gouverneur Morris would have it read: "The importation of slaves into North Carolina, South Carolina, and Georgia, shall not be prohibited," etc. [17] This emendation was, however, too painfully truthful for the doctrinaires, and was, amid a score of objections, withdrawn. The taxation clause also was manifestly too vague for practical use, and Baldwin of Georgia wished to amend it by inserting "common impost on articles not enumerated," in lieu of the "average" duty. [18] This minor point gave rise to considerable argument: Sherman and Madison deprecated any such recognition of property in man as taxing would imply; Mason and Gorham argued that the tax restrained the trade; while King, Langdon, and General Pinckney contented themselves with the remark that this clause was "the price of the first part." Finally, it was unanimously agreed to make the duty "not exceeding ten dollars for each person." [19]

Southern interests now being safe, some Southern members attempted, a few days later, to annul the "bargain" by restoring the requirement of a two-thirds vote in navigation acts. Charles Pinckney made the motion, in an elaborate speech designed to show the conflicting commercial interests of the States; he declared that "The power of regulating commerce was a pure concession on the part of the Southern States." [20] Martin and Williamson of North Carolina, Butler of South Carolina, and Mason of Virginia defended the proposition, insisting that it would be a dangerous concession on the part of the South to leave navigation acts to a mere majority vote. Sherman of Connecticut, Morris of Pennsylvania, and Spaight of North Carolina declared that the very diversity of interest was a security. Finally, by a vote of 7 to 4, Maryland, Virginia, North Carolina, and Georgia being in the minority, the Convention refused to consider the motion, and the recommendation of the committee passed. [21]

When, on September 10, the Convention was discussing the amendment clause of the Constitution, the ever-alert Rutledge, perceiving that the results of the laboriously settled "bargain" might be endangered, declared that he "never could agree to give a power by which the articles relating to slaves might be altered by the states not interested in that property." [22] As a result, the clause finally adopted, September 15, had the proviso: "Provided, that no amendment which may be made prior to the year 1808 shall in any manner affect the 1st and 4th clauses in the 9th section of the 1st article." [23]

36. Settlement by the Convention. Thus, the slave-trade article of the Constitution stood finally as follows: —

"Article I. Section 9. The Migration or Importation of such Persons as any of the States now existing shall think proper to admit, shall not be prohibited by the Congress prior to the Year one thousand eight hundred and eight, but a Tax or duty may be imposed on such Importation, not exceeding ten dollars for each Person."

This settlement of the slavery question brought out distinct differences of moral attitude toward the institution, and yet differences far from hopeless. To be sure, the South apologized for slavery, the Middle States denounced it, and the East could only tolerate it from afar; and yet all three sections united in considering it a temporary institution, the corner-stone of which was the slave-trade. No one of them had ever seen a system of slavery without an active slave-trade; and there were probably few members of the Convention who did not believe that the foundations of slavery had been sapped merely by putting the abolition of the slave-trade in the hands of Congress twenty years hence. Here lay the danger; for when the North called slavery "temporary," she thought of twenty or thirty years, while the "temporary" period of the South was scarcely less than a century. Meantime, for at least a score of years, a policy of strict *laissez-faire*, so far as the general government was concerned, was to intervene. Instead of calling the whole moral energy of the people into action, so as gradually to crush this portentous evil, the Federal Convention lulled the nation to sleep by a "bargain," and left to the vacillating and unripe judgment of the States one of the most threatening of the social and political ills which they were so courageously seeking to remedy.

Notes

1. Moncure D. Conway, *Omitted Chapters of History disclosed in the Life and Papers of Edmund Randolph* (New York, 1888), ch. ix.
2. *Ibid., p.* 78.
3. Jonathan Elliot, ed., *The Debates in the Several State Conventions on the Adoption of the Federal Constitution,* I (Washington, 1827), p. 227.
4. Cf. Conway, *Life and Papers of Edmund Randolph,* pp. 78–9.
5. For the following debate, Madison's notes (Elliot, *Debates,* V. 457 ff.) are mainly followed.
6. Cf. Elliot, *Debates,* V., *passim.*
7. By Charles Pinckney.
8. By John Dickinson.
9. Mentioned in the speech of George Mason.
10. Charles Pinckney. Baldwin of Georgia said that if the State were left to herself, "she may probably put a stop to the evil": Elliot, *Debates,* V. 459.
11. *Affirmative:* Connecticut, New Jersey, Maryland, Virginia, North Carolina, South Carolina, Georgia, — 7. *Negative:* New Hampshire, Pennsylvania, Delaware, — 3. *Absent:* Massachusetts, — 1.
12. *Negative:* Connecticut and New Jersey.

13. Luther Martin's letter, in Elliot, *Debates*, I. 373. Cf. explanations of delegates in the South Carolina, North Carolina, and other conventions.
14. Elliot, *Debates*, V. 471.
15. Saturday, Aug. 25, 1787.
16. Elliot, *Debates*, V. 477.
17. *Ibid.* Dickinson made a similar motion, which was disagreed to: *Ibid.*
18. *Ibid.*, V. 478.
19. *Ibid.*
20. Aug. 29: *Ibid.* V. 489.
21. *Ibid.*, V. 492.
22. *Ibid.*, V. 532.
23. *Ibid.*, I. 317.

12. Women and the Framers

Sylvia A. Law

Sylvia A. Law, professor of law at New York University School of Law, is the author of *The Rights of the Poor* (1973; rev. ed. 1980), "Economic Justice," in Norman Dorsen, ed., *Our Endangered Rights* (1984), "Rethinking Sex and the Constitution," *University of Pennsylvania Law Review* 132 (1984), "The Founders on Families," *University of Florida Law Review* 39 (1987), and other works, and is the coauthor of *Political and Civil Rights in the United States* (1973; rev. ed. 1981). Her litigation for women's rights includes the amicus brief for American Historians in *Webster v. Reproductive Health Services* U.S. (1989).

The following essay is reprinted from "Women: From the Framers, a Deafening Silence" (New York) *Newsday*, 17 August 1987, 47.

Today many constitutional controversies involve conflicting visions of the family and the meaning of sexual equality. Answers, however, will not be found in the original intent of the Framers. Their dominant conceptions of families denied the liberty, equality and even personhood of women.

Silence—absolute and deafening—is the central theme of the Founders' discussions of women and families. The Constitution does not mention them. *The Federalist Papers'* only reference to women is Hamilton's warning that the intrigues of courtesans and mistresses can threaten the safety of the state.

The philosophers of the Enlightenment, who influenced our Constitution, assumed that the male-headed family was the basic unit of the political structure. John Locke, for example, challenged the absolute patriarchal rule of kings. Yet he thought it natural and inevitable that men were dominant in the home and represented the family in politics.

The Founders' ideology assumed that behind each man—that is each individual—was a family. This is no trivial matter. It was not just that women were unfairly excluded from public life. They were assigned at birth to perform essential work in the home. The ordinary law of the time assumed, with the philosophers, that when a woman married; her legal identity merged into that of her husband; she was civilly *dead*.

She couldn't sue, be sued, enter into contracts, make wills, keep her own earnings, or control her own property. Her husband had the right to chastise her, restrain her freedom and force sex upon her.

In American political theory, political rights were limited to those who owned a stake in the community property. Thus married women could not vote. By this logic, unmarried adult women property owners should have been allowed to vote. But they were not.

Families were profoundly different then. More than 90 percent of the people lived outside of the few cities. Mother, father and children worked together. Prevailing ideology condemned any sexual relationship except procreative sex within marriage. Patriarchal family life was enforced by the formal legal rules, by the family, by the churches and by neighbors. Custom and law strongly encouraged family formation. New England colonies prohibited "solitary living" to ensure that everyone would be "subject to the governance of family life." Fathers were entitled to control children's choice of a marital partner.

The average white woman in the late 18th Century bore more than seven children. Black women, whose masters could increase their human property simply by encouraging their female slaves' fertility, bore 10 or 11 children. Pregnancy and care of the children must have been exhausting, especially when combined with production of clothing and food, time-consuming food preparation and preservation, candle and soap making and doing laundry in iron pots over open fires, with water carried by hand from the nearest well or stream.

Understandably, many women were dissatisfied. Discontent was rooted not simply in the necessity of hard work, but also in the invariable routine of domestic labor and women's low social status.

It is possible, however, to tell a different story about the Founders, families and women—a story of increasing gender equality and sexual liberty. It too is a part of our constitutional legacy.

Against a long tradition in which legitimacy and power flowed down from God and the monarch, our Founders were truly revolutionary in asserting that the people are sovereign. Nonetheless, the power of the state is strictly limited, no matter what the will of the majority, according to the precepts of a constitutional structure.

That the Founders' culture blinded them from seeing that these principles also apply within families does not eradicate the centrality of their commitment to equality and individual liberty. Women and other groups excluded from the Constitution have for 200 years appealed to these grand ideas in seeking to improve their situation.

Even in the Revolutionary era, many women and families did not fit the mold ascribed to them. The traditional schoolbook narrative of the Revolution depicts a series of pitched battles between uniformed armies. But in fact the Revolution was a civil war involving the entire population. With men away in the army, white American women managed farms and businesses and dealt with the dangers of epidemics of small pox and dysentery. As active fighting drew near, women decided whether to attempt to flee to safety or to stay and protect their homes.

Women also made Revolutionary boycotts work. Mobs of women attacked the property of merchants who hoarded or stocked British goods. Patriotic women gathered in spinning bees, saved rags for paper making and bandages, turned in lead weights from windows to be melted down for bullets and saved family urine for saltpeter.

The Revolution generated the first women's political organization. In Philadelphia in 1779 Revolutionary women issued a proclamation and collected funds door to door to support Washington's army. Many women no longer accepted the convention that their sphere of concern was solely domestic. They followed public events and expressed their political observations in letters and conversation.

Husbands and wives worked jointly in the farms and small businesses that dominated the economy. Courts of the post-Revolutionary era increasingly recognized married women's property interests.

Increased mobility, the disestablishment of the Protestant church, the growth of cities and commercial agriculture all weakened the interlocking control that community, family and church previously exerted over individual social and sexual relationships. Enlightenment ideas supported a new concept of marriage as serving individual happiness, not simply the duty to procreate or to fulfill obligations. For the first time in our history, sexual relationships outside of marriage became possible, as a practical matter.

Premarital pregnancy rates rose sharply in the late 18th Century. Parents increasingly permitted children to choose their own mates. Within marriage, evidence of falling birth rates suggests that in the 1780s, precisely as our Founders drafted the Constitution, married couples began to practice contraception. This represented a new willingness to make family size a matter of choice, rather than a fate determined by God. No breakthrough in contraceptive technology explained the birthrate. As women developed a sense of themselves as people, contraceptive practices that depended upon cooperation became possible.

Today a broad moral and political consensus recognizes that women are full human beings. Yet both conservatives and liberals invoke the original intent to support particular positions on the meaning of the Constitution.

As a dramatic example, the courts have upheld the power of the state to punish two people of the same sex who engage in private, consensual sexual activity. Both Supreme Court Justice Byron White and Judge Robert Bork have rejected arguments that such prosecution violated individual interests in liberty, privacy, expression and equality. Both purport to rely on the intent of the Framers.

While the Framers' parochial assumptions about family denied the full personhood of both gay people and women, our Constitution also articulated more visionary concepts of liberty and equality. Even though sexism was pervasively rooted in the specific intent of our constitutional founders, the Supreme Court has correctly recognized that sexist laws are inconsistent with our more general constitutional commitment to individual liberty and equality.

The Constitution, like any political document, is the product of compromise and is bound by the culture of its time. It incorporates departures from its own best principles. It has provided a language and process within which we have engaged in passionate debates about our identities, values and visions. For most of our history the voices of women have been excluded from these debates. Yet, women have always played a full and equally vital role in constructing our nation.

Our challenge is to envision constitutional and cultural arrangements that read the words "We the People" quite literally, even though that was not originally intended.

13. The Voice of Madison

Daniel De Leon

Socialist Daniel De Leon (1852–1914) was involved with Edward Bellamy's Nationalist reform movement before becoming a leader of the Socialist Labor Party. His writings include the pamphlets *What Means This Strike?* (1898), *Two Pages From Roman History* (1903), and *Socialist Reconstruction of Society* (1905).

The following selection is reprinted from "The Voice of Madison," *Nationalist* 1 (August 1889).

The wrongs on which the social movement in this country has fixed attention have finally, thanks to unremitting agitation, become matters of such undisputed authenticity, that there is now a perceptible diminution of the refutations once attempted by those who, with book and candle, were, and to a certain extent still are, wont to formulate alleged scientific dicta in opposition to glaring facts. This sort of argument is now yielding to another which, in legal parlance, may be termed of confession and avoidance. It consists in admitting the ills complained of, but denying their connection with anything inherent in our economic system, and attributing them in some unexplained way to a departure from the wholesome lines originally laid down by the Revolutionary Fathers. [1] Accordingly, exhortations to return to old-time ways are becoming no uncommon thing; and, in proportion as this sort of declamation approaches the level of 4th of July orations, we find it festooned with flowery phrases on the fertility of our soil, with encomiums on the radical political advantages enjoyed by the inhabitants of this over those of any other country, and with random quotations from the Revolutionary Fathers intended to show that they considered the principles established by them sufficient to insure to American industry the rewards of its labor, and to free the American people from the afflictions and problems that disturb the happiness of others.

A study of the works left to us by the Revolutionary Fathers reveals, however, that they were not the visionary beings their well-meaning admirers would make them, but indeed the giant intellects Pitt pronounced them to be. Peculiarly interesting among these statesmen on the social conditions of their days, and the future problems with which they thought the people would come to be confronted was James Madison, whom to study is to revere. Madison was no hireling scribbler, catering to a self-seeking constituency; no sycophantic pedagogue talking for place or pelf. He was an honest, as well as earnest and profound thinker, peering deep into the future in order to foresee his country's trials, and, if possible, smooth her path. Let us then enrich the discussion with the learning of this distinguished Revolutionary Father, and give ear to the voice of Madison.

The question of the suffrage was one to which Madison justly attached critical importance. He understood it to be the point where political and economic conditions meet and react one upon the other. With pains, himself and his contemporary statesmen had devised our present duplex system of small and large constituencies intended to be a check on popular impulses, and, at the same time, a concession to republican instincts. This system met with Madison's approval. His reliance on its efficacy was, however, grounded upon the actual distribution of property in the United States, and the universal hope of acquiring it. [2] Those conditions, Madison argued, lay at the root of, inspired, and nurtured among the people a sentiment of sympathy with the rights of property. Again and again he declared that sentiment essential to the stability of a republican government. And he pointed with gratification to that social and economic peculiarity as among the happiest contrasts in the situation of the new-born states to that of the Old World, where no anticipated change in that respect could generally inspire a like sentiment of sympathy with the rights of property. But would the principles established by the revolution insure the permanence of that happy contrast?—and Madison's face grew overcast with apprehension as, searching the answer, his thoughts traveled whither economic and historic reasoning pointed the way.

Madison accepted the natural law touching the capacity of the earth to yield, under a civilized cultivation, subsistence for a large surplus of consumers beyond those who own the soil, or other equivalent property; he realized the great lengths to which improvements in agriculture, and other labor-saving arts were tending, and measured their effect upon the production of wealth; the laws of increasing population with the increasing productivity of labor were no secret to him; he succumbed to no hallucination on the score of the freedom of our political institutions; and, finally, gauging the effect of the individual system of production, or competitive struggle for existence, he drew from these combined premises, and declared the conclusions, that the class of the propertyless in the United States would increase from generation to generation; that, from being a minority it would eventually swell into a majority; that it would be reduced to lower and lower wages affording the bare necessities of life; and that, thus gradually sinking in the scale of happiness and well-being, the large majority of the people of this country would finally touch the point where they would be, not only without property, but *without even the hope of acquiring it.* [3]

It was then no immutable state of happiness, but a steady progress towards poverty that this eminent Revolutionary Father, for one, foresaw and foretold as the inevitable sequel of the forces at work under the economic system that lay at the foundation of the country. All the causes he enumerates as productive, by their combined agencies, of a majority of hopeless poor have been at work among us with an intensity beyond his forecast. The pitiable stage when the masses of the people would be, not only without property, but without even the hope of acquiring it, Madison calculated would be reached by the United States before the nation numbered a population greater than that of England or France. Our population is now double that of either; and Madison's gloomy prophecy is, accordingly, realized by us in its deepest colors. Our property holders have become an actual, ever decreasing minority; the propertyless are today the overwhelming majority; the wages of these have declined until they afford the bare means for a pinched subsistence; chance or intrigue, cautious crime or toadying, may, but no degree of honest toil can any longer, under the prevailing system, insure property or the just rewards of their labor to the myriad wealth-producing workers with brain or brawn; the few among them, with whom the spark of hope still glimmers, hold to a straw that must soon disabuse them; with most all hope in this direction is totally extinct; starvation, plus work, is creating by the thousands the genus "tramp," which prefers starvation minus work; and, as the certain consequence of grinding poverty and its concomitant extravagant wealth, immorality, as well as corruption, is rampant among the people, and breaks out in the government. Not, then, by reason of any degeneration, not by reason of any departure from, but closely adhering to the lines laid down by the Revolutionary Fathers, have the people reached the present shocking state against which the Nationalist movement is enlisted. The vulnerable point was the competitive system of production which the American revolution left extant. The present conditions are its logical result. [4]

On a notable occasion, John Adams, another Revolutionary Father, had uttered the sentence, that where the working poor were paid in return for their labor only as much money as would buy them the necessaries of life, their condition was identical with that of the slave, who received those necessaries at short hand; the former might be called "freemen," the latter "slaves," but the difference was imaginary only. Madison grasped the bearing of this profound thought in all its fulness. As his own reasoning revealed to him the eventual destitution of the masses, the conclusion was self-evident that their condition would become virtually that of slavery. A minority of slaves might be kept under; but a large majority—and that made up of the races to which the world owes its progress—Madison realized would not long submit to the galling yoke. Accordingly, he descried in the not distant future a serious conflict between the class with and the class without property; the fated collapse of the system of suffrage he had helped to rear; and, consequently, the distinct outlines of a grave national problem.

The solution of this problem, which presented itself to Madison in the guise of a question of suffrage, involved, however, the economic question: What should be done with that unfavored class, who toiling in hopeless poverty—slaves in fact, if not in name—would constitute the majority of the body social? This question Madison proposed, but vainly labored to find in the various methods of checks and balances an answer that was either adequate to the threatened emergency, or satisfactory to his judgment. To exclude the class without property from the right of suffrage he promptly rejected, as no republican government could be expected to endure that rested upon a portion of the society having a numerical and physical force excluded from and liable to be turned against it, unless kept down by a standing military force fatal to all parties. To confine the right of suffrage for one branch of the legislature to those with, and for the other branch to those without property, he likewise set aside as a regulation calculated to lay the foundation for contests and antipathies not dissimilar to those between the patricians and plebians at Rome. And again, he shrewdly detected dangers lurking in a mixture of the two classes in both branches.

Thus the question of the suffrage brought Madison unconsciously face to face with the social question. His talent saved him from falling into a reactionary plan, or even resorting to a temporary make-shift; but likewise did the limitations of his age prevent him from hitting upon the scheme which alone could solve both the problem that preoccupied him, and the graver one into which his spirit had projected. He gave the matter over; but not without first bestowing upon it a parting flash of genius by the significant avowal that the impending social changes would necessitate a proportionate change in the institutions and laws of the country, and would bespeak all the wisdom of the wisest patriot.

Karl Marx stops in the midst of his analysis of the law of values to render tribute to the genius of Aristotle for discovering in the expression of the value of commodities the central truth of political economy which only the peculiar system of society in which he lived prevented him from accepting and carrying to its logical conclusion. How much more brilliant and deserving of tribute the genius of Madison that enabled him to take so long a look ahead; calculate with such nicety the results of political and economic forces; foresee with such accuracy the great coming problem of our country, and state it with such clearness; weigh with such breadth of judgement the methods known to him in order to meet and solve it, and discard them one after the other with so much acumen; rise to such height of statesmanship by boldly declaring the problem could be dealt with in no way other than by adapting the laws and institutions of the country to the social changes that may take place; and, finally, commend the task to, and invoke for its performance, the wisdom of the future patriot!

That the wisdom of the Revolutionary Fathers and their teachings are not lost upon their successors, the appearance and growth of the Nationalist movement demonstrate. The voice of Madison has reached our generation. The patriots in the revolution now impending and equally important with that of a hundred years ago will be on hand.

Notes

1. The centennial sermon of Bishop Potter is the latest, most notable, and curious instance of this new departure. [For a transcript of Potter's address, delivered at the New York City celebration of the 100th anniversary of George Washington's inauguration as the first president of the United States, see the *New York Times*, 1 May 1889, p. 9.—EDS.].
2. Even as late as the year 1829, a majority of the people in the United States were property-holders, or the heirs and aspirants of property.
3. It should be noted that in this reasoning Madison altogether leaves out of his calculation the additional cause of immigration. Without this cause, a cause to

which our so-called statisticians love to turn with predilection, Madison justly arrives at the conclusion upon which the present social movement rests, and from which it starts.

4. It does not necessarily follow from this that a blunder was committed by the Revolutionary Fathers. History seems to show that the competitive stage is a requisite step in the evolution of society. But whether this be so or not, today the competitive system is only productive of mischief.

14. Social Forces and the Constitution

Algie Simons

Algie Simons (1870–1950) was a founder of the Socialist Party of America and editor of the *International Socialist Review*. He later split with the party by endorsing U.S. involvement in World War I. He translated works by the German socialists Karl Kautsky and Werner Sombart and wrote the pamphlets *The American Farmer* (1902) and *Class Struggles in America* (1903). The latter was later expanded into *Social Forces in American History* (1911).

The following selection is excerpted from *Social Forces in American History*. (New York: Macmillan, 1911), 81–93 and 99.

Formation of the Government

The surrender of Cornwallis in America was followed by a Whig victory in Parliament. On the 27th of February, 1782, this resolution was carried in the House of Commons:—

"That it is the opinion of this House that a further prosecution of offensive war against America would, under present circumstances, be the means of weakening the efforts of this country against her European enemies, and tend to increase the mutual enmity so fatal to the interests both of Great Britain and America."

One month later the Tory ministry fell, and the English allies of the American army came into power in the home country. In some ways the English Whigs were more consistent and more revolutionary than those who had fought under the Continental flag. They curbed the power of the king and the House of Lords, made the House of Commons supreme, and laid the foundations for a much more truly democratic government than this country has yet enjoyed. One reason for this is to be found in the existence in England of a powerful landed interest which was in such sharp antagonism to the rising industrial capitalists that the latter felt keenly the need of continuous curbing of their opponents.

No such condition existed in America. Here the antagonism of classes was rather between the industrial and mercantile creditors on the coast and the farmer debtors of the interior. These latter were apt to make an alliance with the wageworkers of the larger cities, although these were too little developed to play an important part. Consequently the richer class in the colonies did not feel the need of any democratic measures in order to secure allies from the poorer classes in a fight against a crown and landed nobility, as was the case in England.

We see the effect of this condition in the character of the state governments formed during the Revolution. Practically all of these were supposed to be modeled after the British government. But there was an important difference. Since the colonists had left England the crown and the House of Lords had ceased to hold a dominant position in the English government, and their importance was decreased still further by the parliamentary conflict which was being waged simultaneously with the Revolutionary War in America.

In the state governments which were formed during the war to take the place of the old colonial establishments, the second chamber, corresponding to the House of Lords, was given equal power with the lower House. Moreover, this upper House, instead of being representative of a particular form of property relation, and that a declining one, was made representative of property alone, through very high property requirements for membership and suffrage. Property qualifications for voting were characteristic of all the state constitutions adopted during the Revolution, with the single exception of Pennsylvania. This would seem to show that all the fine talk about the rights of men and "taxation without representation" and "all men are created equal" was intended only to secure popular support with which to pull some very hot chestnuts out of the fire for the ruling class of the colonies.

The nature of these state governments gives an idea of the political forms desired by ruling class interests at the time of the Revolution. The national government was too filmy a thing to tell any story clearly. And yet it is possible that this very indefiniteness tells an equally clear story, for it corresponded very closely to the lack of a general industrial life. There were very few interests common to all the colonies, and these few were not of a kind to overcome the immediate separatist ones.

At the outbreak of the war there was, of course, no central government.

For the revolutionary forces its place was taken by the conspiratory "Committees of Correspondence." From these sprang the "Continental Congress," which took to itself more and more power as the Revolution continued. [1]

It was this body that controlled the movements of the army, gave Washington his commission, declared independence, made alliances with France, Spain, and Holland, borrowed money and pledged the credit of the combined colonies for its repayment, issued an inconvertible currency, granted letters of marque and reprisal, built a navy, and carried on peace negotiations when the war was ended. Yet this body had no legal existence, no definite powers, none of the things which are supposed to be the essential foundation of a legislative body until the war was over, its important work completed, and its life about to end. The Articles of Confederation, which for the first time provided these things, were not adopted by the various states until 1781, and by that time the Continental Congress, to which those articles for the first time gave a legal sanction, had ceased to play any important function.

Just as the Confederation was born, however, it was saved from the calamity of complete insignificance by being made a property holder. One of the obstacles to all efforts looking toward even so loose a union as that of the Confederation had been the possession by several of the states of great tracts of western land. This land was claimed under old royal grants, all of which were drawn before anything was known about the internal geography of the country, and several of which read "from sea to sea." Some of the smaller states, Maryland in particular, insisted that these lands must be surrendered as a prelude to any plan of confederation. This was at last agreed to, and Maryland made possible the formation of the Confederation in 1781. This action ultimately assured the existence of a national government. The Confederation now had a territory to govern outside the boundaries of the federated states. This territory, although thinly populated, was almost as large as all the thirteen original states. Finally, when Manasseh Cutler appeared before the Continental Congress with a proposition to purchase large tracts of this land, and it began to appear not simply in the light of a territory to be governed, but also as a source of income, Congress roused from its lethargy to almost its only important action since it had been legally constituted, — the passing of the [Northwest] Ordinance of 1787.

This ordinance providing for the organization and government of the great territory between the Ohio, the Mississippi, the Great Lakes, and the Alleghenies contains some remarkable provisions. There is, of course, the famous one upon which the thirteenth amendment to the national Constitution was afterward based, providing that "There shall be neither slavery nor involuntary servitude in the said territory, otherwise than in the punishment of crimes, whereof the party shall have been duly convicted." But there is also a complete "bill of rights," providing for religious liberty, the right of *habeas corpus*, and trial by jury, representative government, bail for all save capital offenses, moderate fines, no cruel and unusual punishments, and also for the foundation of a public school system. This latter provision was to be little heeded until a movement of the working class should force this issue upon the people. These provisions, however, when contrasted with the proceedings of the constitutional convention, show that the Continental Congress had become much more of a popular body than was the one that wrote the present fundamental law of the United States.

During the time of the Revolution, in spite of this one very important action by the Continental Congress, the real governing power in the country had been the group of individuals who were in the midst of events and were making history rather than recording its results in legislation. These were the men who best incarnated the spirit of the rising social class. They were willing that the work of legislation, like the work of fighting in the ranks, should be done by others, providing their hands were upon the levers that moved the social machinery. [2]

The American Revolution, like most wars, was fought by those who had least interest in its outcome. The workers and "embattled farmers," who as "minute men" at Concord "fired the shot heard round the world," and left the imprint of their bleeding feet at Valley Forge and Yorktown, found themselves at the close of the war hopelessly indebted to the mercantile and financial class of the coast cities. The Continental currency, with which the government had paid for supplies, had now become valueless in the hands of the producers of wealth. One hundred and twelve million dollars had been thus extorted from the people. Taxes were most inequitably distributed, the poll tax being one of the most common methods of taxation. In Massachusetts it was proposed to collect over five million dollars by this method from 90,000 taxpayers. The fisheries were almost wiped out during the war and only slowly revived with the coming of peace. [3] McMaster says of Vermont: "One half of the community was totally bankrupt, the other half plunged in the depths of poverty." Of another state he says: "It was then the fashion of New Hampshire, as indeed it was everywhere, to lock men up in jail the moment they were so unfortunate as to owe their fellows a sixpence or shilling. Had this law been rigorously executed in the autumn of 1785, it is probable that not far from two thirds of the community would have been in the prisons."

The burden of debt had been multiplied by the depreciation of currency, and the attempt to collect it in specie. To again quote McMaster: "Civil actions were multiplied to a degree that seems scarcely credible. The lawyers were overwhelmed with cases. The courts could not try half that came before them."[4]

The wealthy citizens who had sent their money to war that it might breed and multiply found their bonds would be of little value unless taxes could be squeezed from the workers. The Confederacy had no power to levy taxes, or to collect money in any way save by the sale of lands and bonds and the issuance of paper money. There were no purchasers for any of these commodities.

The manufacturers who had revolted against British tariffs were now looking for a national government to assist them with tariff legislation. The Revolution, by almost completely stopping importations, had acted on the budding manufacturers like a prohibitive tariff. Moreover, the exigencies of war created an abnormal demand for certain articles, and the Continental Congress devoted no small portion of its energies to efforts to encourage domestic manufactures. The moment the war ended, on the other hand, there was a flood of importations. British manufacturers, especially, were accused of "dumping" goods upon the market at less than London prices for the especial purpose of preventing the growth of American manufactures. We are not surprised to learn that "By no class of the community was the formation of the new government, and its general adoption by the states, more zealously urged than by the friends of American manufactures."[5]

The paramount interest of the time was commercial, and it was fitting that commerce should play the largest part in the formation of the new government. Commerce demanded a powerful central government. No other could afford protection in foreign ports, provide for uniform regulations throughout the country, make and enforce commercial treaties, and maintain the general conditions essential to profitable trading. As Fisher Ames said in the first Congress:—

"I conceive, sir, that the present constitution was dictated by commercial necessity, more than any other cause. The want of an efficient government to secure the manufacturing interests, and to advance our commerce, was long seen by men of judgment, and pointed out by patriots solicitous to promote the general welfare."[6]

All of these interests were confined to the New England and Middle states. Unless a class could be found in the South that was also interested in a centralized government, there could be little hope of forming a union. In the North the farmers were opposed to a central government and the merchants were its friends. In the South the reverse was true. There the great planters, who were the social rulers, favored the formation of the union. The explanation of this is found in the fact that the planters of the South did their own exporting, but did it through English merchants. The latter were driving a profitable trade through their control of importations and the channels of export. The merchants were growing rich and the planters poor. The latter saw a possibility of relief in an internal commerce and in the development of domestic shipping with the opening of the West Indian trade through commercial treaties. [7]

To collect debts, public and private, to levy a tariff for the benefit of "infant industries," to protect the fisheries and pay bounties to the fishers, to assist the Southern planter in marketing his crops, and to secure commercial treaties and guard commercial interests in all parts of the world a centralized government was needed. Those who desired such a government were, numerically speaking, an insignificant minority of the population, but, once more, they were the class whose interests were bound up with progress toward a higher social stage. In advancing their interests this wealthy class of planters, merchants, and manufacturers was really building for future progress.

The wageworking, farming, and debtor class naturally had no desire for a strong central government. These desired above all relief from the crushing burden of debt. They sought this relief in new issues of paper money, in "stay laws" postponing the collection of debts, and in restrictions on the powers of the courts. In regard to government they cried out for economy and low taxes. The ever recurring populistic feud between frontier debtors and coast creditors made its appearance. The former were in an overwhelming majority, but they lacked cohesion, collective energy, and intelligence, — in short, class consciousness.

It was in Massachusetts that the struggle became especially violent. The populistic debtors elected a legislature pledged to carry out their program. When the legislature met, influences were brought to bear upon it by the creditor class of Boston that caused its members to break their pledges. Angered at this anarchistic defeat of the popular will, the farmers began to defy and intimidate the courts. As almost invariably happens, when a working class rises, collectivist ideas found expression. General Knox, then Secretary of War, who was sent by the Continental Congress to investigate the situation, reported that

"Their creed is that the property of the United States has been protected from the confiscation of Britain by the joint exertions of all, and therefore ought to be the common property of all."[8]

When the courts attempted to force the collection of debts from those who had nothing, the desperate debtors rallied to arms under the leadership of Daniel Shays, a veteran of the Revolution, and captured some of the smaller cities. Although there was no money in the treasury of Massachusetts with which to carry on the functions of government, yet the militia was called out to shoot down these starving veterans of the Revolution, and the wealthy merchants and bankers of Boston advanced the money with which to pay the troops. [9]

There was a similar situation in Rhode Island, with the difference that in this state the debtors were able to seize the legislature and force it to do their will. The result was something very like civil war, with the debtors trying to force their creditors to accept the paper money that had been issued. Here, also, we find the collectivist idea, coupled with a crude sort of state socialism which, as populism, became familiar on the western prairies more than a century later.

"A convention of all the towns in Providence county met at Smithfield to consult upon further measures of hostility toward the merchants, whom they accused of exporting specie, and thus causing the distresses of the State. A plan of 'State trade' was proposed, to be submitted to the General Assembly, and the Governor was requested to call a special session for that purpose. The plan was for the State to provide vessels and import goods on its own account, under direction of a committee of the legislature; that produce, lumber, and labor, as well as money, should be received in payment of taxes, and thus furnish cargoes in return for which specie and goods could be obtained. Interest certificates were no longer to be received in payment of duties, but the private importers were to be compelled to pay them in money. The act making notes of hand negotiable was to be repealed, and the statute of limitation shortened to two years."[10]

These uprisings gave the final jar that was necessary to solidify the forces working for a national government. Until the threat arose of the capture of two or more states by the masses, there were many even of the wealthy classes who were inclined to think that their interests might be best furthered by several separate states.

"But the rebellion of Shays broke out. In an instant public opinion changed completely. Stern patriots, who, while all went well, talked of the dangers of baneful aristocracies, soon learned to talk of the dangers of baneful democracies."[11]

There are few things more striking than this complete change of front by the budding capitalists of Revolutionary times in obedience to material class interests. In 1776 they were all for paper money, restriction of the power of the courts, "natural rights," and the whole string of democratic principles. By 1786 they had rejected all these principles and were defending most of the positions of the English government of King George, while the prerevolutionary principles were left for debt-ridden farmers and workingmen. It is at least interesting to learn that the ruling class had even the same demagogues to secure popular support, and that Sam Adams was now an ardent defender of the creditor class. [12]

The framing of the Constitution under these conditions took on much of the character of a secret conspiratory *coup d'état*, such as most historians congratulate America on having escaped. The little group of individuals who best represented the ruling class, and who had dominated throughout the Revolution, were, to a large extent, losing their control. They now set about recapturing it through a secret counter-revolution.

. . . To sum up: the organic law of this nation was formulated in secret session by a body called into existence through a conspiratory trick, and was forced upon a disfranchised people by means of a dishonest apportionment in order that the interests of a small body of wealthy rulers might be served. This should not blind us to the fact that this small ruling class really represented progress, that a unified government was essential to that industrial and social growth which has made this country possible. It also should not blind us to the fact that there was nothing particularly sacred about the origin of this government which should render any attempt to change it sacrilegious.

Notes

1. John Fiske, *The Critical Period of American History* (Boston: Houghton, 1888), pp. 92–93.
2. Woodrow Wilson, *History of the American People*, Vol. III (New York: Harper

and Brothers, 1902–1908), p. 22: "The common affairs of the country had therefore to be conducted as the revolution had in fact been conducted, — not by the authority or the resolutions of the Congress, but by the extraordinary activity, enterprise, and influence of a few of the leading men in the States who had union and harmonious common effort at heart."

3. *American State Papers: Documents, Legislative and Executive, of the Congress of the United States*, Vol. I: *Commerce and Navigation* (Washington: Gales and Seaton, 1832–1861), pp. 6–21.

4. John Bach McMaster, *History of the People of the United States*, Vol. I (New York: Appleton, 1883–1900), p. 302.

5. James Leander Bishop, *History of American Manufactures*, Vol. I (Philadelphia: Young, 1867), p. 422.

6. *Annals of Congress*, Vol. I (Washington: Gales and Seaton, 1834–1856), p. 230. See also William Thomas Davis, ed., *Professional and Industrial History of Suffolk County, Massachusetts*, Vol. II (Boston: Boston History Company, 1894), p. 84; and William Clarence Webster, A *General History of Commerce* (Boston: Ginn, 1903), p. 341.

7. McMaster, *History of the People of the United States*, Vol. I, pp. 272–273.

8. Washington Irving, *Life of Washington*, Vol. IV (New York: Putnam, 1855–1859), p. 451.

9. McMaster, *History of the People of the United States*, Vol. I, pp. 318–319; George Richards Minot, *History of the Insurrection in Massachusetts in 1786*, 2d ed. (Boston: Burdett, 1810).

10. Samuel Greene Arnold, *History of the State of Rhode Island and Providence Plantations, 1636–1790*, Vol. II (New York: Appleton, 1859–1860), p. 524.

11. McMaster, *History of the People of the United States*, Vol. I, p. 391.

12. James Kendall Hosmer, *Sam Adams, The Man of the Town Meeting* (Baltimore: Johns Hopkins University, 1884), p. 51.

15. The Founding Finaglers

Gustavus Myers

Gustavus Myers (1872–1964), an independent socialist and one of the original muckrakers, is best known as the author of *History of the Great American Fortunes* (1910; rev. ed. 1936). Other works include *History of Tammany Hall* (1901), *History of Canadian Wealth* (1914), *The History of American Idealism* (1925), *The Ending of Hereditary American Fortunes* (1939), and *History of Bigotry in the United States* (1943).

The following selection, from a chapter originally entitled "The Real Forces of the Revolution and the Drafters of the Constitution," is excerpted by permission from *History of the Supreme Court of the United States* (Chicago: Charles H. Kerr, 1912), 129–34.

Constitutional Convention Held in Secrecy

With an understanding of the facts, both retrospective and anticipatory, herein presented, no explanation is needed as to why it was that the Federal Constitutional Convention held its deliberations and proceedings behind locked doors, as Luther Martin, Attorney-General of Maryland and a delegate to the Convention, indignantly reported to the Maryland Legislature. No delegate, Martin wrote, was allowed to correspond with his constituents; taking of notes was permitted only by special consent; the utmost precautions were exercised to prevent the debates and acts from reaching the public.

"So solicitous," wrote Martin, "were they that their proceedings should not transpire, that the members were prohibited even from taking copies of resolutions, on which the Convention was deliberating, or extracts from any of the journals, without formally moving for, and obtaining permission, by a vote of the convention for that purpose."[1]

Here was the epochal spectacle of a Constitutional Convention delegated in solemn meeting apparently to establish a Republican democracy, yet not daring to trust the very people for whom the Republic was theoretically founded with any knowledge of its proceedings. Not until long after were the debates published. It was not that the delegates lacked trust in the intelligence of the people; they feared the results if their betrayal of the popular demands should become known.

When they did become known, after the Federal Convention had adopted the Constitution, and before the different States had taken action, there was a blaze of popular anger. The various eminent delegates whose handiwork it was hastened to exert every possible influence to bring about its adoption by the State Conventions: Gorham and Gerry in Massachusetts; Wilson, Robert Morris and McKean in Pennsylvania; Washington in Virginia; Daniel Carroll and Samuel Chase in Maryland; William Livingston and Jonathan Dayton in New Jersey; and Livingston's son-in-law, John Jay, and Alexander Hamilton in New York. In Delaware and Pennsylvania John Dickinson, a member of the Federal Constitutional Convention, was energetic for the adoption of that instrument; Dickinson had inherited the vast estate of "Crosia—dore," granted to Walter Dickinson in 1659; he had represented the Penn Proprietors and had obtained for them $580,000 during the Revolution when their land was declared forfeited; and he had been President of the Supreme Council of Pennsylvania. In Connecticut Oliver Ellsworth argued stoutly for the Constitution; the presiding officer of the Connecticut Convention which ratified the Constitution was Matthew Griswold, who had inherited a baronial estate in that colony, and was a man of great wealth. But it is quite needless to enumerate other examples.

In the Pennsylvania Convention Wilson appeared as the principal defender of the Constitution; he admitted that the popular view of that instrument was that it was designed to perpetuate the powers of the aristocracy, and he devoted his arguments to attempting to counteract that belief. . . .

These men held constant secret conclaves, or corresponded regularly; they issued essays and publications filled with alluring arguments to influence the public mind. During the publication of the *Federalist*, the work so largely of Hamilton and Jay, the workingmen of New York City showed their feelings by a street demonstration. In trying with Hamilton to quell it, Jay so exasperated his auditors that a stone was hurled at him striking him on the head; he was left for dead but recovered.

All the great power of the land magnates was used to avert the threatened danger of the Constitution being rejected. The Livingstons, Van Rennselaers and Schuylers in New York; the Carrolls—the largest landowners in Maryland, and estimated one of the very richest families in the country—these, and all the rest of the landed class combined to beat into line such antagonistic dependents as there were of every stripe—lawyers, clergy, college professors, tradesmen, workers and newspaper editors.

The banks controlled by Hamilton, Wilson, Robert Morris, Gouverneur Morris and other delegates[2] exercised the most effective influence upon tradesmen by the threat of withdrawing credit or by harassing them should they fail to support the adoption of the Constitution.[3]

Whom the Constitution Pleased

These methods succeeded throughout the colonies. Writing from New York to Livingston, January 14, 1788, as to the pending question of whether the Constitution was likely to be adopted in Massachusetts, General Henry Knox wrote that "the commercial part of the State, to which are added all the men of considerable property, the clergy, the lawyers, including all of the officers of the late army, and also all the neighborhood of all the great towns" favored its adoption. "Perhaps," added Knox, "many of them would have been still more pleased with the new Constitution, had it been more analogous to the British Constitution."[4]

On the other hand, there were not lacking exponents of the popular hostility; one of these, writing under the name of "Brutus," expressed the opposing view. Pointing out that "the farmer, merchant, mechanic and other various orders of the people ought to be represented [in Congress] according to their respective weight and numbers," he went on:

"According to the common course of human affairs, the natural aristocracy of the country will be elected. Wealth always creates influence, and this is generally increased in large family connections; this class in society will forever have a great number of dependents; besides they will always favor each other. It is to their interest to combine—they will therefore constantly unite their efforts to procure men of their own rank to be elected. . . . It is probable that few of the merchants, and those of the most opulent and ambitious, will have a representation from their body. . . . The great body of the yeomen [the small farmers] of the country cannot expect any of their order in this assembly. . . . The mechanics of every branch must expect to be excluded from a seat in this body; . . . so that in reality there will be no part of the people represented but the rich, even in that branch of the Legislature called democratic. The well-born, and highest orders in life, as they term themselves, will be ignorant of the sentiments of the middling class," etc., etc. The representation, continued the paper, "is merely nominal—a mere burlesque, and that no security is provided against corruption and undue influence."[5]

Of the whole Constitution the people at large were suspicious to a degree little comprehended now. They saw that it was the product of a convention composed mostly of manorial lords or their attorneys and mouthpieces. They feared that the so-called democratic representation in Congress would resolve itself into a continuation of the old rule by the great land owners and traders; and that they were right events quickly proved.

But what especially aroused fears was the judiciary. During the Revolution only one of the royal judges in Massachusetts, for example, had espoused the popular cause, and this particular one—Cushing—did not do so until he was virtually compelled to give an expression of opinion; he then became one of the most stalwart and time-serving of the band of reactionaries. During more than a century the judges had acted arrogantly and often corruptly; they had usurped powers never granted to them, and had assumed the right to void laws as much as they pleased. In the Revolutionary period some judges were attacked by armed bodies of indignant patriots outraged by the actions of those judicial reactionaries. The people had long seen the landholders or their retainers put on the bench; and then, by the expedient of irresponsible judicial construction, those judges had validated titles obtained by fraud and corruption.

The greatest popular bitterness manifested itself against the courts. This feeling, grounded on the experience of centuries of oppression, was not to be allayed by smooth explanations on the part of the advocates of the Constitution. Of this popular sentiment the makers of the Constitution were fully aware. By adroitly dwelling upon the principle of representation in Congress, and by arguing and counter-arguing about it, and emphasizing it, those advocates succeeded, to a considerable extent, in diverting the popular mind from the tremendous potential power that the Constitution had lodged in a small, omnipotent body, appointed for life. This handful of judicial rulers was the Supreme Court of the United States.

Notes

1. Jonathan Elliot, ed., *The Debates in the Several State Conventions on the Adoption of the Federal Constitution*, Vol. I (Philadelphia: J. B. Lippincott, 1881), p. 345.
2. The history of these banks is given in Chap. IV [of Gustavus Myers' *History of the Supreme Court*].
3. It should not be imagined that elections then were "pure and undefiled." Far from it. The buying of votes in New York was an old story. And as far back as March 11, 1752, the Legislature of Pennsylvania had passed an act "for the prevention of bribery and corruption in the election of Sheriffs and coroners within this province." *Laws of the Commonwealth of Pennsylvania*, Vol. I (Philadelphia: Carey and Bioren, 1803), p. 328.
4. *Debates and Proceedings in the Convention of the Commonwealth of Massachusetts* (Boston: W. White, 1856), p. 399. Gen. Knox's wife, it may be said, had inherited a large share of the great Waldo estate, in what is now the State of Maine.
5. Brutus, Essay III, *Ibid.*, pp. 389–391.

16. The People's Two Bodies:
The Declaration and the Constitution

Sheldon S. Wolin

Sheldon S. Wolin, professor of political science at Princeton University, is the author of *Politics and Vision: Continuity and Innovation in Western Political Thought* (1960), *Hobbes and the Epic Tradition of Political Thought* (1970), and *The Presence of the Past: State and Constitution in America* (1989), editor of the radical democratic quarterly *democracy: A Journal of Political Renewal and Radical Change* (1981–1983), and coeditor of *The Berkeley Student Revolt* (1965).

The following selection is excerpted by permission from an essay originally entitled "The People's Two Bodies," *democracy* 1 (January 1981): 11–19.

The current crisis is widely proclaimed to be a crisis of governmental power, but it may be wider and deeper than that. To ask, what have we become? we must first ask, what kind of people did we conceive ourselves to be?

Our starting point is the eighteenth century, when the sovereign position of monarchs was challenged by revolutionary movements and when, in some countries, the sovereignty of the people was proclaimed and the political theories of the day began to refer to "the body of the people." I want to suggest that in the American political tradition, the people has had two "bodies," with each standing for a different conception of collective identity, of power, and of the terms of power. In one of these bodies the people was conceived to be politically active, while in the other it was essentially, though not entirely, passive. The one collectivity was political and democratic and can be called a body politic; the other was primarily economic and intentionally antidemocratic and it can be called a political economy. Each of these bodies has a long tradition of theory and practice.

The classic statement of the body politic was the Declaration of Independence, its charter, the Articles of Confederation. The conception of political economy is more composite: the Constitution, *The Federalist* papers, and Hamilton's great state papers dealing with finance, manufacturing, and the interpretation of the powers of the national government. The first American body politic was formed by the revolution of 1776, the second by the ratification of the Constitution.

On the first: revolution is the most radical action that a people can undertake collectively. Revolution means rejecting an established mode of authority, withdrawing the power that flows to it, and snapping the continuity between past and future. The gravity of the act requires a people to ask themselves who they are as a collectivity, what justifies the destruction of their prior identity, and who they hope to become by reconstituting themselves.

The greatness of the Declaration of Independence was its sensitivity to these questions and its attempt to capture a new and emergent identity. For about ten years the colonists had been arguing and protesting about their status within the British Empire. The Declaration caught and preserved the moment when Americans renounced their status as colonial dependents who were required to accept and obey a system of political authority over which they exerted little control and in which they did not directly participate. In the words of the Declaration, the revolutionaries had determined "to dissolve the political bands which . . . connected them" with the mother country, and "to assume among the powers of the earth the separate and equal station to which the laws of nature and of nature's God entitle them." The Declaration conceived of a new kind of political being, not the colonial subject of an empire, or even the "citizen," who demanded "the rights of Englishmen" and especially the right not to be taxed by some distant authority. ". . . All men are created equal . . . with certain unalienable rights. . . . to secure these rights, governments are instituted among men, deriving their just powers from the consent of the governed. . . ." The new conception went beyond even Aristotle's political man, who knew how to rule and be ruled in turn. The Declaration envisaged a being who would not just participate in politics, but would join in actually creating a new political identity, to "institute," "alter," or "abolish" governments, to lay a "foundation" and to organize power. The "self-evident truths" of the Declaration were not, as later generations often assumed, abstract and ideal constructions with no basis in experience, but a recapitulation of nearly one hundred years of practice. Not only had the colonists been practicing something close to self-government for over a century before the revolution, but in the years immediately preceding its outbreak they had telescoped and compressed that experience in novel ways. About two years before the Declaration, the committees of correspondence and the Continental Congress had been invented to coordinate the resistance of the colonies, and in May of 1776, the Congress instructed the colonial assemblies to undertake the one political act that alone compares in significance to the act of revolution: the founding of new governments that would "best conduce to the happiness and safety of their constituents. . . ."

The Declaration summarized a political identity in the making, one that stretched back to the Mayflower compact and to seventeenth-century ideas about political and religious associations as voluntary unions. That identity was perpetuated and strengthened in the eighteenth century by two profound political experiences, those of revolutionary struggle and of the construction of new political orders. Both experiences were experiences of action, of ordinary people acting together to order their common existence. Thus the Declaration had a profoundly political conception of collective identity and a profoundly democratic conception of power; power was grounded in the deliberations of the governed and exercised within a structure that had been democratically organized.

Throughout most of the 1780s, the states operated under the loose system of authority set up by the Articles of Confederation. Save for certain powers relating to war and diplomacy, the Confederation clearly favored a decentralized condition in which the states were the major political entities. It represented a widespread belief that democracy and equality had an appropriate scale. The political discourse of the day was full of references to the affection and loyalty commanded by the states and towns. From reading these documents, it is apparent that the colonists recognized that democracy depended upon making political experience—the true basis of equality—accessible to all.

The conception of the body politic as participatory, democratic, and egalitarian did not mean that economic relations were ignored. The emphasis upon political participation was directly related to the great economic controversies of the 1770s and 1780s concerning debtor laws, paper money, interest rates, and taxes. Those who formed the body politic and opposed the new Constitution tended to be small farmers who suffered from shortages of money and credit, and hence were frequently in debt. They believed that it was natural and desirable for their government to "interfere" in the economy. The economy was not a sacred object, but a set of relationships that might have to be amended when the good of the members required it.

All of the notions of a body politic were challenged throughout the 1780s by a gathering movement among the higher social classes and the more powerful economic interests. It produced the Constitution, with its very different conception of collectivity and power. The framers of the Constitution made no secret of the fact that representative government was designed, as Madison put it, "to preserve the spirit and form of popular government" but to take away its substance, so that an "unjust and interested majority" could not invade the rights and freedom of the propertied classes.[1] The new Constitution aimed to reverse the direction of the country, to set it against the democratic and participatory politics flourishing in the states. This was to be accomplished by two wide-sweeping changes. One was to construct a national government that would be based on the principle of representation instead of on democracy. Except for the House of Representatives, no officer of the new government would be directly elected by the people. "We the people" were acclaimed as "the pure original foundation of all legitimate authority" (Hamilton),[2] but this was a formula to give the Constitution a legitimate basis, not to encourage an active citizenry.

The second change was aimed at breaking the power of the states where the democratic tradition of the body politic had taken hold. The Constitution created a centralized system of government with strong powers to tax, regulate, legislate, and coerce citizens who, hitherto, had been the objects of the state legislatures. Thus the citizen was placed in an entirely new set of relationships—with a government that was almost as remote as the British Parliament. At the same time, the state governments, to which the citizen stood closest, were forced to surrender or share many of the powers they had exercised during the era of the Articles of Confederation—powers over currency, commerce, and taxes.

Hamilton saw that the new Constitution would take hold only if it were able to attract the loyalties of citizens away from their state governments and local institutions and change democratic citizens into beings disposed to render "a due obedience to [the federal government's] authority."[3] The transformation of the citizenry would come about, he reasoned, if the activities of the national government were to penetrate the states and localities so as to become part of "the common occurrences of . . . political life." The role of a strong state would be to promote, regulate, and protect the economic interests crucial to state power—manufacturing, commerce, banking, and agriculture—"those objects which touch the most sensible chords and put into motion the most active springs of the human heart. . . ." In appealing to self-interest and economic motives, Hamilton hoped to promote a new set of civic dispositions that would strengthen "the authority of the Union and the affections of the citizens towards it."[4]

The nature of these "dispositions"—Hamilton himself used the word—and their potential for producing power were associated by Hamilton with the division of labor and specialization. "The results of human exertion," he observed,

may be immensely increased by diversifying its objects. When all the different kinds of industry obtain in a community, each individual can find his proper element, and can call into activity the whole vigor of his nature. And the community is benefitted by the services of its respective members in the manner in which each can serve it with most effect.[5]

These dispositions ran squarely against the ones incorporated into the Declaration's conception of a body politic, for the "community" that he conjured up was not an association of equals or of sharers. By "diversifying" the "objects" set before man, the division of labor encouraged "the diversity of talents and dispositions which discriminate men from each other." While it could be claimed that human potentialities were thus being encouraged, there is no doubt that this was not Hamilton's main aim. "The addition of a new energy to the general stock of effort" had as its end "the wealth of a nation,"[6] that is, the foundation of the material basis of national power. Hamilton's concern with the human dispositions that generate power was part of a larger strategy to make economic activity the basis of political order. "The possession" of the "means of subsistence, habitation, clothing, and defense" is, he wrote,

necessary to the perfection of the body politic, to the safety as well as to the welfare of the society; the want of either is the want of an important organ of political life and motion. . . .[7]

The strategy was based on two assumptions, that the collectivity was symbolized in the state, not in the citizenry, and that state power was derived from the structure of the economy.[8] A political economy, in which the state would be grounded in economic relationships and act mainly through its administrative branch, was to be promoted by a system of subsidies and incentives. This vision was later incorporated into Hamilton's program for the national government to assume the war debts of the states, to establish a national bank ("a political machine of the greatest importance to the state"),[9] and to encourage "infant" industries. The dynamics of economic growth that would be unleashed by encouraging self-interest was expected to produce "the momentum of civil power necessary to . . . a great empire."[10]

The emphasis upon the capacity of the new national political economy to generate great power was not an incidental consideration, but was central to a bold conception of the Constitution that envisaged a political society that would stretch from the Atlantic coast far into the unexplored westward regions. "Civil power properly organized and exerted is capable of diffusing its force to a very great extent; and can in a manner reproduce itself in every part of a great empire . . ." (Hamilton).[11] The founders clearly understood that a large, expanding state was inconsistent with a participatory body politic, but they knew as well that there had to be concessions to the democratic tradition of "free government," in which, as one of its anti-Federalist defenders put it, "the people is the sovereign and their sense or opinion is the criterion of every public measure."[12] They opted for a representative government because, as a system capable of being extended almost indefinitely, it fitted more snugly with an economy that was conceived in dynamic terms. At the same time, westward expansion was expected to dilute political passions and to frustrate popular political action. Enlarging the scope would increase the number of competing interests and thereby make it difficult for a majority will to form among such a widely scattered people. "Extend the sphere and . . . you make it less probable that a majority of the whole will . . . discover their own strength and act in unison with each other."[13] Thus the aim of the Federalists was not only to found a strong state, but also to depoliticize the people. They posed a choice to Americans between "pure democracy," in which "a small number of citizens . . . assemble and administer the Government in person," and an extended republic, in which there was "the delegation of the Government . . . to a small number of citizens elected by the rest."[14] The choice was between participatory democracy, with its inherent inability to generate sufficient power—a vision of America that Hamilton ridiculed as "an infinity of little, jealous, clashing, tumultuous commonwealths, the wretched nurseries of unceasing discord . . ."[15]—and, on the other hand, a powerful republic, "one great American system, superior to the control of all trans-atlantic forces or influence, and able to dictate the terms of the connection between the old and the new world."[16]

The two bodies coexisted throughout the nineteenth century. The democratic and participatory body politic found expression at the local levels—in the westward movement that saw Americans founding communities along the way and improvising political forms to meet their needs, and in the great Populist movements of farmers and workers after the Civil War. But it was the political economy that displayed the greater vitality. Its political component, the state, became more centralized and acquired a professional bureaucracy. Under the pressures of the world wars of the twentieth century and the Great Depression, the American state grew in size, power, and functions. Its economic basis radically changed in nature, evolving from a society of small-scale producers and small farmers into an integrated economy dominated by large corporations and monopolies and characterized by the concentration of economic wealth and power in a small number of giant firms. Despite ritual conflicts between "government and business," the union of the polity and the economy became ever tighter, as the antidemocratic, antipolitical implications of the terms of power under this form of collectivity became clearer. . . .

These enlarged notions of the scope of American power signified the end of the Hamiltonian political economy with its vision of a powerful and autonomous nation-state grounded in a national economy and preoccupied with the development of its own territory. The new age would see the imperial state attempt to derive its power from and to assert its mastery over an international economy. That change would undermine the political settlement established by the original Constitution of the Federalists. The institutions of representative government, including the party system that was developed to lend plausibility to the legitimation process of popular elections, would weaken and decline. The successors to Hamilton would take his case one step further. While careful to continue his tirade against democracy for arousing unrealistic expectations among ordinary people and for encouraging them to question the superior wisdom of elites, the new men would also turn against representative government itself. They had to find a new basis of legitimacy to replace the political compact that had drawn the original colonies and their citizens into "a more perfect union." One was found in a form of agreement, a *social* contract, that would signal the demise of the political citizen and the emergence of the American voter. In return for the surrender of their political power, and along with it the practice of the arts of the citizen, Americans would be rewarded with purchasing power and "consumer sovereignty."

Notes

1. *The Federalist*, ed. Jacob E. Cooke (Middletown, Conn.: Wesleyan University Press, 1961), no. 22, p. 64.
2. Ibid., p. 146.
3. Ibid., no. 27, p. 174.
4. Ibid., p. 173.
5. "Report on Manufactures," in *Papers on Public Credit, Commerce and Finance by Alexander Hamilton*, ed. Samuel McKee, Jr. (New York: Columbia University Press, 1934), p. 195.
6. Ibid., p. 196.
7. *The Papers of Alexander Hamilton*, ed. H. S. Syrett, 26 vols. (New York: Columbia University Press, 1961–1979), vol. 10, p. 291.
8. See Hamilton's discussion in McKee, ed., *Papers on Public Credit*, pp. 227, 231.
9. "Report on a National Bank," in Syrett, ed., *Papers of Alexander Hamilton*, vol. 7, pp. 305 ff.
10. *The Federalist*, no. 13, p. 81.
11. Ibid.
12. *The Anti-Federalists*, ed. Cecilia M. Kenyon (Indianapolis: Bobbs Merrill, 1966), p. 7.
13. *The Federalist*, no. 10, p. 64.
14. Ibid., pp. 61–62.
15. Ibid., no. 9, pp. 52–53.
16. Ibid., no. 12, p. 73.

III. STRUGGLES OVER CONSTITUTIONAL INTERPRETATION AND PRACTICE

17. The Constitution as an Elitist Document

Michael Parenti

Political scientist Michael Parenti is the author of *Power and the Powerless* (1978), *Inventing Reality: The Politics of the Mass Media* (1986), *Democracy for the Few* (5th ed. 1987), *The Sword and the Dollar: Imperialism, Revolution, and the Arms Race* (1989), and other works. He is currently completing *Make Believe Media*, a book on the politics of Hollywood film and television. Parenti resides in Washington, D.C., and lectures widely.

The following selection is reprinted, with emendations by the author for this edition, by permission of the American Enterprise Institute for Public Policy Research, from "The Constitution as an Elitist Document," in Robert A. Goldwin and William A. Schambra, eds., *How Democratic Is the Constitution?* (Washington, D.C.: American Enterprise Institute, 1980), 39–58.

How democratic is the Constitution? Not as democratic as we have been taught to believe. I will argue that the intent of the framers of the Constitution was to *contain* democracy, rather than give it free rein, and dilute the democratic will, rather than mobilize it. In addition, their goal was to construct a centralized power to serve the expanding interests of the manufacturing, commercial, landowning, and financial classes, rather than the needs of the populace. Evidence for this, it will be shown, can be found in the framers' opinions and actions and in the Constitution they fashioned. Finally, I will argue that the elitist design of the Constitution continues to function as intended, serving as a legitimating cloak and workable system for the propertied interests at the expense of the ordinary populace.

Class and Power in Early America

It is commonly taught that in the eighteenth and nineteenth centuries men of property preferred a laissez-faire government, one that kept its activities to a minimum. In actuality, they were not against a strong state but against state restrictions on business enterprise. They never desired to remove civil authority from economic affairs but to ensure that it worked *for*, rather than against, the interests of property. This meant they often had to move toward new and stronger state formations.

Adam Smith, who is above suspicion in his dedication to classical capitalism, argued that, as wealth increased in scope, government would have to perform still greater services on behalf of the propertied class. "The necessity of civil government," he wrote, "grows up with the acquisition of valuable property."[1] More importantly, Smith argued seventy years before Marx, "Civil authority, so far as it is instituted for the security of property, is in reality instituted for the defense of the rich against the poor, or of those who have some property against those who have none at all."[2]

Smith's views of the purposes of government were shared by the rich and the wellborn who lived in America during the period between the Revolution and the framing of the Constitution. Rather than keeping their distance from government, they set the dominant political tone.

Their power was born of place, position, and fortune. They were located at or near the seats of government and they were in direct contact with legislatures and government officers. They influenced and often dominated the local newspapers which voiced the ideas and interests of commerce and identified them with the good of the whole people, the state, and the nation. The published writings of the leaders of the period are almost without exception those of merchants, of their lawyers, or of politicians sympathetic with them.[3]

The United States of 1787 has been described as an "egalitarian" society free from the extremes of want and wealth which characterized the Old World, but there were landed estates and colonial mansions that bespoke an impressive munificence. From the earliest English settlements, men of influence had received vast land grants from the crown. By 1700, three-fourths of the acreage in New York belonged to fewer than a dozen persons. In the interior of Virginia, seven persons owned a total of 1,732,000 acres.[4] By 1760, fewer than 500 men in five colonial cities controlled most of the commerce, banking, mining, and manufacturing on the eastern seaboard and owned much of the land.[5]

Here and there could be found farmers, shop owners, and tradesmen who, by the standards of the day, might be judged as comfortably situated. The bulk of the agrarian population were poor freeholders, tenants, squatters, and indentured and hired hands. The cities also had their poor—cobblers, weavers, bakers, blacksmiths, peddlers, laborers, clerks, and domestics, who worked long hours for meager sums.[6]

As of 1787, property qualifications left perhaps more than a third of the white male population disfranchised.[7] Property qualifications for holding office were so steep as to prevent most voters from qualifying as candidates. Thus, a member of the New Jersey legislature had to be worth at least 1,000 pounds, while state senators in South Carolina were required to possess estates worth at least 7,000 pounds, clear of debt.[8] In addition, the practice of oral voting, the lack of a secret ballot, and an "absence of a real choice among candidates and programs" led to "widespread apathy."[9] As a result, men of substance monopolized the important offices. "Who do they represent?" Josiah Quincy asked of the South Carolina legislature. "The laborer, the mechanic, the tradesman, the farmer, the husbandman or yeoman? No, the representatives are almost if not wholly rich planters."[10]

Dealing with Insurgency

The Constitution was framed by financially successful planters, merchants, lawyers, and creditors, many linked by kinship and marriage and by years of service in Congress, the military, or diplomatic service. They congregated in Philadelphia in 1787 for the professed purpose of revising the Articles of Confederation and strengthening the powers of the central government. They were impelled by a desire to do something about the increasingly insurgent spirit evidenced among poorer people. Fearful of losing control of their state governments, the framers looked to a national government as a means of protecting their interests. Even in a state like South Carolina, where the propertied class was distinguished by the intensity of its desire to avoid any strong federation, the rich and the well-born, once faced with the possibility of rule by the common people" and realizing that a political alliance with conservatives from other states would be a safeguard if the radicals should capture the state government . . . gave up 'state rights' for 'nationalism' without hesitation."[11] It swiftly became their view that a central government would be less accessible to the populace and would be better able to provide the protections and services that their class so needed.

The landed, manufacturing, and merchant interests needed a central government that would provide a stable currency; impose uniform standards for trade; tax directly; regulate commerce; improve roads, canals, and harbors; provide protection against foreign imports and against the discrimination suffered by American shipping; and provide a national force to subjugate the Indians and secure the value of western lands. They needed a government that would honor at face value the huge sums of public securities they held and would protect them from paper-money schemes and from the large debtor class, the land-hungry agrarians, and the growing numbers of urban poor.

The nationalist conviction that arose so swiftly among men of property during the 1780s was not the product of a strange transcendent inspiration; it was not a "dream of nation-building" that suddenly possessed them as might a collective religious experience. (If so, they were remarkably successful in keeping it a secret in their public and private communications.) Rather, their newly acquired nationalism was a practical and urgent response to material conditions affecting them in a most immediate way. Gorham of Massachusetts, Hamilton of New York, Morris of Pennsylvania, Washington of Virginia, and Pinckney of South Carolina had a greater identity of interest with each other than with debt-burdened neighbors in their home counties. Their like-minded commitment to a central government was born of a common class interest stronger than state boundaries.

The rebellious populace of that day has been portrayed as irresponsible and parochial spendthrifts who never paid their debts and who believed in nothing more than timid state governments and inflated paper money. Little is said by most scholars of the period about the actual plight of the common people, the great bulk of whom lived at a subsistence level. Farm tenants were burdened by heavy rents and hard labor. Small farmers were hurt by the low prices merchants offered for their crops and by the high costs for merchandised goods. They often bought land at inflated prices, only to see its value collapse and to find themselves unable to meet their mortgage obligations. Their labor and their crops usually were theirs in name only. To survive, they frequently had to borrow money at high interest rates. To meet their debts, they mortgaged their future crops and went still deeper into debt. Large numbers were caught in that cycle of rural indebtedness which is the common fate of agrarian peoples in many countries to this day. The artisans, small tradesmen, and workers (or "mechanics," as they were called) in the towns were not much better off, being "dependent on the wealthy merchants who ruled them economically and socially." [12]

During the 1780s, the jails were crowded with debtors. Among the people, there grew the feeling that the revolution against England had been fought for naught. Angry, armed crowds in several states began blocking foreclosures and sales of seized property, and opening up jails. They gathered at county towns to prevent the courts from presiding over debtor cases. In the winter of 1787, farmers in western Massachusetts led by Daniel Shays took up arms. But their rebellion was forcibly put down by the state militia after some ragged skirmishes.[13]

Containing the Spread of Democracy

The specter of Shays' Rebellion hovered over the delegates who gathered in Philadelphia three months later, confirming their worst fears about the populace. They were determined that persons of birth and fortune should control the affairs of the nation and check the "leveling impulses" of that propertyless multitude which composed "the majority faction." "To secure the public good and private rights against the danger of such a faction," wrote James Madison in *Federalist* No. 10," and at the same time preserve the spirit and form of popular government is then the great object to which our inquiries are directed." Here Madison touched the heart of the matter: how to keep the *spirit* and *form* of popular government with only a minimum of the *substance*, how to provide the appearance of republicanism without suffering its leveling effects, how to construct a government that would win mass acquiescence but would not tamper with the existing class structure, a government strong enough both to service the growing needs of an entrepreneurial class while withstanding the egalitarian demands of the poor and propertyless.

The framers of the Constitution could agree with Madison when he wrote in the same *Federalist* No. 10 that "the most common and durable source of factions has been the various and unequal distribution of property. Those who hold and those who are without property have ever formed distinct interests in society." They were of the opinion that democracy was "the worst of all political evils," as Elbridge Gerry put it. Both he and Madison warned of "the danger of the leveling spirit." "The people," said Roger Sherman, "should have as little to do as may be about the Government." And according to Alexander Hamilton, "All communities divide themselves into the few and the many. The first are the rich and the well-born, the other the mass of the people. . . . The people are turbulent and changing; they seldom judge or determine right."[14]

The delegates spent many weeks debating their interests, but these were the differences of merchants, slave owners, and manufacturers, a debate of haves versus haves in which each group sought safeguards within the new Constitution for its particular concerns. Added to this were the inevitable disagreements that arise over the best means of achieving agreed-upon ends. Questions of structure and authority occupied a good deal of the delegates' time: How much representation should the large and small states have? How might the legislature be organized? How should the executive be selected? What length of tenure should exist for the different officeholders? *Yet, questions of enormous significance, relating to the new government's ability to protect the interests of property, were agreed upon with surprisingly little debate.* For on these issues, there were no dirt farmers or poor artisans attending the convention to proffer an opposing viewpoint. The debate between haves and have-nots never occurred.

The portions of the Constitution giving the federal government the power to support commerce and protect property were decided upon after amiable deliberation and with remarkable dispatch considering their importance. Thus all of Article I, Section 8 was adopted within a few days.[15] This section gave to Congress the powers needed by the propertied class for the expansion of its commerce, trade, and industry, specifically the authority to (1) regulate commerce among the states and with foreign nations and Indian tribes, (2) lay and collect taxes and impose duties and tariffs on imports but not on commercial exports, (3) establish a national currency and regulate its value, (4) "borrow Money on the credit of the United States"—a measure of special interest to creditors,[16] (5) fix the standard of weights and measures necessary for trade, (6) protect the value of securities and currency against counterfeiting, (7) establish "uniform Laws on the subject of Bankruptcies throughout the United States," and (8) "pay the Debts and provide for the common Defense and general Welfare of the United States."

Some of the delegates were land speculators who expressed a concern about western holdings; accordingly, Congress was given the "Power to dispose of and make all needful Rules and Regulations respecting the Territory or other Property belong to the United States. . . ." Some delegates speculated in highly inflated and nearly worthless Confederation securities. Under Article VI, all debts incurred by the Confederation were valid against the new government, a provision that allowed speculators to make generous profits when their securities were honored at face value.[17]

In the interest of merchants and creditors, the states were prohibited from issuing paper money or imposing duties on imports and exports or interfering with the payment of debts by passing any "Law impairing the Obligation of

Contracts." The Constitution guaranteed "Full Faith and Credit" in each state "to the Acts, Records, and judicial Proceedings" of other states, thus allowing creditors to pursue their debtors more effectively.

The property interests of slave owners were looked after. To give the slave-owning states a greater influence, three-fifths of the slave population were to be counted when calculating the representation deserved by each state in the lower house. The importation of slaves was allowed until 1808. Under Article IV, slaves who escaped from one state to another had to be delivered to the original owner upon claim, a provision unanimously adopted at the convention.

The framers believed the states acted with insufficient force against popular uprisings, so Congress was given the task of "organizing, arming, and disciplining the Militia" and calling it forth, among other reasons, to "suppress Insurrections." The federal government was empowered to protect the states "against domestic Violence." Provision was made for "the Erection of Forts, Magazines, Arsenals, dock-Yards and other needful Buildings" and for the maintenance of an army and navy for both national defense and to establish an armed federal presence within the potentially insurrectionary states—a provision that was to prove a godsend a century later when the army was used repeatedly to break strikes by miners, railroad employees, and factory workers.

In keeping with their desire to contain the majority, the founders inserted "auxiliary precautions" *designed to fragment power without democratizing it.* By separating the executive, legislative, and judiciary functions and then providing a system of checks and balances among the various branches, including staggered elections, executive veto, Senate confirmation of appointments and ratification of treaties, and a bicameral legislature, they hoped to dilute the impact of popular sentiments. They also contrived an elaborate and difficult process for amending the Constitution. *To the extent that it existed at all, the majoritarian principle was tightly locked into a system of minority vetoes, making sweeping popular actions nearly impossible.*

The propertyless majority, as Madison pointed out in *Federalist* No. 10, must not be allowed to concert in common cause against the established economic order.[18] First, it was necessary to prevent unity of public sentiment by enlarging the polity and then compartmentalizing it into geographically insulated political communities. The larger the nation, the greater the "variety of parties and interests" and the more difficult it would be for a majority to find itself and act in unison. As Madison argued, "A rage for paper money, for an abolition of debts, for an equal division of property, or for any other wicked project will be less apt to pervade the whole body of the Union than a particular member of it. . . ." An uprising of impoverished farmers could threaten Massachusetts at one time and Rhode Island at another, but a national government would be large and varied enough to contain each of these and insulate the rest of the nation from the contamination of rebellion.

Political Diversity

Contemporary political scientists have said different things about the concept of political diversity. Some presume that a wide variety of interests produces moderation and compromise, it being argued that the "cross-pressured" lawmaker and voter and the multigroup polity are more likely to avoid the "extremist" solutions that are presumed to inflict those possessed of a single-minded, homogeneous political interest. In contrast, Madison welcomed diversity because it would produce not compromise but division. It would keep the mass of people divided against each other, unable to concert against the opulent class.

Political scientists have also feared that too great a multiplicity of interests makes compromise impossible, leading to the kind of factionalism and instability that supposedly result when a vast array of irreconcilable demands are made on the polity. Here too, Madison was of a different mind. For him, the danger was centripetal, not centrifugal. The problem was not factionalism, as such, but democracy. His concern was that the people might *not* be riddled with divisions, that they might unify in common cause as an oppressive majority "faction."

Here I would enter a qualification. A close reading of *Federalist* No. 10 actually uncovers two themes. The first is the one just mentioned, the one that occupied Madison's thoughts before and during the convention: the relation between the propertyless and the propertied, the division that was "the most common and durable source of factions," factions which "ever formed distinct interests in society." But in the same paragraph of that same great essay, Madison introduced another theme, shifting the focus from the divisions between the propertied and the propertyless to the divisions *among* the propertied. "A landed interest, a manufacturing interest, a mercantile interest, a moneyed interest grow up of necessity in civilized nations. . . ." For all his supposed concern for "factions," Madison was not too worried about *these* factions. Unlike the factionalism between the propertied and propertyless that necessitated the whole great effort in Philadelphia and the need for a central government, the minority factions of propertied interests caused him no alarm.

True, these minority factions might occasionally be a nuisance; they might "clog the administration" and even "convulse the society." But for some unstated reason, they would never be able "to sacrifice . . . the public good and the rights of other citizens," nor could any propertied faction "mask its violence under the forms of the Constitution." Only the majority faction was capable of such evils. Only the propertyless majority was capable of "improper and wicked projects" against property. The propertied interests, whatever their particular differences, would never advocate "an abolition of debts" or "an equal division of property"; they would never jeopardize the institution of property and wealth and the untrammeled uses thereof, which in their eyes—and Madison's—constituted the essence of "liberty."

There was, then, no need to impose constitutional checks upon the haves. If a larger polity would make it difficult for the populace to coalesce, it would do just the opposite for the propertied elites, allowing them to organize a centralized force to protect themselves from the turbulent plebeians within the various states. They would do well to settle their particular differences and work in unison to defend their common class interests. Indeed, in large part, that was what the Philadelphia convention was all about. Madison wanted what every elite has ever wanted, unity of purpose within his own class and divisions and conflicts within the other, larger one.

By focusing on Madison's second theme, the diversity of supposedly self-regulating propertied interests, modern-day political scientists discovered pluralism. By ignoring his first and major theme, the conflict between haves and have-nots, they have yet to discover class conflict.

It is interesting to note that Madison did not advocate minority rights as some abstract principle, although some of the language in the *Federalist Papers* seems to suggest so. He was concerned about protecting the *propertied* minority and not regional, racial, ethnic, or state minorities. In fact, on the question of representation he took a hardline majoritarian position. As a Virginian he repeatedly argued against giving the small states an equal voice in the Senate with the large ones. Representation should be proportional to population with no special provisions for the less populous states. On this question he evidenced not the slightest fear of majoritarian dominance, no difficulty in brushing aside the anxieties of representational minorities in smaller states. To repeat, Madison's fear in Philadelphia was not of some abstract majority but of a particular *class* majority, a democracy.[19]

Besides preventing the people from finding *horizontal* cohesion, the Constitution was designed to dilute their *vertical* force, blunting its upward thrust upon government by interjecting indirect and staggered forms of representation. Thus, the senators from each state were to be elected by their respective state legislatures and were to have rotated terms of six years. The chief executive was to be selected by an electoral college voted by the people but, as anticipated by the framers, composed of men of substance and prominence who would gather in their various states and choose a president of their own liking. The Supreme Court was to be elected by no one, its justices being appointed to life tenure by the president and confirmed by the Senate.[20]

This system of checks would be the best safeguard against "agrarian attempts" and "symptoms of a leveling spirit," observed Madison at the convention. In those same remarks, he opposed a six-year term for the Senate, preferring a nine-year one because he believed the Senate should be composed of "a portion of enlightened citizens whose limited number and firmness might seasonably interpose against" popular impetuosity.[21] Exactly who were the "enlightened citizens"? Certainly not the tenants and squatters, nor even the average freeholder. Only the men of substance. If wealth were not a sufficient cause of enlightenment, it was almost always a necessary condition for Madison and his colleagues. Who else would have the breeding, education, and experience to govern? While often treated as an abstract virtue, "enlightened" rule had a real class meaning.

The only portion of government directly elected by the people was the House of Representatives. Many of the delegates would have preferred excluding the public entirely from direct representation. John Mercer observed that he found nothing in the proposed Constitution more objectionable than "the mode of election by the people. The people cannot know and judge of the characters of Candidates. The worst possible choice will be made." Others were concerned that demagogues would ride into office on a populist tide only to pillage the treasury and wreak havoc on all. "The time is not distant," warned Gouverneur Morris, "when this Country will abound with mechanics and manufacturers [industrial workers] who will receive their bread from their employers. Will such men be the secure and faithful Guardians of liberty? . . . Children do not vote. Why? Because they want prudence, because they have no will of their own. The ignorant and dependent can be as little trusted with the public interest."[22]

Several considerations softened the framers' determination to contain democracy. First and most important, the delegates recognized that there were limits to what the states would ratify. They also understood that if the federal government were to have any kind of stability, it must gain some measure of popular acceptance. Hence, for all their class biases, they were inclined to "leave something for the People," even if it were only "the *spirit* and *form* of popular government," to recall Madison's words. In addition, some delegates feared not only the tyranny of the many but the machinations of the few. It was Madison who reminded his colleagues that in protecting themselves from the multitude, they must not reintroduce a "cabal" or a monarchy, thus erring in the opposite direction.

Plotters or Patriots?

The question of whether the founders were motivated by financial or national interest has been debated since Charles Beard published *An Economic Interpretation of the Constitution* in 1913. It was Beard's view that the delegates were guided by their class interests. Arguing against Beard's thesis are those who believe that the framers were concerned with higher things than lining their purses and protecting their property. True, they were moneyed men who profited directly from policies initiated under the new Constitution, but they were motivated by a concern for nation building that went beyond their particular class interests, the argument goes.[23] To paraphrase Justice Holmes, these men invested their belief to make a nation; they did not make a nation because they had invested. "High-mindedness in not impossible to man," Holmes reminded us.

That is exactly the point: High-mindedness is one of man's most common attributes even when, or especially when, he is pursuing his personal and class interest. The fallacy is to presume that there is a dichotomy between the desire to build a strong nation and the desire to protect property and that the delegates could not have been motivated by both. In fact, like most other people, they believed that what was good for themselves was ultimately good for the entire society. Their universal values and their class interests went hand in hand; to discover the existence of the "higher" sentiment does not eliminate the self-interested one.

Most persons believe in their own virtue. The founders never doubted the nobility of their effort and its importance for the generations to come. Just as many of them could feel dedicated to the principle of "liberty for all" and at the same time own slaves, so could they serve both their nation and their estates. The point is not that they were devoid of the grander sentiments of nation building but that there was nothing in the concept of nation which worked against their class interest and a great deal that worked for it.

People tend to perceive things in accordance with the position they occupy in the social structure; that position is largely—although not exclusively—determined by their class status. Even if we deny that the framers were motivated by the desire for personal gain that moves others, we cannot dismiss the existence of their class interest. They may not have been solely concerned with getting their own hands in the till, although enough of them did, but they were admittedly preoccupied with defending the propertied few from the propertyless many—for the ultimate benefit of all, as they understood it. "The Constitution," as Staughton Lynd noted, "was the settlement of a revolution. What was at stake for Hamilton, Livingston, and their opponents, was more than speculative windfalls in securities; it was the question, what kind of society would emerge from the revolution when the dust had settled, and on which class the political center of gravity would come to rest."[24]

The small farmers, tradesmen, and debtors who opposed a central government have been described as motivated by self-serving parochial interests—as opposed to the supposedly higher-minded statesmen who journeyed to Philadelphia and others of their class who supported ratification. How or why the propertied rich became visionary nation builders is never explained. In truth, it was not their minds that were so much broader but their economic interests. Their motives were neither higher nor lower than those of any other social group struggling for place and power in the United States of 1787–1789. They pursued their material interests as single-mindedly as any small freeholder—if not more so. Possessing more time, money, information, and organization, they enjoyed superior results. How could they have acted otherwise? For them to have ignored the conditions of governance necessary for the maintenance of their enterprises would have amounted to committing class suicide—and they were not about to do that. They were a rising bourgeoisie rallying around a central power in order to advance their class interests. Some of us are quite willing to accept the existence of such a material-based nationalism in the history of other countries, but not in our own.

Among the mass of ordinary people there were some who supported the new Constitution. For instance some northern workers in cities like New York supported the provisions for stronger manufacturing and shipping protections.[25] This point has been made by latter-day apologists who wish to emphasize that the framers' work had popular support. Apparently suggestions that some *workers* supported the Constitution from direct economic interest is an acceptable datum, but to suggest that merchants, manufacturers, landowners, speculators, and creditors did so is a contention bred of the crudest economic determinism.

Finally, those who argue that the founders were motivated primarily by high-minded objectives consistently overlook the fact that the delegates repeatedly stated their intention to erect a government strong enough to protect the haves from the have-nots. They gave voice to the crassest class prejudices and never found it necessary to disguise the fact—as have latter-day apologists—that their uppermost concern was to diminish popular control and resist all tendencies toward class equalization (or "leveling," as it was called). Their opposition to democracy and their dedication to the propertied and moneyed interests were unabashedly and openly avowed. Their preoccupation was so pronounced that one delegate, James Wilson, did finally complain of hearing too much about how the purpose of government was to protect property. He wanted it noted that the ultimate objective of government was the ennoblement of mankind—a fine sentiment that evoked no opposition from his colleagues as they continued about their business.

An Elitist Document

More important than conjecturing about the framers' motives is to look at the Constitution they fashioned, for it tells a good deal about their objectives. It was, and still is, largely an elitist document, more concerned with securing property interests than personal liberties. Bills of attainder and ex post facto laws are expressly prohibited, and Article I, Section 9, assures us that "the Privilege of the Writ of Habeas Corpus shall not be suspended, unless when in Cases of Rebellion or Invasion the public Safety may require it," a restriction that leaves authorities with a wide measure of discretion. Other than these few provisions, the Constitution that emerged from the Philadelphia Convention gave no attention to civil liberties.

When Colonel Mason suggested to the Convention that a committee be formed to draft "a Bill of Rights"—a task that could be accomplished "in a few hours"—the representatives of the various states offered little discussion on the motion and voted almost unanimously against it. The Bill of Rights, of course, was ratified only after the first Congress and president had been elected.

For the founders, liberty meant something different from democracy; it meant liberty to invest and trade and carry out the matters of business and enjoy the security of property without encroachment by king or populace. The civil liberties designed to give all individuals the right to engage actively in public affairs were of no central concern to the delegates and, as noted, were summarily voted down.

When asking how democratic the Constitution is, we need look not only at the Constitution but also at what we mean by "democracy," for different definitions have been ascribed to the term. Let us say that democracy is a system of governance that represents, both in form *and content*, the desires and interests of the ruled. This definition is more meaningful for the twentieth century—and at the same time somewhat closer to the eighteenth-century one—than the currently propagated view that reduces democracy to a set of procedures and "rules of the game." Democracy is a *social order* with a social class content—which is why the framers so disliked it. What they feared about democracy was not its forms but its content, the idea that the decisions of government might be of substantive benefit to the popular class at the expense of their own.

In a democracy, the people exercise a measure of control by electing their representatives and by subjecting them to the check of periodic elections, open criticism, and removal from office. In addition, a democratic people should be able to live without fear of want, enjoying freedom from economic, as well as political, oppression. In a real democracy, the material conditions of people's lives should be humane and roughly equal. It was this democratic vision that loomed as a nightmare for the framers and for so many of their spiritual descendants today.

Some people argue that democracy is simply a system of rules for playing the game, which allows some measure of mass participation and government accountability, and that the Constitution is a kind of rule book. One should not try to impose, as a precondition of democracy, particular class relations, economic philosophies, or other substantive arrangements on this open-ended game. This argument certainly does reduce democracy to a game. It presumes that formal rules can exist in a meaningful way independently of substantive realities. Whether procedural rights are violated or enjoyed, whether one is treated by law as pariah or prince, depends largely on material realities that extend beyond a written constitution or other formal guarantees of law. Whether a political system is democratic depends not only on its procedures but on its substantive outputs, that is, the actual material benefits and costs of policy and the kind of social justice, or injustice, that is propagated. By this view, a government that pursues policies that by design or neglect are so inequitable as to deny people the very conditions of life, is not fully democratic, no matter how many competitive elections it holds.

The twentieth-century concept of social justice, involving something more than procedural liberties, is afforded no place in the eighteenth-century Constitution. The Constitution says nothing about those conditions of like that have come to be treated by many people as essential human rights—for instance, freedom from hunger; the right to decent housing, medical care, and education regardless of ability to pay; the right to gainful employment, safe working conditions, and a clean, nontoxic environment. Under the Constitution, equality is treated as a *procedural* right without a *substantive* content. Thus, "equality of opportunity" means equality of opportunity to move ahead competitively and become unequal to others; it means a chance to get in the game and best others rather than to enjoy an equal distribution and use of the resources needed for the maintenance of community life.

If the founders sought to "check power with power," they seemed chiefly concerned with restraining mass power, while assuring the perpetuation of their own class power. They supposedly had a "realistic" opinion of the self-interested and rapacious nature of human beings—readily evidenced when they talked about the common people—yet they held a remarkably sanguine view of the self-interested impulses of their own class, which they saw as being inhabited by industrious, trustworthy, and virtuous men. Recall Hamilton's facile reassurance that the rich will "check the unsteadiness" of the poor and will themselves "ever maintain good government" by being given a "distinct permanent share" in it. Power corrupts others but somehow has the opposite effect on the rich and the wellborn.

If the Constitution is so blatantly elitist, how did it manage to win enough popular support for ratification? First, it should be noted that it did not have a wide measure of support, initially being opposed in most of the states. But the same superiority of wealth, leadership, organization, control of the press, and control of political office that allowed the rich to monopolize the Philadelphia Convention worked with similar effect in the ratification campaign. Superior wealth also enabled the Federalists to bribe, intimidate, and, in other ways, pressure and discourage opponents of the Constitution. At the same time, there were some elements in the laboring class, especially those who hoped to profit from employment in shipping and export trades, who supported ratification. [26]

Above all, it should be pointed out that the Constitution never was submitted to popular ratification. There was no national referendum and none in the states. Ratification was by state convention composed of elected delegates, the majority of whom were drawn from the more affluent strata. The voters who took part in the selection of delegates were subjected to a variety of property restrictions. In addition, the poor, even if enfranchised, carried all the liabilities that have caused them to be underrepresented in elections before and since: a lack of information and organization, illiteracy, a sense of being unable to have any effect on events, and a feeling that none of the candidates represented their interests. There were also the problems of relatively inaccessible polls and the absence of a secret ballot. Even if two-thirds or more of the adult white males could vote for delegates, as might have been the case in most states, probably not more than 20 percent actually did. [27]

In sum, the framers laid the foundation for a national government, but it was one that fit the specifications of the propertied class. They wanted protection from popular uprisings, from fiscal uncertainty and irregularities in trade and currency, from trade barriers between states, from economic competition by more powerful foreign governments, and from attacks by the poor on property and on creditors. The Constitution was consciously designed as a conservative document, elaborately equipped with a system of minority checks and vetoes, making it hard to enact sweeping popular reforms or profound structural changes, and easy for entrenched interests to endure. It provided ample power to build the services and protections of state needed by a growing capitalist class but not the power for a transition of rule to a different class or to the public as a whole.

Democratic Concessions

For all its undemocratic aspects, the Constitution was not without its historically progressive features. [28] Consider the following:

1. The very existence of a written constitution with specifically limited powers represented an advance over more autocratic forms of government.
2. No property qualifications were required for any federal officeholder, unlike in England and most of the states. And salaries were provided for all officials, thus rejecting the common practice of treating public office as a voluntary service, which only the rich could afford.
3. The President and all other officeholders were elected for limited terms. No one could claim a life tenure on any office.
4. Article VI reads: "No religious Test shall ever be required as a Qualification to any Office or public Trust under the United States," a feature that represented a distinct advance over a number of state constitutions which banned Catholics, Jews, and nonbelievers from holding office.
5. Bills of attainder, the practice of declaring by legislative fiat a specific person or group of people guilty of an offense, without benefit of a trial, were made unconstitutional. Also outlawed were ex post facto laws, the practice of declaring an act a crime and punishing those who had committed it *before* it had been unlawful.
6. As noted earlier, the framers showed no interest in a Bill of Rights, but supporters of the new Constitution soon recognized their tactical error and pledged the swift adoption of such a bill as a condition for ratification. So in the first session of Congress, the first ten amendments were swiftly passed and then adopted by the states; these rights included freedom of speech and religion; freedom to assemble peaceably and to petition for redress of grievances; the right to keep arms; freedom from unreasonable searches and seizures, self-incrimination, double jeopardy, cruel and unusual punishment, and excessive bail and fines; the right to a fair and impartial trial; and other forms of due process.
7. The Constitution guarantees a republican form of government and explicitly repudiates monarchy and aristocracy; hence, Article I, Section 9 states: "No title of Nobility shall be granted by the United States . . ." According to James McHenry, a delegate from Maryland, *at least 21 of the 55 delegates favored some form of monarchy.* Yet few dared venture in that direction out of fear of popular opposition. Furthermore, delegates like Madison believed that stability for their class order was best assured by a republican form of government. The time had come for the bourgeoisie to rule directly without the baneful intrusions of kings and nobles.

Time and again during the Philadelphia convention, this assemblage of men who feared and loathed democracy found it necessary to show some regard for popular sentiment (as with the direct election of the lower house). If the Constitution was going to be accepted by the states and if the new government was to have any stability, it had to gain some measure of popular acceptance; hence, the founders felt compelled to leave something for the people. While the delegates and their class dominated the events of 1787–89, they were far from omnipotent. The class system they sought to preserve was itself the cause of marked restiveness among the people.

Land seizures by the poor, food riots, and other violent disturbances occurred throughout the eighteenth century in just about every state and erstwhile colony.[29] This popular fomentation spurred the framers in their effort to erect a strong central government *but it also set a limit on what they could do.* The delegates "gave" nothing to popular interests; rather—as with the Bill of Rights—they reluctantly made concessions under the threat of democratic rebellion. They kept what they could and grudgingly relinquished what they felt they had to, driven not by a love of democracy but by a fear of it, not by a love of the people but by a prudent desire to avoid popular uprisings. The Constitution, then, was a product not only of class privilege but of class struggle—a struggle that continued and intensified as the corporate economy and the government grew.

With some democratizing changes, including the direct election of the Senate and the enfranchisement of women, the Constitution fashioned in 1787 has served its intended purpose. During the industrial strife of the late nineteenth century, when the state militias proved unreliable and state legislatures too responsive to the demands of workers, the military power of the federal government was used repeatedly to suppress labor insurgency. Where would the robber barons have been without a Constitution that provided them with the forceful services of the U.S. Army?[30]

Similarly, for over seventy years, the Supreme Court wielded a minority veto on social welfare, unionization, and taxation, preventing reform legislation that had been enacted in European countries decades earlier. The Court became—and with momentary exceptions remains—what the founders intended it to be, a nonelective branch staffed by persons of elitist political, legal, and business backgrounds, exercising a preponderantly conservative influence as guardian of existing class and property relations.

The Senate today qualifies as the "tinsel aristocracy" that Jefferson scorned, composed mostly of persons with large financial holdings, many of them millionaires, who vote their own interests with shameless regularity. The House is subdivided into a network of special-interest subcommittees, dominated by the concerns of banking, agribusiness, and big corporations, in what has become almost a parody of Madison's lesson on how to divide power in order to fragment mass pressures and protect the propertied few.[31]

The system of popular elections, an institution most of the founders never liked, has been safely captured by two political parties that are financed by moneyed interests and dedicated to the existing corporate social order. In modern times, especially at the national level, men of property have demonstrated their adeptness at financing elections, running for office, getting elected, and influencing those who are elected, in ways that would warm the heart of the most conservative Federalist. Electoral politics is largely a rich man's game and the property qualifications—as translated into campaign costs—are far steeper today than in 1787.

The endeavor the framers began in Philadelphia, for a stronger central government to serve the commercial and industrial class, has continued and accelerated. As industrial capitalism has expanded at home and abroad, the burden of subsidizing its endeavors and providing the military force needed to protect its markets, resources, and client states has fallen disproportionately on that level of government which is national and international in scope— the federal—and on that branch which is best suited to carry out the necessary technical, organizational, and military tasks—the executive. The important decisions increasingly are being made in federal departments and corporate boardrooms and in the advisory committees that are linked to the upper echelons of the executive branch, staffed by public policy makers and private representatives of the major industries. I described this in an earlier work:

One might better think of ours as a dual political system. First, there is the *symbolic* political system centering around electoral and representative activities including party conflicts, voter turnout, political personalities, public pronouncements, official role-playing and certain ambiguous presentations of some of the public issues which bestir Presidents, governors, mayors and their respective legislatures. Then there is the *substantive* political system, involving multibillion-dollar contracts, tax write-offs, protections, rebates, grants, loss compensations, subsidies, leases, giveaways and the whole vast process of budgeting, legislating, advising, regulating, protecting and servicing major producer interests, now bending or ignoring the law on behalf of the powerful, now applying it with full punitive vigor against heretics and "troublemak-ers." The symbolic system is highly visible, taught in the schools, dissected by academicians, gossiped about by newsmen. The substantive system is seldom heard of or accounted for.[32]

By offering well-protected havens for powerful special interests, by ignoring substantive rights and outcomes, by mobilizing the wealth and force of the state in a centralizing and property-serving way, by making democratic change difficult, the Constitution has served well an undemocratic military-indus-trial corporate structure. The rule of the "minority faction," the "persons of substance," the "propertied interest," the "rich and the well-born"—to men-tion a few of the ways the founders described their class—has prevailed. The delegates would have every reason to be satisfied with the enduring nature of their work.

Notes

1. Adam Smith, *An Inquiry into the Nature and Causes of the Wealth of Nations* (Chicago: Encyclopaedia Britannica, Inc., 1952), p. 309.
2. Ibid., p. 311.
3. Merrill Jensen, *The New Nation* (New York: Random House, 1950), p. 178.
4. Sidney H. Aronson, *Status and Kinship in the Higher Civil Service* (Cambridge, Mass.: Harvard University Press, 1964), p. 35.
5. Ibid., p. 41.
6. Ibid., passim.
7. This is Beard's estimate regarding New York. Charles A. Beard, *An Economic Interpretation of the Constitution of the United States* (New York: Macmillan, 1935), pp. 67–68. In a few states like Pennsylvania and Georgia, suffrage was more widespread; in others it was even more restricted than New York; see Arthur Ekrich, Jr., *The American Democratic Tradition* (New York: Macmillan, 1963). For a pioneer work on this subject, see A. E. McKinley, *The Suffrage Franchise in the Thirteen English Colonies in America* (Philadelphia: B. Franklin, 1969, originally published 1905). Robert E. Brown makes the argument that Massachusetts was close to being both an economic and political democracy—which would have been alarming news to the Boston aristocracy of manufacturers, merchants, and large property holders. He conjectures that property requirements of a 40 shilling freehold could be easily met and that rural underrepresentation (during the same period that produced Shays' Rebellion) was due more to indifference than to disenfranchisement. See his *Middle-Class Democracy and the Revolution in Massachusetts* (Ithaca, N.Y.: Cornell University Press, 1955).
8. Beard, *An Economic Interpretation*, pp. 68, 70.
9. Aronson, *Status and Kinship*, p. 49.
10. Ibid., p. 49.
11. Merrill Jensen, *The Articles of Confederation* (Madison: University of Wisconsin Press, 1948), p. 30.
12. Ibid., pp. 9–10. "In addition to being frequently in debt for their lands," Beard noted, "the small farmers were dependent upon the towns for most of the capital to develop their resources. They were, in other words, a large debtor class, to which must be added, or course, the urban dwellers who were in a like unfortunate condition." Beard, *An Economic Interpretation*, p. 28.
13. For a study of this incident, see Monroe Stearns, *Shays' Rebellion, 1786–7: Americans Take Up Arms Against Unjust Laws* (New York: Franklin Watts, 1968).
14. The quotations by Gerry, Madison, Sherman, and Hamilton are taken from

Max Farrand, ed., *Records of the Federal Convention* (New Haven: Yale University Press, 1927), vol. 1, passim. For further testimony by the Founding Fathers and other early leaders, see John C. Miller, *Origins of the American Revolution* (Boston: Little, Brown, 1943), pp. 491 ff. and Andrew C. McLaughlin, *A Constitutional History of the United States* (New York: Appleton-Century, 1935), pp. 141–144.

15. John Bach McMaster, "Framing the Constitution," in his *The Political Depravity of the Founding Fathers* (New York: Farrar, Straus, 1964, originally published in 1896), p. 137. Farrand refers to the consensus for a strong national government that emerged after the small states had been given equal representation in the Senate. Much of the work that followed "was purely formal" albeit sometimes time-consuming. See Max Farrand, *The Framing of the Constitution of the United States* (New Haven: Yale University Press, 1913), pp. 134–135.

16. The original working was "borrow money and emit bills." The latter phrase was deleted after Gouverneur Morris warned that "the Monied interest" would oppose the Constitution if paper notes were not prohibited. There was much strong feeling about this among creditors. In any case, it was assumed that the borrowing power would allow for "safe and proper" public notes should they be necessary. See Farrand, *The Framing of the Constitution*, p. 147.

17. See Beard, *An Economic Interpretation*, passim. The profits accrued to holders of public securities were in the millions. On the question of speculation in western lands, Hugh Williamson, a North Carolina delegate, wrote to Madison a year after the convention: "For myself, I conceive that my opinions are not biassed by private Interests, but having claims to a considerable Quantity of Land in the Western Country, I am fully persuaded that the Value of those Lands must be increased by an efficient federal Government." Ibid., p. 50. Critiques of Beard have been made by Robert E. Brown, *Charles Beard and the American Constitution* (Princeton, N.J.: Princeton University Press, 1956) and Forrest McDonald, *We the People—The Economic Origins of the Constitution* (Chicago: Chicago University Press, 1958).

18. *Federalist* No. 10 can be found in any of the good editions of *The Federalist Papers*. It is one of the most significant essays on American politics ever written. With clarity and economy of language, it explains, as do few other short works, how a government may utilize the republican principle to contain the populace and protect the propertied few from the propertyless many. It confronts, if not solves, the essential question of how government may reconcile the tensions between liberty, authority, and dominant class interest. In effect, the Tenth *Federalist* Paper maps out a method, relevant to this day, for preserving the existing undemocratic class structure under the legitimizing cloak of democratic forms.

19. See his lengthy comments of June 28 and July 14, 1787, in Madison's *The Debates in the Federal Convention of 1787 Which Framed the Constitution of the United States of America*, ed. Gaillard Hunt and James Brown Scott (New York: Oxford University Press, 1920), pp. 177–180, 256–258.

20. In time, of course, the electoral college proved to be something of a rubber

stamp, and the Seventeenth Amendment, adopted in 1913, provided for the popular election of the Senate.

21. Madison's speech of June 26, 1787, in *The Debates in the Federal Convention*, p. 167.

22. Farrand, *Records of the Federal Convention*, vol. 2, pp. 200 ff.

23. For some typical apologistic arguments on behalf of the "Founding Fathers" see Broadus Mitchell and Louise Pearson Mitchell, *A Biography of the Constitution of the United States* (New York: Oxford University Press, 1964), pp. 46–51, and David G. Smith, *The Convention and the Constitution* (New York: St. Martin's Press, 1965), chap. 3. Smith argues that the framers had not only economic motives but "larger" political objectives, as if the political had no relation to the economic or as if the economic interests were less selfish because they were national in financial scope.

24. Staughton Lynd, *Class Conflict, Slavery and the United States Constitution* (Indianapolis: Bobbs-Merrill, 1967), selection in Irwin Unger, ed., *Beyond Liberalism: The New Left Views American History* (Waltham, Mass.: Xerox College Publishing, 1971), p. 17. For discussions of the class interests behind the American Revolution, see Alfred F. Young, ed., *The American Revolution: Explorations in the History of American Radicalism* (DeKalb, Ill.: Northern Illinois University Press, 1976).

25. Beard, *An Economic Interpretation*, pp. 44–45.

26. See Jackson Turner Main, *The Antifederalists* (Chapel Hill: University of North Carolina Press, 1961).

27. See the studies cited by Beard, *An Economic Interpretation*, p. 242 ff.

28. This section on the progressive features of the Constitution is drawn from Herbert Aptheker, *Early Years of the Republic* (New York: International Publishers, 1976), pp. 71 ff. and passim.

29. Howard Zinn, *A People's History of the United States* (New York: Harper and Row, 1980), chapter 3.

30. See William Preston, Jr., *Aliens and Dissenters* (Cambridge, Mass.: Harvard University Press, 1963).

31. For a fuller exposition of these points see my *Democracy for the Few*, 5th ed. (New York: St. Martin's Press, 1987).

32. Ibid.

18. The Second American Revolution

Gore Vidal

Gore Vidal's writings include the historical novels *Burr* (1973), *1876* (1976), *Lincoln* (1984), and *Empire* (1987), and the collections of criticism, *Homage to Daniel Shays* (1972), *Matters of Fact and Fiction* (1977), *The Second American Revolution* (1982), and *At Home* (1988).

The following essay, a review of muckraker Ferdinand Lundberg's *Cracks in the Constitution*, is reprinted with permission from *The New York Review of Books.* Copyright © 1981 Nyrev, Inc.

Future generations, if there are any, will date the second American Revolution, if there is one, from the passage of California's Proposition 13 in 1978, which obliged the managers of that gilded state to reduce by more than half the tax on real estate. Historically, this revolt was not unlike the Boston Tea Party, which set in train those events that led to the separation of England's thirteen American colonies from the crown and to the creation, in 1787, of the First Constitution. And in 1793 (after the addition of the Bill of Rights) of the Second Constitution. And in 1865 of the Third Constitution, the result of those radical alterations made by the Thirteenth, Fourteenth, and Fifteenth amendments. Thus far we have had three Constitutions for three quite different republics. Now a Fourth Constitution—and republic—is ready to be born.

The people of the United States (hereinafter known forever and eternally as We) are deeply displeased with their government as it now malfunctions. Romantics who don't read much think that all will be well if we would only return, somehow, to the original Constitution, to the ideals of the founders, to a strict construction of what the Framers (nice word) of the First Constitution saw fit to commit to parchment during the hot summer of 1787 at Philadelphia. Realists think that an odd amendment or two and better men in government (particularly in the Oval Office, where too many round and square pegs have, in recent years, rattled about) would put things right.

It is taken for granted by both romantics and realists that the United States is the greatest country on earth as well as in the history of the world, with a government that is the envy of the lesser breeds just as the life-style of its citizens is regarded with a grinding of teeth by the huddled masses of old Europe—while Africa, mainland Asia, South America are not even in the running. Actually, none of the hundred or so new countries that have been organized since World War II has imitated our form of government— though, to a nation, the local dictator likes to style himself the president. As for being the greatest nation on earth, the United State's hegemony of the known world lasted exactly five years: 1945 to 1950. As for being envied by the less fortunate (in a *Los Angeles Times* poll of October 1, 1980, 71 percent of the gilded state's citizens thought that the United States had "the highest living standard in the world today"), the United States has fallen to ninth place in per-capita income while living standards are higher for the average citizen in many more than eight countries.

Although this sort of information is kept from the 71 percent, they are very much aware of inflation, high taxes, and unemployment. Because they know that something is wrong, Proposition 13, once a mere gleam in the eye of Howard K. Jarvis, is now the law in California and something like it has just been enacted in Massachusetts and Arkansas. Our ancestors did not like paying taxes on their tea; we do not like paying taxes on our houses, tradition- ally the only form of capital that the average middle-class American is allowed to accumulate.

Today, thanks to the efforts of the National Taxpayers Union, thirty state legislatures have voted in favor of holding a new constitutional convention whose principal object would be to stop the federal government's systematic wrecking of the economic base of the country by requiring, somewhat na- ïvely, a balanced federal budget and, less naïvely, a limitation on the federal government's power to print money in order to cover over-appropriations that require over-borrowing, a process (when combined with a fifteen-year decline in industrial productivity) that has led to double-digit inflation in a world made more than usually dangerous by the ongoing chaos in the Middle East from which the West's oil flows—or does not flow.

Even the newspapers that belong to the governing establishment of the republic are beginning to fret about that national malaise which used to trouble the thirty-ninth Oval One. Two years ago, *The New York Times* printed three articles, more in sorrow than in anger, on how, why, where, when did it all go wrong? "The United States is becoming increasingly difficult to govern," the *Times* keened, "because of a fragmented, inefficient system of authority and procedures that has developed over the last decade and now appears to be gaining strength and impact, according to political leaders, scholars and public interest groups across the country."

Were this not an observation by an establishment newspaper, one would think it a call for a Mussolini: "difficult to govern . . . inefficient system of authority. . . ." Surely, We the People govern, don't we? This sort of dumb sentiment is passed over by the *Times*, which notes that "the national political parties have continued to decline until they are little more than frameworks for nominating candidates and organizing Congress and some state legislatures." But this is all that our political parties have ever done (honorable exceptions are the first years of the Republican party and the only years of the Populists). The Framers did not want political parties—or factions, to use their word. So what has evolved over the years are two pieces of electoral machinery devoted to the acquiring of office—and money. Since neither party represents anything but the interests of those who own and administer the country, there is not apt to be much "choice" in any election.

Normally, *The New York Times* is perfectly happy with any arrangement of which the *Times* is an integral part. But a series of crazy military adventures combined with breathtaking mismanagement of the economy (not to mention highly noticeable all-out corruption among the politicos) has thrown into bright relief the failure of the American political system. So the thirty-ninth Oval One blames the people while the people blame the lousy politicians and wish that Frank Capra would once more pick up the megaphone and find us another Gary Cooper (*not* the second lead) and restore The Dream.

Serious establishment types worry about the Fragmentation of Power. "Our political system has become dominated by special interests," said one to the *Times*, stars falling from his eyes like crocodile tears. After all, our political system is—and was—the invention of those special interests. The government has been from the beginning the *cosa nostra* of the few and the people at large have always been excluded from the exercise of power. None of our rulers wants to change this state of affairs. Yet the heirs of the Framers are getting jittery; and sense that something is going wrong somewhere. But since nothing can ever be their fault, it must be the fault of a permissive idle electorate grown fat (literally) before our eyes, which are television. So give the drones less wages; more taxes; and put them on diets.

But the politician must proceed warily; if he does not, that 71 percent which has been conned into thinking that they enjoy the highest standard of living in the world might get suspicious. So for a while the operative word was "malaise" in political circles; and no effort was made to change anything. Certainly no one has recognized that the principal source of all our problems is the Third Constitution, which allows the big property owners to govern pretty much as they please, without accountability to the people or to anyone else, since for at least a century the Supreme Court was perhaps the most active—even reckless—part of the federal machinery, as we shall demonstrate.

There is more than the usual amount of irony in the fact that our peculiar Constitution is now under siege from those who would like to make it either more oppressive (the Right-to-Lifers who want the Constitution to forbid abortion) or from those sly folks who want to make more and more money out of their real estate shelters. But no matter what the motive for change, change is now very much in the air; and that is a good thing.

This autumn, the counsel to the president, Mr. Lloyd N. Cutler, proposed some basic changes in the Constitution.[1] Although Mr. Cutler's approach was tentative and highly timid (he found no fault at all with the Supreme Court—because he is a partner is a Washington law firm?), he does think that it is impossible for a president to govern under the present Constitution because the separation of powers has made for a stalemate between executive and legislative branches. Since "we are not about to revise our own Constitution so as to incorporate a true parliamentary system," he proceeded to make a number of suggestions that would indeed give us a quasi-parliamentary form of government—president, vice president, and representative from each congressional district would all be elected at the same time for a four-year term (Rep. Jonathan Bingham has such a bill before the House); half the Cabinet to be selected from the Congress where they would continue to sit—and answer questions as in England; the president would have the power, once in his term, to dissolve the Congress and hold new elections—and the Congress would have the power, by a two-thirds vote, to call for a new presidential election; et cetera. Mr. Cutler throws out a number of other notions that would involve, at most, amendments to the Constitution; he believes that a new constitutional convention is a "non-starter" and so whatever change that is made must originate in the government as it now is even though, historically, no government has ever voluntarily dissolved itself.

Mr. Cutler also suffers from the malaise syndrome, contracted no doubt while serving in the Carter White House: "The public—and the press—still expect the President to govern. But the President cannot achieve his overall program, and the public cannot fairly blame the President because he does not have the power to legislate and execute his program." This is perfect establishment nonsense. The president and the Congress together or the president by himself or the Supreme Court on its own very special power trip can do virtually anything that they want to do as a result of a series of usurpations of powers that have been taking place ever since the Second Constitution of 1793.

When a president claims that he is blocked by Congress or Court, this usually means that he does not want to take a stand that might lose him an election. He will then complain that he is stymied by Congress or Court. In 1977, Carter could have had an energy policy *if* he had wanted one. What the president cannot get directly from Congress (very little if he knows how to manage those princes of corruption), he can often obtain through executive order, secure in the knowledge that the House of Representatives is not apt to exercise its prerogative of refusing to fund the executive branch: after all, it was nearly a decade before Congress turned off the money for the Vietnam War. In recent years, the presidents have nicely put Congress over a barrel through the impounding of money appropriated for projects displeasing to the executive. Impounded funds combined with the always vast Pentagon budget and the secret revenues of the CIA give any president a plump cushion on which to rest his Pharaonic crook and flail.

Obviously, a president who does not respect the decent opinion of mankind (namely, *The New York Times*) can find himself blocked by the Court and impeached by Congress. But the Nixon misadventure simply demonstrated to what extremes a president may go before his money is turned off—before the gates of Lewisberg Federal Penitentiary, like those to Hell or Disneyland, swing open.

Carter could have given us gas rationing, disciplined the oil cartels, encouraged the development of alternative forms of energy. He did none of those things because he might have hurt his chances of reelection. So he blamed Congress for preventing him from doing what he did not want to do. This is a game that all presidents play—and Congress, too. Whenever the

Supreme Court strikes down a popular law which Congress has been obliged to enact against its better judgment, the Supreme Court gets the blame for doing what the Congress wanted to do but dared not. Today separation of powers is a useful device whereby any sin of omission or commission can be shifted from one branch of government to another. It is naïve of Mr. Cutler to think that the president he worked for could not have carried out almost any program *if he had wanted to*. After all, for eight years Johnson and Nixon prosecuted the longest and least popular war in American history by executive order. Congress' sacred and exclusive right to declare war was ignored (by Congress as well as by the presidents) while the Supreme Court serenely fiddled as Southeast Asia burned. Incidentally, it is startling to note that neither Congress nor the Court has questioned the *principle* of executive order, even in the famous steel seizure case.

What *was* the original Constitution all about? I mean by this, what was in the document of 1787 as defended in the Federalist Papers of 1787–1788 by Madison, Hamilton, and Jay. Currently, Ferdinand Lundberg's *Cracks in the Constitution* is as good a case history of that Constitution (and its two successors) as we are apt to get this troubled season. Lundberg is the latest— if not the last—in the great line of muckrakers (TR's contemptuous phrase for those who could clean with Heraclean zeal the national stables which he, among others, had soiled) that began with Steffens and Tarbell. Luckily for us, Lundberg is still going strong.

The father of the country was the father if not of the Constitution of the convention that met in May 1787, in Philadelphia. Washington had been troubled by the civil disorders in Massachusetts in particular and by the general weakness of the original Articles of Confederation in general. From Mount Vernon came the word; and it was heard—and obeyed—all around the states. Quick to respond was Washington's wartime aide Alexander Hamilton, who knew exactly what was needed in the way of a government. Hamilton arrived at Philadelphia with a scheme for a president and a senate and a supreme court to serve for life—while the state governors would be appointed by the federal government.

Although neither John Adams nor John Jay was present in the flesh at Philadelphia, Jay's handiwork, the constitution of New York State (written with Gouverneur Morris and R. R. Livingston), was on view as was that of John Adams, who wrote nearly all of the Massachusetts state constitution; these two charters along with that of Maryland were the basis of the conven-

tion's final draft, a curious document which in its separation of powers
seemed to fulfill not only Montesquieu's cloudy theories of separation of
powers but, more precisely, was a mirror image of the British tripartite
arrangement of crown, bicameral legislature, and independent judiciary.
Only the aged Franklin opted for a unicameral legislature. But the other
Framers had a passion for England's House of Lords; and so gave us the
Senate.

Lundberg discusses at some length just who the Framers were and where
they came from and how much money they had. The state legislatures
accredited seventy-four men to the convention. Fifty-five showed up that
summer. About half drifted away. Finally, "no more than five men provided
most of the discussion with some seven more playing fitful supporting roles."
Thirty-three Framers were lawyers (already the blight had set in); forty-four
were present or past members of Congress; twenty-one were rated rich to very
rich—Washington and the banker Robert Morris (soon to go to jail where
Washington would visit him) were the richest; "another thirteen were affluent
to very affluent"; nineteen were slave owners; twenty-five had been to college
(among those who had *not* matriculated were Washington, Hamilton, Robert
Morris, George Mason—Hamilton was a Columbia dropout). Twenty-seven
had been officers in the war; one was a twice-born Christian — the others
tended to deism, an eighteenth-century euphemism for agnosticism or
atheism.

All in all, Lundberg regards the Framers as "a gathering of routine
politicians, eyes open for the main chance of a purely material nature. . . .
What makes them different from latter-day politicians is that in an age of few
distractions, many—at least twenty—were readers to varying extents in law,
government, history and classics."

Lundberg does not accept the traditional American view that a consortium
of intellectual giants met at Philadelphia in order to answer once and for all
the vexing questions of how men are to be governed. Certainly, a reading of
the *Federalist Papers* bears out Lundberg. Although writers about the Constitution like to mention Locke, Hume, Montesquieu and the other great
savants of the Enlightenment as godfathers to the new nation, Montesquieu
is quoted only four times in the *Federalist Papers*; while Hume is quoted just
once (by Hamilton) in a passage of ringing banality. Locke is not mentioned.
Fans of the Framers can argue that the spirit of Locke is ever-present; but
then non-fans can argue that the prevailing spirit of the debate is that of the
never-mentioned but always felt Hobbes. There is one reference each to

Grotius, Plato, and Polybius. There are three references to Plutarch (who wrote about great men) and three to Blackstone (who showed the way to greatness—or at least the higher solvency—to lawyers). God is mentioned three times (in the Thank God sense) by Madison, a clergyman's son who had studied theology. Jesus, the Old and New Testaments, abortion, and women's rights are not alluded to. The general tone is that of a meeting of the trust department of Sullivan and Cromwell.

Lundberg quotes Merrill Jensen as saying, "Far more research is needed before we can know, if ever, how many men actually voted for delegates to the state conventions [which chose the Framers]. An old guess that about 160,000 voted—that is, not more than a fourth or fifth of the total adult (white) male population—is probably as good as any. About 100,000 of these men voted for supporters of the Constitution and about 60,000 for its opponents." It should be noted that the total population of the United States in 1787 was about 3,000,000, of which some 600,000 were black slaves. For census purposes, each slave would be counted as three-fifths of a person within the First Republic.

The Framers feared monarchy and democracy. In order to prevent the man who would be king from assuming dictatorial powers and the people at large from seriously affecting the business of government, the Framers devised a series of checks and balances within a tripartite government that would, they hoped (none was very optimistic: they were practical men), keep the people and their passions away from government and the would-be dictator hedged 'round with prohibitions.

In the convention debates, Hamilton took on the romantic notion of the People: "The voice of the people has been said to be the voice of God; and however generally this maxim has been quoted and believed, it is not true in fact. The people are turbulent and changing; they seldom judge or determine right. Give therefore to [the rich and wellborn] a distinct, permanent share in the government." The practical old Tory Gouverneur Morris took the same view, though he expressed himself rather more serenely than the fierce young man on the make: "The rich will strive to establish their dominion and enslave the rest. They always did. They always will. The proper security against them is to form them into a separate interest." Each was arguing for a Senate of lifetime appointees, to be chosen by the state legislatures from the best and the richest. It is curious that neither envisioned political parties as the more natural way of balancing economic interests.

Since Hamilton's dark view of the human estate was shared rather more than less by the Framers ("Give all power to the many, they will oppress the few. Give all power to the few, they will oppress the many"), the House of Representatives was intended to be the principal engine of the tripartite government. Like the British Parliament, the House was given (in Hamilton's words) "The exclusive privilege of originating money bills. . . . The same house will possess the sole right of instituting impeachments; the same house will be the umpire in all elections of the President. . . ." And Hamilton's ultimate defense of the new Constitution *(Federalist Paper* No. 60) rested on the ingenious way that the two houses of Congress and the presidency were chosen: "The House of Representatives . . . elected immediately by the people, the Senate by the State legislatures, the President by electors chosen for that purpose by the people, there would be little probability of a common interest to cement these different branches in a predilection for any particular class of electors."

This was disingenuous: the electoral franchise was already so limited in the various states that only the propertied few had a hand in electing the House of Representatives and the state legislatures. Nevertheless, this peculiar system of government was a success in that neither the mob nor the dictator could, legally at least, prevail. The turbulent "democratic" House would always be reined in by the appointed senators in combination with the indirectly elected president and his veto. The Constitution gave the oligarch, to use Madison's word, full possession of the government—the object of the exercise at Philadelphia. Property would be defended, as George Washington had insisted that it should be. Since Jefferson's teeth were set on edge by the word property, the euphemism "pursuit of happiness" had been substituted in the Declaration of Independence. Much pleased with this happy phrase, Jefferson recommended it highly to the Marquis de Lafayette when he was Rights of Man-ing it in France.

The wisest and shrewdest analysis of how the House of Representatives would evolve was not provided by the would-be aristo Hamilton but by the demure James Madison. In *Federalist Paper* No. 59, Madison tried to set at ease those who feared that popular gathering in whose horny hands had been placed the national purse. Madison allowed that as the nation increased its population, the House would increase its membership. But, said he with perfect candor and a degree of complacency, "The people can never err more than in supposing that by multiplying their representatives beyond a certain limit they strengthen the barrier against the government of the few. Experience will forever admonish them that . . . they will counteract their own views by every addition to their representatives. The countenance of the government may become more democratic, but the soul that animates it will be more oligarchic" because "the greater the number composing [a legislative assembly] the fewer will be the men who will in fact direct their proceedings." Until the present—and temporary—breakdown of the so-called lower House, this has proved to be the case.

By May 29, 1790, the Constitution had been ratified by all the states. The need for a bill of rights had been discussed at the end of the convention but nothing had been done. Rather than call a second convention, the Bill of Rights was proposed—and accepted—as ten amendments to the new Constitution. A principal mover for the Bill of Rights was George Mason of Virginia, who had said, just before he left Philadelphia, "This government will set out [commence] a moderate aristocracy: it is at present impossible to foresee whether it will, in its operation, produce a monarchy, or a corrupt, tyrannical [oppressive] aristocracy: it will most probably vibrate some years between the two, and then terminate in the one or the other." The words in brackets were supplied by fellow Virginian—and notetaker—Madison. As the ancient Franklin observed brightly, sooner or later every republic becomes a tyranny. They liked reading history, the Framers.

But the wild card in the federal apparatus proved not to be the predictable Congress and the equally predictable presidency whose twistings and turnings any reader of Plutarch might have anticipated. The wild card was the Supreme Court.

Lundberg calls attention to the following language of Article III of the Constitution.

"The Supreme Court shall have appellate jurisdiction, both as to law and fact, *with such exceptions, and under such regulations as the Congress shall make.*"
The preceding twelve words [he continues] are emphasized because they are rarely alluded to in discussions about the Court. They bring out that, under the Constitution, the Supreme Court is subject to regulation by Congress, which may make exceptions among the types of cases heard, individually or by categories. Congress, in short, is explicitly empowered by the Constitution to regulate the Court, not *vice versa.*

Certainly, the Court was never explicitly given the power to review acts of Congress. But all things evolve and it is the nature of every organism to expand and extend itself.

In 1800, the outgoing Federalist President John Adams made a last-minute appointment to office of one William Marbury. The incoming

Republican President Jefferson ordered his secretary of state Madison to deny Marbury that office. Marbury based his right to office on Section 13 of Congress' Judiciary Act of 1789. Federalist Chief Justice John Marshall responded with marvelous cunning. In 1803 *(Marbury v. Madison)* he found unconstitutional Section 13, the work of Congress; therefore, the Court was unable to go forward and hear the case. The partisan Jefferson was happy. The equally partisan Marshall must have been secretly ecstatic: he had set a precedent. In passing, as it were, Marshall had established the right of the Supreme Court to review acts of Congress.

The notion of judicial review of the Executive or of Congress was not entirely novel. Hamilton had brought up the matter in 1787 *(Federalist Paper* No. 78). "In a monarchy [the judiciary] is an excellent barrier to the depotism of the prince; in a republic it is a no less excellent barrier to the encroachments and representations of the representative body." But the other Framers did not accept, finally, Hamilton's view of the Court as a disinterested umpire with veto power over the legislative branch. Yet Hamilton had made his case most persuasively; and he has been much echoed by subsequent upholders of judicial review.

Hamilton believed that the judiciary could never be tyrannous because it lacked real power; he does admit that "some perplexity respecting the rights of the courts to pronounce legislative acts void because contrary to the Constitution, has arisen from an imagination that the doctrine would imply a superiority of the judiciary to the legislative power. It is urged that the authority which can declare the acts of another void must necessarily be superior to the one whose acts must be declared void." Since this is true and since the Constitution that Hamilton is defending does *not* give judicial review to the Supreme Court, Hamilton does a most interesting dance about the subject. The Constitution is the "fundamental law" and derives from the people. If the legislative branch does something unconstitutional it acts against the people and so a disinterested court must protect the people from their own Congress and declare the act void.

Nor does this conclusion by any means suppose a superiority of the judicial to the legislative power. It only supposes that the power of the people is superior to both, and that where the will of the legislature, declared in its statutes, stands in opposition to that of the people, declared in the Constitution, the judges ought to be governed by the latter rather than the former.

This is breathtaking, even for Hamilton. He has now asserted that a court of life appointees (chosen from the rich and wellborn) is more interested in the rights of the people than the House of Representatives, the only more or less democratically elected branch of the government. But Hamilton is speaking with the tongue of a prophet who knows which god he serves. The future in this, as in so much else, was what Hamilton had envisaged, constitutional or not. Characteristically, by 1802, he had dismissed the Constitution as "a frail and worthless fabric."

Marshall was most sensitive to the charge of judicial usurpation of congressional primacy; and during the rest of his long tenure on the bench, he never again found an act of Congress unconstitutional. But Marshall was not finished with republic-shaping. Although he shared the Framers' passion for the rights of property, he did not share the admittedly subdued passion of certain Framers for the rights of the citizens. In 1833, Marshall proclaimed (speaking for a majority of his Court in *Barron* v. *City of Baltimore*) that the Bill of Rights was binding only upon the federal government and not upon the states. In order to pull off this caper, Marshall was obliged to separate the amendments from the Constitution proper so that he could then turn to Article VI, Paragraph 2, where it is written that this Constitution (pre–Bill of Rights) "shall be the supreme law of the land . . . any thing in the Constitution or laws of any state to the contrary not withstanding." Apparently, the first ten amendments were not an integral part of "this Constitution."

The result of Marshall's decision was more than a century of arbitrary harassment of individuals by sheriffs, local police, municipal and state governing bodies—to none of whom the Bill of Rights was held to apply. As for the federal government, the Supreme Court was only rarely and feebly willing to enforce the rights of citizens against it. It is startling to think that the Supreme Court did not seriously begin to apply the Bill of Rights to the states until the 1930s despite the Fourteenth Amendment (1868), which had spelled out the rights of citizens. Gradually, over the last thirty years, an often grudging court has doled out to the people of the United States (including Mr. Brown) most of those rights which George Mason had wanted them to have in 1793.

Fifty-four years after *Marbury* v. *Madison*, the Supreme Court found a second act of Congress unconstitutional. In order to return property to its owner (the slave Dred Scott to his master Dr. Emerson), the Supreme Court declared unconstitutional the Missouri Compromise; and made inevitable the Civil War. It was ironic that the Court which Hamilton had so Jesuitically proposed as a defender of the people against a wicked legislature should, in its anxiety to protect property of any kind, have blundered onto a stage where it had neither competence nor even provenance. (Article IV: "The Congress shall have power to dispose of and make all needful rules and regulations respecting the territory or other property belonging to the United States. . . .") But the wild card had now been played. Judicial review was a fact. The Court was now ready—give or take a Civil War or two—to come into its unconstitutional own.

In 1864, the Court struck down the income tax, denying Congress its absolute power to raise revenue; and not until the passage of the Sixteenth Amendment (1913) did Congress get back its right, in this instance, to raise taxes—which it can never *not* have had, under the Constitution. But as Lundberg says, "The Court had gained nearly eighteen years of tax-free bliss for its patrons although it was shown to be out of harmony with the thinking of the country as well as that of the framers, previous courts, and legal scholars—and the Constitution."

From March 9, 1865 (when the management of the reigning Republican party became almost totally corrupt), to 1970, ninety acts of Congress were held void in whole or in part. Most of these decisions involved property, and favored large property owners. As of 1970, the Court had also managed to overrule itself 143 times. Plainly, the Constitution that the justices keep interpreting and reinterpreting is a more protean document than the Framers suspected. "The trouble with the Constitution of the United States," wrote the *London Chronicle* a century ago, "is that nobody has ever been able to find out what it means." Or, put another way, since everybody knows what it means, much trouble must be taken to distort the meaning in order to make new arrangements for the protection of property.

Lundberg takes the position that, by and large, the Court's behavior is the result of a tacit consensus among the country's rulers: that two percent of the population—or one percent, or sixty families, or those *active* members of the Bohemian Club—owns most of the wealth of a country that is governed by the ruler's clients in the three branches of government. On those occasions when their Congress is forced by public opinion to pass laws that they do not want enacted, like the income tax of 1864, they can count either on their president's veto or on the Court's invocation of the Constitution to get Congress off the hook. The various courts are so devised, Lundberg writes, as to "rescue the legislatures and executives from their own reluctant acts."

Except for the passing of the Sixteenth Amendment, Congress has made only two serious attempts to reclaim its constitutional primacy over the Court (as opposed to a lot of unserious attempts). The first was in 1868. The House

Judiciary Committee, fearful that the Court would strike down a number of Reconstruction acts, reported a bill requiring that two-thirds of a court's judges must concur in any opinion adverse to the law. This bill passed the House but died in the Senate. In the same year, the House did manage to pass a law (over presidential veto) to limit certain of the Court's appellate powers. On March 19, 1869, the Court unanimously bowed to Congress, with a sideswipe to the effect that although the Constitution did vest them with appellate powers, the clause that their powers were conferred "with such exceptions and under such Regulations as Congress shall make" must be honored.

This is one of the few times that Congress has asserted directly its constitutional primacy over a Court that for the next seventy years took upon itself more and more the powers not only to review any and all acts of Congress but to make law itself, particularly when it came to preventing the regulation of corporations or denying rights to blacks. During the last forty years, although the Court has tended to stand aside on most economic matters and to intervene on racial ones, the Court's record of self-aggrandizement has been equaled only by that of the Johnny-come-lately wild card, the president.

The first fifteen presidents adjusted themselves to their roomy constitutional cage and except for an occasional rattling of the bars (the Alien and Sedition Acts) and one break-out (the Louisiana Purchase) they were fairly docile prisoners of Article II. In 1860, the election of the sixteenth president caused the Union to collapse. By the time that Abraham Lincoln took office, the southern states had organized themselves into what they called a confederacy, in imitation of the original pre-Constitution republic. As Lincoln himself had declared in 1847, any state has the moral and, implicitly, constitutional right to govern itself. But permissive Congressman Lincoln was not stern President Lincoln. Firmly he put to one side the Constitution. On his own authority, he levied troops and made war; took unappropriated money from the Treasury; suspended habeas corpus. When the aged Chief Justice Taney hurled the Constitution at Lincoln's head, the president ducked and said that, maybe, all things considered, Congress ought now to authorize him to do what he had already done, which Congress did.

Lincoln's constitutional defense for what he had done rested upon the oath that he had sworn to "preserve, protect and defend the Constitution" as well as to see to it "that the law be faithfully executed." Lincoln proved to be a satisfactory dictator; and the Union was preserved. But the balances within the constitution of the Second Republic had been forever altered. With the adoption of the Thirteenth, Fourteenth and Fifteenth Amendments extending the vote to blacks (and, by 1920, to women and, by 1970, to eighteen- to twenty-year-olds) while ensuring, yet again, that no state can "deprive any person of life, liberty, or property without the process of law; nor deny to any person within its jurisdiction the equal protection of the laws," the Bill of Rights was at last, officially at least, largely applicable to the people who lived in the states that were again united.

Needless to say, the Supreme Court, often witty if seldom wise, promptly interpreted the word "person" to mean not only a human being but a corporate entity as well. During the next fifty years, the Court continued to serve the propertied interests against any attack from the other branches of government while ignoring, as much as possible, the rights of actual persons. Any state that tried to curb through law the excesses of any corporation was sure to be reminded by the Court that it had no such right.

But the Third Republic had been born; the electorate had been expanded; and civil rights were on the books if not engraved in letters of fire upon the hearts of the judiciary. Although the presidents pretty much confined themselves to their constitutional duties, the memory of Lincoln was—and is—a constant stimulus to the ambitious chief magistrate who knows that once the nation is at war his powers are truly unlimited, while the possibilities of personal glory are immeasurable.

At the turn of the century Theodore Roosevelt nicely arranged a war for his president, McKinley, who did not particularly want one. In 1917 Wilson arranged a war which neither Congress nor nation wanted. Since then the presidents have found foreign wars irresistible. With the surrender of Japan in 1945, the last official war ended. But the undeclared wars—or "police actions"—now began with a vengeance and our presidents are very much on the march. Through secret organizations like the CIA, they subvert foreign governments, organize invasions of countries they do not like, kill or try to kill foreign leaders while spying, illegally, on American citizens. The presidents have fought two major wars—in Korea and Vietnam—without any declaration of war on the part of Congress.

Finally, halfway through the executives' war in Vietnam, the sluggish venal Congress became alarmed—not to mention hurt—at the way they had been disregarded by Johnson Augustus. The Senate Committee on Foreign Relations began to ask such questions as, by what inherent right does a president make war whenever he chooses? On March 8, 1966, the president (through a State Department memorandum) explained the facts of life to Congress: "since the Constitution was adopted there have been at least 125 instances in which the President has ordered the armed forces to take action or maintain positions abroad without obtaining prior Congressional authorization, starting with the 'undeclared war' with France (1798–1800). . . ." Congress surrendered as they had earlier when the inexorable Johnson used a murky happening in the Tonkin Bay to ensure their compliance to his war. It was not until many thousands of deaths later that Congress voted to stop funds for bombing the Indochinese.

How did the president break out of his cage? The bars were loosened by Lincoln, and the jimmy that he used was the presidential oath, as prescribed by the Constitution: "I do solemnly swear that I will faithfully execute the Office of President of the United States, and will to the best of my ability, preserve, protect, and defend the Constitution of the United States." Lincoln put the emphasis on the verb "defend" because he was faced with an armed insurrection. Later presidents, however, have zeroed in on the verb "execute" —as broad a verb, in this context, as any president on the loose could wish for. From this innocuous-seeming word have come the notions of inherent executive power and executive privilege, and that astonishing fact with which we have been obliged to live for half a century, the executive order.

Congress and Court can be bypassed by an executive order except on very odd occasions such as Truman's unsuccessful seizure of the steel mills. When Wilson's request to arm merchant American ships was filibustered to death by the Senate in 1917, Wilson issued an executive order, arming the ships. Later, still on his own, Wilson sent troops to Russia to support the czar; concluded the armistice of 1918; and introduced Jim Crow to Washington's public places. In 1936 Franklin Roosevelt issued a secret executive order creating what was later to become, in World War II, the OSS, and then in peacetime (sic) the CIA. This vast enterprise has never been even moderately responsive to the Congress that obediently funds it. The CIA is now the strong secret arm of the president and no president is about to give it up.

For all practical purposes the Third Republic is now at an end. The president is a dictator who can only be replaced either in the quadrennial election by a clone or through his own incompetency, like Richard Nixon, whose neurosis it was to shoot himself publicly and repeatedly in, as they say, the foot. Had Nixon not been helicoptered out of the White House, men in white would have taken him away. The fact that we are living in an era of one-term presidents does not lessen, in any way, the formidable powers of the executive.

The true history of the executive order has yet to be written. As of December 31, 1975, the presidents had issued 11,893 executive orders. The Constitution makes no allowances for them. In fact, when an order wages war or spends money, it is unconstitutional. But precedents can always, tortuously, he found for the president to "execute his office." In 1793, Washington proclaimed that the United States was neutral in the war between England and France, in contravention of the treaty of 1778 which obliged the United States to come to France's aid. In 1905 the Senate declined to approve a treaty that Theodore Roosevelt wanted to make with Santo Domingo. Ever brisk and pugnacious, TR made an agreement on his own; and a year later the Senate ratified it. In 1940 Franklin Roosevelt gave England fifty destroyers that were not his to give. But three years earlier, the Supreme Court had validated the principle of the executive *agreement (U.S. v. Belmont)*; as a result, the executive agreement and the executive order are now for the usurper president what judicial review has been for the usurper Court.

Law by presidential decree is an established fact. But, as Lundberg notes, it is odd that there has been no effective challenge by Congress to this usurpation of its powers by the executive. Lundberg quotes the late professor Edward S. Corwin of Princeton, a constitutional scholar who found troubling the whole notion of government by decree: "It would be more accordant," wrote Corwin in *Court Over Constitution*,[2] "with American ideas of government by law to require, before a purely executive agreement to be applied in the field of private rights, that it be supplemented by a sanctioning act of Congress. And that Congress, which can repeal any treaty as 'law of the land or authorization' can do the same to executive agreements would seem to be obvious." Obvious—but ignored by a Congress more concerned with the division of the contents of the pork barrel than with the defense of its own powers.

Between a president ruling by decrees, some secret and some not, and a Court making policy through its peculiar powers of judicial review, the Congress has ceased to be of much consequence. Although a number of efforts were made in the Congress during the Fifties to put the president back in his cage and to deflect the Court from its policymaking binges, nothing substantive was passed by a Congress which, according to Lundberg, "is no more anxious to restrict the president than it is to restrict the Supreme Court.

Congress prefers to leave them both with a free hand, reserving the right at all times to blame them if such a tactic fits the mood of the electorate." When Congress rejected Carter's energy program, it was not blocking a president who might well have got around it with an executive order. Congress was simply ducking responsibility for a gasoline tax just as the president had ducked it by maliciously including them in the process. Actually, Congress does, from time to time, discipline presidents, but it tends to avoid collisions with the principle of the executive order when wielded by the lonely Oval One. So does the Supreme Court. Although the Court did stop President Truman from seizing the steel mills in the course of the Korean (by executive order) War, the Court did not challenge the principle of the executive order per se.

Since the main task of government is the collection of money through taxes and its distribution through appropriations, the blood of the Third Republic is the money-labor of a population which pays taxes to support an executive establishment of some ten million people if one includes the armed forces. This is quite a power base, as it includes the Pentagon and the CIA —forever at war, covertly or overtly, with monolithic communism. "Justice is the end of government," wrote Madison (*Federalist Paper* No. 52). "It is the end of civil society. It ever has been and ever will be pursued until it is obtained, or until liberty be lost in the pursuit." Time to start again the hard pursuit.

It was the wisdom of Julius Caesar and his heir Octavian to keep intact the ancient institutions of the Roman republic while changing entirely the actual system of government. The new dynasty reigned as traditional consuls, not as kings. They visited regularly their peers in the Senate—in J.C.'s case once too often. This respect for familiar forms should be borne in mind when We the People attend the second constitutional convention. President, Senate, House of Representatives must be kept as familiar entities just as their actual functions must be entirely altered.

Thomas Jefferson thought that there should be a constitutional convention at least once a generation because "laws and institutions must go hand in hand with the progress of the human mind. As that becomes more developed, more enlightened, as new discoveries are made, new truths disclosed, and manners and opinions change with the change of circumstances, institutions must advance also, and keep pace with the times. We might as well require a man to wear still the coat which fitted him as a boy, as a civilized society to remain ever under the regimen of their barbarous ancestors." Jefferson would be amazed to see how the boy's jacket of his day has now become the middle-aged man's straitjacket of ours. The amended Constitution of today is roomier than it was, and takes into account the national paunch; but there is little freedom to move the arms because, in Herder's words, "The State is happiness for a group" and no state has ever, willingly, spread that happiness beyond the group which controls it. The so-called "iron law of oligarchy," noted by James Madison, has always obtained in the United States.

Ten years ago Rexford Guy Tugwell, the old New Dealer, came up with Version XXXVII of a constitution that he had been working on for some years at the Center for the Study of Democratic Institutions at Santa Barbara. Tugwell promptly makes the mistake that Julius Caesar and family did not make. Tugwell changes names, adds new entities. Yet the old unwieldy tripartite system is not really challenged and the result is pretty conventional at heart because "I believe," said Tugwell, explaining his new arrangements, "in the two-party system." One wonders why.

The Framers wanted no political parties—or factions. It was their view that all right-minded men of property would think pretty much alike on matters pertaining to property. To an extent, this was—and is—true. Trilateral Commissions exist as shorthand symbols of this meeting of minds and purses. But men are hungry for political office. Lincoln felt that if the United States was ever destroyed it would be by the hordes of people who wanted to be office-holders and to live for nothing at government expense—a vice, he added dryly, "from which I myself am not free."

By 1800 there were two political parties, each controlled by a faction of the regnant oligarchy. Today, despite close to two centuries of insurrections and foreign wars, of depressions and the usurpations by this or that branch of government of powers not accorded, there are still two political parties, each controlled by a faction of the regnant oligarchy. The fact that the country is so much larger than it was makes for an appearance of variety. But the substance of the two-party system or non-system is unchanged. Those with large amounts of property control the parties which control the state which takes through taxes the people's money and gives a certain amount of it back in order to keep docile the populace while reserving a sizable part of tax revenue for the oligarchy's use in the form of "purchases" for the defense department, which is the unnumbered, as it were, bank account of the rulers.

As Walter Dean Burnham puts it, "The state is primarily in business to promote capital accumulation and to maintain social harmony and legitimacy." But expensive and pointless wars combined with an emphasis on the consumption of goods at the expense of capital creation has called into question the legitimacy of the oligarchy's government. Even the dullest consumer has got the point that no matter how he casts his vote for president or for Congress, his interests will never be represented because the oligarchy serves only itself. It should be noted that this monomania can lead to anomalies. In order to buy domestic tranquility, Treasury money in the form of transfer-payments to the plebes now accounts for some 79 percent of the budget—which cannot, by law, be cut back.

In the 1976 presidential election 45.6 percent of those qualified to vote did not vote. According to Burnham, of those who did vote, 48.5 percent were the blue-collar and service workers. Of those who did not vote, 75 percent were blue-collar and service workers. The pattern is plain. Nearly 70 percent of the entire electorate are blue-collar and service workers. Since only 20 percent of this class are unionized, natural interest requires that many of these workers belong together in one party. But as 49 percent of the electorate didn't vote in 1980, the "two-party system" is more than ever meaningless and there is no chance of a labor party—or of any party other than than of the status quo.

The regnant minority is genuinely terrified of a new constitutional convention. They are happier with the way things are, with half the electorate permanently turned off and the other half mildly diverted by presidential elections in which, despite a semblance of activity, there is no serious choice. For the last two centuries the debate has been going on as to whether or not the people can be trusted to govern themselves. Like most debates, this one has been so formulated that significant alternative ideas are excluded at the start. "There are nations," said Herzen, "but not states." He saw the nation-state as, essentially, an evil—and so it has proved most of the time in most places during this epoch (now ending) of nation-states which can be said to have started, in its current irritable megalomaniacal form, with Bismarck in Germany and Lincoln in the United States.

James Madison's oligarchy, by its very nature, cannot and will not share power. We are often reminded that some 25 percent of the population are comprised of (in Lundberg's words) "the superannuated, the unskilled, the immature of all ages, the illiterate, the improvident propagators, the mentally below par or disordered" as well as "another 25 percent only somewhat better positioned and liable at any turn or whirligig of circumstances to find them-selves in the lower category." As Herzen, in an unhappy mood, wrote, "Who that respects the truth would ask the opinion of the first man he meets? Suppose Columbus or Copernicus had put to the vote the existence of America or the movement of the earth?" Or as a successful movie executive, in a happy mood, once put it: "When the American public walks, its knuckles graze the ground."

The constant search for external enemies by the oligarchy is standard stuff. All dictators and ruling groups indulge in this sort of thing, reflecting Machiavelli's wisdom that the surest way to maintain one's power over the people is to keep them poor and on a wartime footing. We fought in Vietnam to contain China, which is now our Mao-less friend; today we must have a showdown with Russia, in order to. . . . One has already forgotten the basis for the present quarrel. No. Arms race. That's it. They are outstripping us in warheads, or something. On and on the propaganda grinds its dismal whine. Second to none. Better to die in Afghanistan than Laguna. We must not lose the will. . . .

There are signs that the American people are beginning to tire of all of this. They are also angry at the way that their money is taken from them and wasted on armaments—although they have been sufficiently conned into thinking that armaments are as good as loafers on welfare and bureaucrats on the Treasury teat are bad. Even so, they believe that too much is being taken away from them; and that too little ever comes back.

Since Lundberg began his career as an economist, it is useful to quote him at length on how the oligarchy operates the economy—acting in strict accordance with the letter if not the spirit of the three constitutions.

The main decision that Congress and the President make that is of steady effect on the citizenry concerns appropriations—that is, how much is to be spent up to and beyond a half-trillion dollars and what for. The proceeds are supposed to come from taxes but here, in response to citizen sensitivity, the government tends to understate the cost. Because the government has taken to spending more than it takes in, the result is inflation—a steady rise in the prices of goods and services.

The difference between what it spends and what it takes in the government makes up by deviously operating the money-printing machine, so that the quantity of money in circulation exceeds the quantity of goods and services. Prices therefore tend to rise and money and money-values held by citizens decline in purchasing value. . . .

All that the government has been doing in these respects is strictly constitutional. For the Constitution empowers it, first, to lay taxes without limit (Article I, Section 8, Paragraph 1). It is empowered in the very next paragraph to borrow money on the credit of the United States—that is, the taxpayers—also without limit. . . . As to inflation, Paragraph 5 empowers the government, through Congress and the President, not only to coin money but to "regulate the value thereof." In other words, under the Constitution a dollar is worth whatever Congress and the President determine it to be by their fiscal decisions, and for nearly three decades officials, Republican and Democratic alike, have decreed that it be worth less. . . .

When Congress and president over-appropriate, the Treasury simply prints

. . . short-term notes and bonds and sends these over to the Federal Reserve Bank, the nation's central bank. In receipt of these securities, the Federal Reserve simply credits the Treasury with a deposit for the total amount. The Treasury draws checks against these deposits. And these checks are new money. Or the Treasury may simply offer the securities for sale in the open market, receiving therefore the checks of buyers.

Since there is no legal way to control either president or Congress under the current system, it is inevitable that there would be a movement for radical reform. The National Taxpayers Union was organized to force the federal government to maintain a balanced budget. In order to accomplish this, it will be necessary to change the Constitution. So the National Taxpayers Union has called for a new constitutional convention. To date, thirty state legislatures have said yes to that call. When thirty-four state legislatures ask for a new convention, there will be one. As Professor Gerald Gunther of Stanford Law School recently wrote:

The convention delegates would gather after popular elections—elections where the platforms and debates would be outside congressional control, where interest groups would seek to raise issues other than the budget, and where some successful candidates would no doubt respond to those pressures. Those convention delegates could claim to be legitimate representatives of the people. And they could make a plausible —and I believe correct—argument that a convention is entitled to set its own agenda. . . .[3]

Those who fear that Milton Friedman's cheerful visage will be swiftly hewn from Dakota rock underestimate the passion of the majority not to be unemployed in a country where the gap between rich and poor is, after France, the greatest in the Western world. Since the welfare system is the price that the white majority pays in order to exclude the black minority from the general society, entirely new social arrangements will have to be made if that system is to be significantly altered.

Predictably, the oligarchs and their academic advisers view with alarm any radical change. The Bill of Rights will be torn to shreds, they tell us.

Abortion will be forbidden by the Constitution while prayers will resonate in the classrooms of the Most Christian Republic. The oligarchs think that the people are both dangerous and stupid. Their point is moot. But we do know that the oligarchs are a good deal more dangerous to the polity than the people at large. Predictions that civil rights would have a rocky time at a new convention ignore the reality that the conglomeration of groups attending it will each have residual ethnic, ideological, religious, and local interests whose expression they will not want stifled. It is by no means clear that civil liberties would be submerged at a new convention; and there is no reason why the delegates should not decide that a Supreme Court of some sort should continue to act as protector of the Bill of Rights—a better protector, perhaps, than the court that recently separated a Mr. Snepp from his royalties.

The forms of the first three republics should be retained. But the presidency should be severely limited in authority, and shorn of the executive order and the executive agreement. The House of Representatives should be made not only more representative but whoever can control a majority will be the actual chief of government, governing through a cabinet chosen from the House. This might render it possible for the United States to have, for the first time in two centuries, real political parties. Since the parliamentary system works reasonably well in the other industrially developed democracies, there is no reason why it should not work for us. Certainly our present system does not work, as the late election demonstrated.

Under a pure parliamentary system the Supreme Court must be entirely subservient to the law of the land, which is made by the House of Representatives; and judicial review by the Court must join the executive order on the junk-heap of history. But any parliamentary system that emerged from a new constitutional convention would inevitably be a patchwork affair in which a special niche could, and no doubt would, be made for a judicial body to protect and enforce the old Bill of Rights. The Senate should be kept as a home for wise men, much like England's House of life-Lords. One of the Senate's duties might be to study the laws of the House of Representatives with an eye to their constitutionality, not to mention rationality. There should be, at regular intervals, national referenda on important subjects. The Swiss federal system provides some interesting ideas; certainly their cantonal system might well be an answer to some of our vexing problems—particularly, the delicate matter of bilingualism.

The First Constitution will be two hundred years old in 1987—as good a date as any to finish the work of the second constitutional convention, which will make possible our Fourth Republic, and first—ah, the note of optimism!—civilization.

Notes

1. *Foreign Affairs*, Fall 1980.
2. Princeton University Press, 1950.
3. "Constitutional Roulette: The Dimensions of the Risk" in *The Constitution and the Budget*, edited by W. S. Moore and Rudolph G. Penner (American Enterprise Institute for Public Policy Research, Washington and London, 1980).

19. Court over Constitution

Ferdinand Lundberg

Ferdinand Lundberg's muckraking writings include *Imperial Hearst* (1936), *America's Sixty Families* (1938), *Who Controls Industry?* (1938), *The Rich and the Super-Rich* (1968), and *The Rockefeller Syndrome* (1975).

The following selection is excerpted by permission from *Cracks in the Constitution* (Secaucus, N.J.: Lyle Stuart, 1980), 202–13 and 215.

For a review article on this book see Gore Vidal's essay in this volume.

The part of the Constitution establishing the Supreme Court, Article III, is the briefest by far of any designating divisions of the government. All it says is that "The judicial power shall be vested in one Supreme Court, and in such inferior courts as the Congress may from time to time ordain and establish. The judges, both of the Supreme Court and inferior courts, shall hold their offices during good behavior, and shall at stated times receive for their services, a compensation, which shall not be diminished during their continuance in office.

"The judicial power shall extend to all cases, in law and equity, arising under this Constitution, the laws of the United States, and treaties made, or which shall be made, under their authority; to all cases affecting ambassadors, other public ministers and consuls; to all cases of admiralty and maritime jurisdiction; to controversies to which the United States shall be a party; to controversies between two or more states; between a State and citizens of another State; between citizens of different States, between citizens of the same state claiming lands under grants of different States, and between a State, or the citizens thereof, and foreign states, citizens or subjects."

This is all, apart from an additional paragraph that gives the Supreme Court original jurisdiction in cases involving diplomats and those to which a state may be a party, and that "the Supreme Court shall have appellate jurisdiction, both as to law and fact, *with such exceptions, and under such regulations as the Congress shall make."*

The preceding twelve words are emphasized because they are rarely alluded to in discussions about the Court. They bring out that, under the Constitution, the Supreme Court is subject to regulation by Congress, which may make exceptions among the types of cases heard, individually or by categories. Congress, in short, is explicitly empowered by the Constitution to regulate the Court, not *vice versa.* Yet the Court more often seems to regulate Congress.

Why is this? First . . . Congress finds it convenient to allow the Court rather than itself to take the blame for unpopular decisions; judges can be removed only with great difficulty and for cause whereas Congressmen are easily removed by the volatile and often quixotic electorate. Second, although individual Congressmen and groups of Congressmen are often volubly wrathful about Court decisions, such wrath being relished by frustrated constituents, it would ordinarily be difficult among 435 members of the lower house and 100 members of the Senate to mobilize enough votes to intervene against the Court. Congressmen are fully sensible of the value of the Court as a scapegoat, deflecting public censure from themselves, and they are in any event usually in great disagreement among themselves.

Only once has Congress seriously moved to trim the claim to final power assumed by the Court, a claim that is itself subject to exceptions. This was in 1868 when the Judiciary Committee of the House reported a bill that prescribed that in any case involving the validity of an act of Congress, two-thirds of the judges must concur in any opinion adverse to the law. Congress could in fact require a unanimous opinion. The bill was passed by 116 to 39. The fear in Congress was that in a pending case the Court was about to hold the post-war Reconstruction acts invalid. The bill died in the Senate. While there was much support for the measure in the country, there was also heated opposition from conservatives. The same year there was another House venture, this one successful, to limit the Court. A Senate bill to extend the Court's appellate jurisdiction to customs and revenue cases came to the House. To it was then tacked an amendment completely repealing the appellate jurisdiction of the Court under the Habeas Corpus Act of 1867 and prohibiting the exercise of any jurisdiction by the Court in this respect on appeals. Back in the Senate the amendment was concurred in with no debate on March 12, 1868, by 32 to 6. The bill was vetoed by President Andrew Johnson but was then repassed over the veto.

The Supreme Court meanwhile delayed hearing what was known as the McCardle case, the one which had provided the strong reaction in Congress. On March 19, 1869, the Court took up the case again on the question of the power of Congress to prohibit it from deciding a pending case and in April unanimously decided that Congress by its statute had in fact, and constitutionally, taken away its jurisdiction in the case and that it could not pronounce judgment.

"Judicial duty", said the Court, "is not less fitly performed by declining ungranted jurisdiction than in exercising firmly that which the Constitution and the laws confer." Although appellate jurisdiction did not stem from acts of Congress but from the Constitution, it said, yet it was conferred "with such exceptions and under such regulations as Congress shall make." [1]

By reason of its power to regulate the Court, only once used, it is clear that the last word in any showdown with respect to the supremacy of Court or Congress under the Constitution lies with Congress, not with the Court. Congress, for its part, is in closer contact with the active political elements of the country than is the Court.

One might say on the basis of what has been said thus far that practically, in nearly all questions, the Court is supreme. Yet even this is not unqualifiedly so. For, contrary to common supposition, the rulings of the Court do not always produce a general rule that is thereupon dutifully followed by everybody. The decisions of the Court apply only to a specific case and may or may not be more broadly applied. Many of its rulings with respect to a single government department for example are simply ignored, not applied, by other government departments. It would be necessary for someone to file another lawsuit in order to get the benefit of the decisive ruling, a tedious proceeding that is not often resorted to, one of the many delays built into the system. The Court cannot direct the entire government.

The country in the case of *Brown v. Board of Education* was shown how an original ruling of the Supreme Court in a controversial case must be followed by a long succession of further court proceedings and peremptory court orders, plus police and military action through a willing executive branch, in specific instances throughout the country. In fact, under *Brown*, the courts, against sullen popular opposition, have had to monitor and direct very precisely the school systems with respect to race in various parts of the country. In many other matters, too, federal judges have taken over the direction of state governments, as in Alabama and elsewhere, with respect to the operation of jails, asylums, shelters and other public facilities where, in the name of local economy or just plain orneriness, the ordinary decent treatment of inmates has been found violated in wholesale fashion.

Where such stringent judicial or legislative follow-ups are not undertaken or where a ruling is not spontaneously embraced all around, a court decision manifestly applies only to the case in question. No general rule is made operative by it.

Many laws on the books, as well as court decisions, are thus much like beautiful roads that extend a distance and then suddenly end on the edge of a desert or a wilderness. They lead, as it is said, to nowhere except in one case where an accommodating path is marked out. Additionally there are equivocal laws, which seem to say one thing but carry within self-cancelling provisions. One example among many such legal mirages was the Corrupt Practices Act of 1925 which, according to the obvious intention of its framers, did not prevent any corrupt practices. It was no more than complicated window-dressing for the naive.

As to what is called judicial review on the part of the Supreme Court, there is no mention of it in the Constitution nor was it authorized by the constitutional convention. A few of the members, judging by their remarks, obviously favored it, and they were not all nationalists. Others were adamantly opposed and said so.

Judicial review is derived by deduction and construction from two separate parts of the Constitution. Article VI, Section 2, three paragraphs from the end, says, "This Constitution, and the laws of the United States which shall be made in pursuance thereof, and all treaties made, or which shall be made, under the authority of the United States, shall be the supreme law of the land; and the judges in every State shall be bound thereby, any thing in the Constitution or laws of any State to the contrary notwithstanding." Combining this section with Article III, Section 1 — "The judicial power shall extend to all cases, in law and equity, arising under this Constitution," etc. — one has the implied basis, constitutionally stated, for judicial review.

Not many persons at the time the Constitution was up for ratification saw the connection. But Judge Robert Yates of New York, a member of the constitutional convention, writing as an experienced jurist under the name of "Brutus," did see it and spelled out what he saw as the dire consequences in a series of notable newspaper articles that impressed Hamilton at least. Under such power to interpret and apply what was a piece of formally unauthorized prior legislation, namely the Constitution, appointed lifetime judges would have a power unprecedented in history: to nullify joint acts of the legislature and the executive made on behalf, theoretically, of the broad constituencies they represented.

A few of the observations made by Judge Yates were as follows:

With respect to the Constitution, "the courts of law, which will be constituted by it, are not only to decide upon the constitution and the laws made in pursuance of it, but by officers subordinate to them to execute all their decisions. The real effect of this system of government, will therefore be brought home to the feelings of the people, through the medium of the judicial power . . ."

Those who are vested with this power

are to be placed in a situation altogether unprecedented in a free country. They are to be rendered totally independent, both of the people and the legislature, both with respect to their offices and salaries. No error they may commit can be corrected by any power above them, if any such power there be, nor can they be removed from office for making ever so many erroneous adjudications . . .

This part of the plan is so modelled, as to authorize the courts, not only to carry into execution the powers expressly given, but where these are wanting or ambiguously expressed, to supply what is wanting by their own decisions . . . A number of hard words and technical phrases are used in this part of the system, about the meaning of which gentlemen learned in the law differ . . .

The cases arising under the constitution must include such, as bring into question its meaning, and will require an explanation of the nature and extent of the powers of the different departments under it.

This article, therefore, vests the judicial with a power to resolve all questions that may arise upon the construction of the constitution, either in law or in equity.

The courts are also given authority

to give the constitution a legal construction, or to explain it according to the rules laid down for construing a law. — These rules give a certain degree of latitude of explanation . . . they are empowered to explain the constitution according to the reasoning spirit of it, without being confined to the word or letter . . . The opinions of the supreme court, whatever they may be, will have the force of law; because there is no power provided in the constitution, that can correct their errors, or control their adjudications. From this court there is no appeal . . . The legislature must be controlled by the constitution, and not the constitution by them . . .

Most of the articles in this system, which convey powers of considerable importance, are conceived in general and indefinite terms, which are either equivocal, ambiguous, or which require long definitions to unfold the extent of their meaning. The two most important powers committed to any government, those of raising money, and of raising and keeping up troops, have already been considered and shewn to be unlimited by any thing but the discretion of the legislature. The clause which vests the power to pass all laws which are proper and necessary, to carry the powers given into execution, it has been shewn, leaves the legislature at liberty, to do everything, which in their judgment is best. It is said, I know, that this clause confers no power on the legislature, which they would not have had without it—though I believe this is not the fact, yet, admitting it to be, it implies that the constitution is not to receive an explanation strictly, according to its letter; but more power is implied than is expressed. And this clause . . . is to be understood as declaring, that in construing any of the articles conveying power, the spirit, intent and design of the clause, should be attended to, as well as the words in their common acceptation.

[The courts] will be interested in using this latitude of interpretation. Every body of men invested with office are tenacious of power; they feel interested, and hence it has become a kind of maxim, to hand down their offices, with all its rights and privileges, unimpaired to their successors; the same principle will influence them to extend their power, and increase their rights; this of itself will operate strongly upon the courts to give such a meaning to the constitution in all cases where it can possibly be done, as will enlarge the sphere of their own authority. Every extension of the power of the general legislature, as well as of the judicial powers, will increase the powers of the courts; and the dignity and importance of the judges, will be in proportion to the extent and magnitude of the powers they exercise. I add, it is highly probable the emoluments of the judges will be increased, with the increase of the business they will have to transact and its importance. From these considerations the judges will be interested to extend the powers of the courts, and to construe the constitution as much as possible, in such a way as to favour it; and that they will do it, appears probable.

Because they will have precedent to plead, to justify them in it. It is well known, that the courts in England, have by their own authority, extended their jurisdiction far beyond the limits set them in their original institution, and by the laws of the land.

This power in the judicial, will enable them to mould the government, in almost any shape they please. —The manner in which this may be effected we will hereafter examine.

Yates by his precisely insightful analysis produced in the "Brutus" articles, published in a New York newspaper prior to the ratification of the Constitution, what amounted to a blueprint of actual future governmental developments under the Constitution.[2] Yates, in brief, wrote much of the scenario for the future, much more so than any other pre-ratification critic or proponent of the Constitution. What he said was publicly denied by pro-ratificationists.

Marbury versus Madison

About this applied judicial power, first clearly asserted by the Court in *Marbury v. Madison* (1803), there was from the beginning much controversy and objection. The controversy recurs from time to time and depends in its magnitude more on the content of each disputed ruling than on the elitist principle of judicial review. Those who approve or benefit from a ruling of the Court believe, for the moment at least, that judicial review is an excellent method. Those who disapprove often go so far as to assert that the Court has usurped its power. They go further and charge that the Court often invents laws, which indeed it does. Approval or disapproval of the work of the Court depends upon whose ox is being gored, which usually leaves the Court in a strong public position as it always has a large or influential section of the public on its side.

The decision of the Court in *Marbury v. Madison*, written by Chief Justice John Marshall, was expressed in a very serpentine way. The apparent issue, about which the new Jefferson administration was unduly excited, concerned the last-minute appointment by outgoing President John Adams under the Judiciary Act of 1801 of some Federalist judges. One of these, William Marbury, was appointed justice of the peace of the District of Columbia. Newly elected President Jefferson ordered Secretary of State James Madison, now very much on his way up in the government, to withhold from Marbury the sealed commission of his appointment, signed by Adams. Here was one President refusing to recognize the legal act of a predecessor.

Marbury sued for a writ of mandamus compelling delivery of the commission. To comply with the request would have brought the Court into a direct confrontation with the irate President and his militant popular party, which was the chief opponent of the Federalist Party to which both Adams and Chief Justice Marshall belonged. In the means he employed to avoid this confrontation, which might well have undermined the Court, Marshall formally placed it on the high theoretical elevation it still enjoys. Marshall declared that Section 13 of the Judiciary Act of 1789, empowering the Court to issue such a writ, was contrary to the Constitution and therefore invalid. He denied Marbury the writ.

In so doing he produced, as it were, a bundle of political dynamite with a long time-fuse attached. But the Jeffersonians were too elated by their victory with respect to Marbury to more than growl, and moved on to have repealed the entire Judiciary Act of 1801 which, in addition to providing more judges also excused Supreme Court judges from doubling as trial judges on circuits, a chore they all found distasteful. The Judiciary Act of 1801 lasted little more than a year and circuit-riding by Supreme Court judges continued for a long time.

What Jefferson got out of the decision was very little. What Marshall and the Federalists and post–Civil War Republicans got was a great deal: a claimed brake on Congress and the President, both elected by the sacred people, although it was far from being the absolute brake that Court cultists at times erroneously make it out to be.

The most interesting aspect of Marshall's decision is that Section 13 of the Judiciary Act was not in fact out of harmony with the Constitution, and Marshall and the Court could have denied Marbury the mandamus he sought simply on the basis of Section 13. But by doing that Marshall would not have obtained what he sought: a precedent of record for declaring an act of Congress and the President void.

Sitting in the Senate when the Judiciary Act was written were twelve out of twenty-four Senators who had been members of the constitutional convention, including outstanding participants such as Ellsworth and Johnson of Connecticut, Paterson of New Jersey, King of New York, and linchpin Robert Morris of Pennsylvania. Eight out of fifty-eight members of the House were recent members of the constitutional convention, including stalwarts Roger Sherman of Connecticut and Madison. And President Washington, chief officer of the convention, signed the act. Epigones such as Marshall and his Court, which included one framer, Paterson, certainly had no better understanding of the Constitution than these men.

The reader may judge for himself whether these men in Congress had inadvertently lapsed from the Constitution they had just put together. Section 13 of the Judiciary Act says that the Supreme Court "shall have power to issue writs of prohibition to the district courts when proceeding as courts of admiralty and maritime jurisdiction, and writs of *mandamus*, in cases warranted by the principles and usages of law, to any courts appointed, or persons holding office, under the authority of the United States."[3]

What Chief Justice Marshall could easily have done was to deny Marbury his request on the ground that his case was not one where a mandamus was "warranted by the principles and usages of law." And this was strictly true as the Supreme Court was an appellate court except in constitutionally designated rare cases where it was a court of original jurisdiction. The writ of mandamus in a court of original jurisdiction is a settled part of the legal routine, and the case brought by Marbury did not fall under one of the classifications allowed by the Constitution as conferring upon the Supreme Court original jurisdiction. Beyond this, at no time in English or American history had a court of any kind been empowered to direct the head of a government in a matter of his official duties. In brief, the mandamus could have been denied simply on the ground that the case was one where the Court had no constitutional jurisdiction. Or, the case need not have been heard at all. But by so adjudicating, the arch-Federalist Marshall would not have been able to make his point about the power of the Court to nullify an act of Congress.

Such a staunch adulator of Marshall and the Court as the historian Charles Warren admits:

> it would have been possible for Marshall, if he had been so inclined, to have construed the language of the section of the Judiciary Act which authorized writs of mandamus, in such a manner as to have enabled him to escape the necessity of declaring the section unconstitutional. The section was, at most, broadly drawn, and was not necessarily to be interpreted as conferring original jurisdiction on the Court . . . Marshall naturally felt that in view of the recent attacks on judicial power it was important to have the great principle [of judicial review] firmly established, and undoubtedly he welcomed the opportunity of fixing the precedent in a case in which his action would necessitate a decision in favor of his political [sic!] opponents. Accordingly, after reviewing the provisions of the Constitution as to the original jurisdiction of the Court, he held that there was no authority in Congress to add to that original jurisdiction, that the [section of the] statute was consequently invalid.[4]

In the United States at the time, the ultimate supremacy of the Court was an unusual claim and had been advanced for a number of years only by a small but growing coterie of lawyers, not all of whom were Federalists. The anti-Court Jeffersonians had earlier clamored to have the Court declare the Alien and Sedition Acts unconstitutional, but these had now changed their tune about the power of the Court.

The Idea of Judicial Supremacy

How the unusual idea of judicial review came to arise at all, an idea that makes the United States Constitution as officially interpreted unique, is itself interesting. There were eight cases of judicial review in the states of the pre-constitutional Confederation—one each in Massachusetts, North Carolina, Rhode Island, Connecticut, New York and New Jersey, and two in Virginia.[5] Such action by these courts however was nowhere formally authorized, just as the legislatures themselves were not formally authorized. Both were *ad hoc* by-products of revolt and secession, the creations of revolutionary juntas.

Where had at least some of the newly independent colonists come upon the idea that a legislature could be judicially overruled? Prior to 1776, in the colonial period, all colonial laws repugnant to English laws were invalid.[6] Here was the very essence of colonial subordination, detested by the revolutionists. Such colonial laws were subject to *administrative* review by the British Board of Trade and by colonial governors, who held office at the pleasure of the King. Hence, at the last resort, all colonial laws existed at the pleasure either of the King or of Parliament, which ruled the Board of Trade. No fewer than 8,563 acts of colonial legislatures were given such review and 469 or 5.5 per cent of them were disallowed.[7] But this was by no means judicial review.

Review in Britain by the Board of Trade began in 1696, prior to which the task fell to the King's Privy Council although that body did not perform it systematically until after 1660. It is thought by many scholars that in this process of essentially foreign administrative review, ideas and principles were developed that in many ways prepared the American mentality for review by permanent judges under the United States Constitution.[8] The judges take the place of the old-style English king and his henchmen.

In a very few cases colonial courts declined to enforce an order of His Majesty in Council because it contradicted the colonial charters, which many colonists, especially lawyers, looked upon as their Constitution. Two such cases were heard in Massachusetts—*Frost v. Leighton* and *Giddings v. Brown*.[9]

The original basis for judicial review, often cited by its proponents, was the pre-colonial decision of Lord Chief Justice Edward Coke in Dr. Bonham's case (1610). The Royal College of Physicians in England had imposed a fine for the illegal practice of medicine and Coke held that according to common law no man can be a judge in his own case.

In the course of his decision he threw out this *obiter dictum*: "It appears in our books that in many cases the common law will control acts of parliament and some times adjudge them to be utterly void; for when an act of parliament is against common right or reason, or repugnant or impossible to be performed, the common law will control it and adjudge such act to be void" (8 Coke 118a).

Leading lawyers of the revolution liked to cite this decision.

In the case of *Rawles v. Mason*, Coke said, "If there be repugnancy in statute or unreasonableness in custom, the common law disallows it and rejects it."[10]

And how does one discover what the common law is, as it is not anywhere recorded? Judges have this pleasant task. As defenders of common law put it, the judges "find" the law in reasonable customs of the people. As critics put it, the judges invent the law, sometimes out of the whole cloth.

Coke as a devotee of the common law was manifestly laying out a large role for judges and has therefore always been an object of admiration by the generality of the legal profession. For very similar reasons Chief Justice Marshall is similarly admired.

At the time of the Bonham case, Coke was in controversy with the repressive Stuart monarchy, which controlled Parliament. He was then, although not always in his career, on the popular side and was the originator of what came to be called "the myth of Magna Carta."[11] Coke, in an age when few people could read and few had access to any books, enjoyed an exaggerated reputation for profound learning in the law; he was not nearly as learned as he professed. Many of his historical doctrines have been found by scholars to be unsound and Coke did not hesitate to invent supposed ancient laws to his own purposes of the moment, some of them personal and profitable. In this respect he was completely unscrupulous and high-handed.

But in 1776 hardly any Americans, high or low, believed in judicial review. "A fact which contributed greatly to the early supremacy of the legislatures was the general assumption during the years 1776–87 that they were the sole judges of their own constitutional powers," says an esteemed Establishment historian. "Few Americans believed that any State court had the right to declare an enactment invalid on the ground that it violated the Constitution. New York, in creating her Council of Revision, implied that whenever a legislative enactment was approved by the Council, it was thenceforth subject to no question . . . The Massachusetts Constitution of 1780 also showed that the State courts were in no instance expected to annul a statute, for it provided that in 1795 there should be a popular vote upon the calling of a Convention to remedy any transgressions of fundamental law . . ."[12]

Nor had public attitudes much changed at the time of the constitutional convention. In the convention opinions were sharply divided on the point so that nobody can cite for his preference what the sacrosanct Founding Fathers thought. Both Madison and James Wilson, chief theoreticians of the convention, were zealously opposed to judicial review and fought for a council of revision that would give prior certification of the constitutionality of every law, thus avoiding the tangle of later expensive litigation with which the country has since been beset. If either judges or President objected to such a certification, it would be subject to overrule by two-thirds vote of Congress; if both judges and the President objected, by three-fourths vote. Delaware, Maryland and Virginia supported this procedure, which was voted down 8 to 3, mainly on the ground that judges should have no hand in legislation.

Charles Pinckney of South Carolina, "opposed the interference of the Judges in the Legislative business," Mercer of Maryland "disapproved of the Doctrine that the Judges as expositors of the Constitution should have authority to declare a law void," Dickinson of Delaware "thought no such power ought to exist," and Sherman of Connecticut "disapproved of Judges meddling in politics and parties." Gouverneur Morris of New York however disagreed and so apparently did Elbridge Gerry.[13]

The convention thereupon, after denying judges participation in the presidential veto, simply made no provision for judicial review of any kind. The absence of any explicit prohibition of something so eccentric as judicial review certainly does not argue that it may be resorted to. For if a constitution had to mention everything not permitted, it would be endless.

Judicial review, then, is just one of the usages of the Constitution that has sprung up in the course of jockeying among the divisions, personalities and factions of the government. It has no sanction from the founders. It was not provided for by the framers in so many words and will be tolerated only as long as it seems useful to political managers or does not produce persistent public objection.

That Marshall was impressed by the growls of disapproval over his pronouncement on Section 13 of the Judiciary Act, which had no immediate practical effect, is suggested by the fact that he never again made a finding of unconstitutionality about an act of Congress although later Courts have found acts of the period unconstitutional. It was not until 1857 [in *Dred Scott*], or 54 years after *Marbury*, that the Supreme Court again used the shotgun Marshall had loaded—with disastrous repercussions upon itself and the nation.

. . . Judicial review, although not without merit, is far from the great procedure that its devotees, mainly lawyers and political conservatives, claim it to be. As often as not its deliverances are unsettling on the spot or productive of deferred profound difficulties. The main objection to it is that it is politically "unnatural", amounting to a basically arbitrary censorship and rescription of the legislative and executive power. A majority of a few judges are no better readers of the Constitution or devisers of legislation than are legislators, presidents or scholars, as the Marbury and Dred Scott cases show. More of whatever the country has to mobilize in the way of wisdom is directed at the legislature than at the courts even though, true enough, a legislature does not always choose the way of wisdom. Nor, as the record shows, do the courts.

Notes

1. *Ex parte McCardle*, 7 Wall. 506. The case is discussed extensively in Charles Warren, *The Supreme Court in United States History*, Little Brown & Co., Boston, 1926, vol. 2, pp. 464–88.
2. The Yates "Letters of Brutus" appeared in the *New York Journal and Weekly Register* in the latter weeks of 1787 and during January, February and March 1788. Numbers 11, 12 and 15 are reproduced in Edward S. Corwin, *Court over Constitution*, Princeton University Press, 1950, pp. 231–62.
3. *The Public Statutes at Large of the United States of America*, 1789–1845. Charles C. Little and James Brown, Boston, 1850, vol. 1, p. 81.
4. Warren, op. cit., vol. 1, pp. 242–3.
5. Charles Grove Haines, *The American Doctrine of Judicial Supremacy*, University of California Press, 1932, pp. 89–121.
6. Ibid., p. 45.
7. Ibid., p. 49.
8. Ibid., p. 45.
9. Ibid., pp. 56–7.
10. Ibid., p. 33.
11. Ibid., p. 34. Edward Jenks in an article titled "The Myth of Magna Carta" in *The Independent Review*, 4:260, pointed out that Coke invented the legend of Magna Carta, the legend that in this document English liberty was born and consecrated. Much research has disclosed this as simply not so. For a succinct and scholarly treatment of Magna Carta and its role in British history see Anne Pallister, *Magna Carta: The Heritage of Liberty*, Oxford University Press, London, 1971. As Pallister points out, only four clauses of thirty-seven paragraphs of the Magna Carta of 1237, which alone was discontinuously operative over any considerable length of time, survive in the British Constitution today. "Yet the validity of three of them is somewhat dubious," the author pointedly remarks (p. 101). The original Magna Carta of 1215, about which American politicians from time to time bawl to the heavens in mock piety, was a dead letter soon after issued and was not known to scholars until the seventeenth century. Magna Carta, as anyone can determine by reading a translation, far from a liberating document, was a yoke for centuries on the British common people who attained

freedom only with its gradual liquidation. The entire Magna Carta story, as commonly told, is a tissue of myth.

12. Allan Nevins, *The American States during and after the Revolution, 1779–1789*, Macmillan Co., N.Y., 1924, pp. 168–9.

13. Max Farrand, ed. *The Records of the Federal Convention of 1787*, revised edition, vol. 2, Yale University Press, 1966, pp. 298–300.

20. The Second American Revolution

Eric Foner

Eric Foner, professor of history at Columbia University, is the author of *Tom Paine and Revolutionary America* (1976), *Free Labor, Free Soil, Free Men: The Ideology of the Republican Party Before the Civil War* (1970), *Politics and Ideology in the Age of the Civil War* (1980), *Nothing but Freedom: Emancipation and Its Legacy* (1983), and *Reconstruction: America's Unfinished Revolution, 1863–1877* (1988) and the editor of *America's Black Past: A Reader in Afro-American History* (1970).

The following selection is reprinted by permission from "The Second American Revolution," *In These Times*, 16–22 September 1987, 12–13.

The Civil War and Reconstruction produced not simply three constitutional amendments—the 13th, 14th and 15th—but a new American constitution. As a result of the greatest crisis in our country's history, it was amended first to abolish slavery, then to establish a national citizenship whose rights, enforced by the federal government, were to be enjoyed equally by blacks and whites and, finally, to enfranchise the nation's black male population.

These were revolutionary changes for a nation whose economy up to 1860 rested in considerable measure on slave labor, whose Constitution included clauses that protected the stability of slavery and the political power of slaveholders and whose laws, from the beginning, were grounded in racism.

The principles engrafted onto the Constitution in the amendments of the era are now so much a part of our political thinking (especially on the left) that it may be difficult to recognize how utterly unprecedented they were before the Civil War. Apart from a few abolitionists, virtually no white Americans before 1860 believed in equality before the law irrespective of race. And on the eve of the Civil War no state accorded blacks the same rights as whites.

Even outside the slave states the majority of blacks could not vote, testify in court against whites or attend public schools. A few Northern states even prohibited blacks by law from entering their territory. In the 1857 *Dred Scott* decision the Supreme Court announced that no black person could be a U.S. citizen (a plausible interpretation of the original Constitution and the subsequent practices of the state and federal governments).

Nor did most Americans before the Civil War look to the federal government to protect citizens' rights. The greatest threats to liberty, most believed, arose not from the abuse of local authority, but from a too-powerful national state. The Bill of Rights reflected this assumption, for it prohibited Congress, but not the states, from abridging citizens' fundamental rights. Nor did any real concept of national citizenship exist before 1860.

Recurring Debate

Indeed, the principles enshrined in the Civil War amendments were so unprecedented that the passionate political debate they inspired has continued to our own time. Only last year Attorney General Edwin Meese chastised the Supreme Court for a series of decisions based on the legal doctrine of "incorporation"—that is, that the 14th Amendment requires the states to respect the prohibitions on abuse of power that the Bill of Rights had originally applied to the federal government.

The justices, Meese argued, had strayed from the "original intent" of the amendment's framers. Meese, in turn, was chastised by Justice William Brennan for attempting to reverse decades of constitutional interpretation.

Neither an assessment of the recent debate nor a broader appreciation of how the Civil War amendments changed the Constitution can be arrived at without a careful look at the crisis of the 1860s. Two developments during the Civil War were crucial to placing the issue of black citizenship on the national agenda. One was the disintegration of slavery—a process initiated by blacks who abandoned their owners' plantations to head for the lines of the Union Army and given political sanction in the Emancipation Proclamation.

The second was the massive enrollment of blacks into the Union armed forces. By the end of the war, some 200,000 black men had served in the Army and Navy. The "logical result" of black military service, one senator observed in 1864, was that "the black man is henceforth to assume a new status among us."

At the same time, the exigencies of war created a profound alteration in the nature of American government. The need to mobilize the North's resources for modern war produced what one Republican called "a new government," with a greatly expanded income, bureaucracy and set of responsibilities.

And the war inspired a broad nationalism, embraced above all by anti-slavery reformers, black and white, and Radical Republicans in Congress. With emancipation, these men and women believed, the federal government had become not a threat to local autonomy and individual liberty, but the "custodian of freedom."

The amendments of the 1860s reflected the intersection of these two Civil War products—the idea of equality before the law and the newly empowered national state. The 13th, adopted by Congress in January 1865 and ratified the following December, not only abolished slavery throughout the Union (including the loyal border slave states to which the Emancipation Proclamation had not applied), but empowerd Congress to enforce abolition with "appropriate legislation."

End as Beginning

"The one question of the age is settled," declared an anti-slavery Congressman, but the amendment closed one question only to open a host of others. Many Republicans envisioned a slaveless nation as one with "one law impartial over all." The amendment, they believed, authorized Congress to eliminate various kinds of discriminations against blacks as "badges of slavery" that must be swept away along with the South's "peculiar institution."

Most forthright in calling for further action on behalf of blacks' rights were the Radical Republicans, led in the House by Thaddeus Stevens of Pennsylvania and in the Senate by Charles Sumner of Massachusetts. The Union's victory in the Civil War, they believed, offered a golden opportunity to purge the nation of "the demon of caste," and to create what Stevens called a "perfect republic" based upon the principle of equality before the law.

Some Radicals, like Stevens, went even further, proposing that the national government confiscate lands belonging to the planter class and distribute them among the former slaves. Most Republicans were unwilling to go this far, but they did insist that blacks should enjoy the same opportunity as whites to compete for advancement in the economic marketplace.

When Congress reconvened in December 1865 the Radicals represented only a minority among Republicans. But events quickly pushed the more numerous moderates in their direction. Lincoln had been succeeded in office by Andrew Johnson of Tennessee. During the summer and fall of 1865, Johnson had initiated his own program of Reconstruction, which in effect placed the old planter class back in control of Southern affairs.

Southern public life was restricted entirely to whites, and the new state governments sought to establish a labor system as close to slavery as possible. Blacks were required by law to sign yearly labor contracts; refusal to do so, or attempting to leave work before a contract expired, meant arrest, a prison term or being leased out to anyone who would pay the culprit's fine. No such regulation applied to white citizens.

These laws, known as the Black Codes, seemed to the North to make a mockery of emancipation. In response, Congress in the spring of 1866 enacted the Civil Rights Act, which became law over Johnson's veto.

This measure defined all persons born in the U.S. (except Indians) as national citizens, and spelled out rights they were to enjoy equally without regard to race—including making contracts, bringing lawsuits, owning property and receiving equal treatment before the courts. No state could deprive an individual of these basic rights; if it did so, state officials would be held accountable in federal court.

In constitutional terms, the Civil Rights Act of 1866 represented the first attempt to give meaning to the 13th Amendment, to define the consequences of emancipation. If states could deny blacks the right to choose their employment, seek better jobs and enforce payment of wages, noted one Congressman, "then I demand to know, of what practical value is the amendment abolishing slavery?" But beyond these specific rights, Republicans also rejected the entire idea of laws differentiating between blacks and whites in access to the courts and penalties for breaches of the law.

Striking Departure

As the first statutory definition of American citizenship, the Civil Rights Act embodied a profound change in federal-state relations. Republican leader James G. Blaine later remarked, before the Civil War only "the wildest fancy of a distempered brain" could have envisioned a law of Congress requiring states to accord blacks "all the civil rights pertaining to a white man." Moreover, the bill invalidated many Northern laws discriminating against blacks. The underlying assumption—that the federal government possessed the power to define and protect citizens' rights—was a striking departure in American law.

One purpose of the 14th Amendment, approved by Congress in June 1866, was to prevent a future Congress from repealing the guarantees in the Civil Rights Act. But the amendment's purposes were broader than this. Its heart was the first section, which declared all persons born or naturalized in the U.S. both national and state citizens, and prohibited the states from abridging their "privileges or immunities," depriving any person of life, liberty or property without "due process of law," or denying them "equal protection of the laws."

For more than a century, politicians, judges, lawyers and scholars have debated the meaning of these elusive terms. The problem of ascertaining the amendment's "original intent" is compounded by the fact that its language was a compromise with which no one seemed "entirely satisfied." Yet despite many drafts, deletions and changes, its central principle remained constant: a national guarantee of equality before the law.

This was now so widely accepted in Republican circles, and had already been so fully discussed, that compared with now-forgotten clauses concerning representation in Congress, the Confederate debt and the disqualification of certain Confederates from office, the first section inspired relatively little debate. One congressman declared it to be "so just that no member of this House can seriously object to it."

Unlike the Civil Rights Act, which listed numerous specific rights a state could not abridge, the 14th Amendment used only broad language. Unlike a statute, it was intended as a statement of principle. Both Radical and moderate Republicans understood phrases like "privileges or immunities" and "equal protection of the laws" as subject to changing interpretation. They preferred to allow Congress and the federal courts maximum flexibility in combatting the multitude of injustices confronting Southern blacks.

Indeed, it is ironic that an attorney general who prides himself on abiding by "original intent" chastises the federal courts for their judicial activism in interpreting the amendment. For Congress intentionally chose to rely on the federal courts for civil-rights enforcement. The alternative would have been either abandoning the freedmen, maintaining a standing army indefinitely in the South or establishing some kind of national police force to oversee Southern affairs.

It is equally apparent that, as Michigan's Sen. Jacob Howard declared, the amendment was intended to prohibit the states from infringing upon liberties guaranteed in the Bill of Rights. Republicans wished to force the states to respect such key provisions as freedom of speech, the right to bear arms, trial by impartial jury and protection against cruel and unusual punishment. In fact, the amendment was deemed necessary, in part, precisely because every one of these rights was being systematically violated in the South in 1866.

The Right to Vote

Transcending boundaries of race and region, the 14th Amendment changed and broadened the definition of freedom for all Americans, for its language challenged legal discrimination throughout the nation. Nonetheless, many reformers were deeply disappointed in the amendment. Republicans in 1866 were divided on the question of black suffrage. The amendment merely threatened to reduce Southern representation in Congress if blacks continued to be denied the franchise.

And, in its representation clause, the amendment for the first time introduced the word "male" into the Constitution. Suffrage restrictions that reduced the number of male voters would cost a state representation; women could continue to be barred from voting without penalty. The result was a split between advocates of blacks' rights and women's rights.

Both ideologically and politically, 19th-century feminism had been tied to abolition. During the war the organized women's movement had put aside the suffrage issue to join in the crusade for the Union and emancipation. Now leaders like Elizabeth Cady Stanton and Susan B. Anthony insisted that if the Constitution were to be changed, the claims of women must not be ignored.

To Radicals and abolitionists who insisted that this was "the Negro's hour," feminists defined it instead as the hour for change—an opportunity that must be seized or another generation might pass "ere the constitutional door will again be opened." In response Radicals, even those sympathetic to the idea of women's suffrage, insisted that tying the issues of black rights and women's suffrage would doom both. A Civil War had not been fought over the status of women, nor had 30 years of prior agitation awakened public consciousness on the issue.

Repudiated by the Southern states and President Johnson, the 14th Amendment became the centerpiece of the political campaign of 1866. When Republicans swept the fall elections, they moved not only to ensure the amendment's ratification, but granted the right to vote to black men in the South and mandated the formation of new Southern governments resting on manhood suffrage. Under this policy of Radical Reconstruction, interracial democracy flourished for several years throughout the South, and blacks probably exercised more genuine power than at any time in our history, before or since.

In 1869 Congress approved the last of the postwar amendments, the 15th, which prohibited the federal or state governments from depriving individuals of the vote on racial grounds. By allowing states to continue to bar women from the polls, it further angered feminist leaders. Moreover, its language left open the possibility of poll taxes, literacy tests and other ostensibly nonracial requirements which could, and would, be used to disfranchise the vast majority of Southern black men.

With the end of Reconstruction in 1877, the egalitarian impulse embodied in the amendments of the 1860s faded from national life. The three amendments remained parts of the Constitution, but as far as blacks were concerned they increasingly became dead letters.

Even in the early 1870s the Supreme Court had begun to restrict the rights protected under the 14th Amendment. After 1877 the federal courts employed their expanded powers primarily to protect corporations from local regulation (on the grounds that corporations were "persons" who could not be deprived of their property rights by state agencies). By 1896, in *Plessy vs. Ferguson*, the court found racial segregation mandated by state law perfectly compatible with the doctrine of equality before the law.

In the 20th century, the court slowly used the 14th Amendment to strike down state laws abridging freedom of speech and other provisions of the Bill of Rights. But only in our own time did a great mass movement and a socially conscious Supreme Court again breathe life into racial egalitarianism, and a broad view of national responsibility for citizens' rights that form the essence of the postwar amendments. If anything, the history of these amendments underscores how fragile individual rights can be, even when protected by the letter of the Constitution.

21. The Third American Revolution

I. F. Stone

Muckraker I. F. Stone (1907–1989), the writer, editor, and publisher of *I. F. Stone's Weekly* (1953–1971), began his newspaper career at age four-teen, when he founded a monthly, the *Progress*. He went on to write for the *Nation, PM*, the *New York Post*, the *Daily Compass*, and other newspapers and magazines. His books include *Business as Usual* (1941), *Underground to Palestine* (1946), *This Is Israel* (1948), *The Hidden History of the Korean War* (1952), *The Truman Era* (1953), *The Haunted Fifties* (1964), *In a Time of Torment* (1967), *Polemics and Prophecies* (1971), *The Killings at Kent State* (1971), *I. F. Stone's Weekly Reader* (1973), and *The Trial of Socrates* (1988).

Stone described himself as "half a Jeffersonian and half a Marxist. I never saw a contradiction between the two, and I still don't."

The following selection is excerpted from *The Court Disposes* (New York: Covici Friede, 1937), 70–79.

The Civil War, historians tell us, was the second American Revolution, shifting power from one class, the planter aristocracy, to an alliance of two other classes, the northern capitalist and the western free-soil farmer.

Between 1890 and 1905 there was a third American Revolution, a revolution by judges, little known, little understood. No property was damaged; no one killed. The *forms* of our government were left undisturbed.

Under the surface in that decade and a half many things changed. The conservative minority on the Supreme Court of the United States became the majority. Jefferson termed the Judiciary the "sappers and miners" of the Constitution. During this period they succeeded in subverting it. The Constitution as it had been interpreted during the first century of our history, was in large part replaced by the cobweb of phrases—"due process," "liberty of contract," "confiscatory rate"—that block economic and social reform in our time. In the face of the rising demand of farmers and workers to curb the growing power of moneyed men and moneyed corporations, the Supreme Court was welded into the instrument American big business needed to evade democratic processes. Behind the veil of legal phrase, the Constitution was remade until it bore little relation, in so far as labor and property relations are concerned, to the document framed at Carpenters' Hall in Philadelphia in 1787, or as expounded by the Supreme Court under Marshall, Taney and Waite.

The Supreme Court began to reign, as the Shoguns of Japan did, in the name of a Mikado that was its prisoner. The Supreme Court ruled in the name of the Constitution, but the Constitution became more truly than ever what the judges say it is.

Many saw in *Munn v. Illinois* a "socialistic" menace to property rights. In November–December of 1890 a distinguished New York lawyer wrote in the *American Law Review* of the new constitutional amendment made necessary by that decision if property in this country was to be secure from "populistic" assaults.

What of the Fourteenth Amendment, and its due process clause? Had that not been in the Constitution since 1873? Was it not all the protection property rights required? One would think so from the vantage point of 1937. In December of 1890 the present use of the "due process" clause as synonymous with laissez faire and an excuse for invalidating any reform legislation the conservatives on the Court dislike could be found only in minority dissenting opinions, beginning with that of Mr. Justice Field in the Louisiana Slaughter House cases in 1873.

A new amendment *was* needed, but the amending was done not by the people but by the judges. The revolution which was to change our Constitution in so far as social and economic legislation is concerned began on March 24, 1890, when in *Chicago, Milwaukee and St. Paul Railroad v. Minnesota*, the Court overturned the rule established in *Munn v. Illinois*, a rule deriving from Marshall, that for the abuse of the regulatory power recourse must be had to the polls and not to the Courts. In 1890 the Court declared that "due process" gave it the right to review rates fixed by Legislature or regulatory commission; and to protect railroads and utilities from "confiscatory rates."

In the next fifteen years the Court was artificially to narrow the "commerce," "police power" and "public interest" concepts developed by Marshall, Taney and Waite, and to turn them into restrictions on, instead of means of widening, legislative power. At the same time they were to substitute a network of corporation lawyer phrases for the Constitution "due process," "liberty of contract" and "confiscatory," and by means of these concepts and by a new use of the Tenth Amendment, drastically to reduce the powers of both federal and state legislatures in dealing with economic and social problems, and vastly to increase the powers of the Court.

Since much of this story must now deal with the "due process" clause, it might be well to glance back at what the Court had always said "due process" meant in the past. In the Slaughter House cases in 1873 counsel objected that the establishment of a regulated slaughter house monopoly in New Orleans was a violation of the Fourteenth Amendment because it deprived other butchers of their property without due process of law. The Court objected that the interpretation placed upon the Amendment "would constitute this court a perpetual censor upon all legislation of the States." The Court in 1873 had no difficulty in disposing of the "due process" plea. The Court referred to "the argument . . . that the defendant's charter deprives the plaintiffs of their property without due process of law, or that it denies to them the equal protection of the law."

The first of these paragraphs has been in the Constitution since the adoption of the Fifth Amendment. . . . It is also to be found in some form of expression in the constitutions of nearly all the States. . . . And it is sufficient to say that under no construction of that provision that we have ever seen, or any that we deem admissible, can the restraint imposed by the State of Louisiana upon the exercise of their trade by the butchers of New Orleans be held to be a deprivation of property within the meaning of that provision.

The Court of the 1890's, in its task of remaking the Constitution to suit Morgans, Goulds, Vanderbilts, Rockefellers, Carnegies, Harrimans, did not let precedents deter it. In 1890 it held that "due process" gave it the right to act as a super-regulatory commission, to review railroad and utility rates. In 1897 it decided for the first time that "due process" protected "liberty of contract"; and later in the same year, though it upheld an eight-hour law for Utah miners as constitutional, it hinted that in the future it would hold any law it considered "unreasonable" a violation of the "due process" clause. In 1905 it went further. It held that a ten-hour law for New York bakers was an "unreasonable" interference with "liberty of contract" and therefore "unconstitutional." In 1897, when the Court first read "liberty of contract" into the Constitution, it merely held that a state had no right to interfere with the liberty of its citizens to contract for insurance *outside* the boundaries of that state. By 1905 the Court ruled that a state could not interfere with "liberty of contract" even within its own borders unless the Supreme Court considered the interference "reasonable." And despite medical testimony it derided the idea that the baker's trade was unhealthy, and limitation of working hours to ten a day reasonable.

In that same year, in the famous case of *Smyth v. Ames*, the 1890 rule that the Courts could protect a railroad or utility against a "confiscatory" rate (*i.e.*, a rate that actually confiscated its property), became a rule that railroads and utilities had a right to a "fair" return on a "fair" valuation, with the Courts to decide what was fair in both cases. Mr. Justice Brewer indicated what he would consider a "fair" valuation. He would include the right to a return on the value of property given to the railroad by states or municipalities. (There were vast grants of this kind to the railroads.)

Nor was that all. Mr. Justice Brewer added:

> If it be said that the rates must be such as to secure to the owners a reasonable per cent on the money invested, it will be remembered that many things have happened to make the investment far in excess of the actual value of the property — injudicious contracts, poor engineering, unusually high cost of material, rascality on the part of those engaged in the construction or management of the property. These, and many other things, as is well known, are factors which have largely entered into the investment with which many railroad properties stand charged.

This was an invitation to bad business practices and dishonesty, with the Court guaranteeing that the public would foot the bill.

The rule laid down by the Court in *Smyth v. Ames* in 1897 has made effective regulation impossible. The problem of valuation has become a nightmare; accounting, a branch of metaphysics. The possibility of appeal to the Courts on both questions of law and fact permit utility companies to enmesh regulatory commissions in endless litigation — at the expense of the public. A few horrible examples were collected by Mr. Justice Brandeis in his dissent in the St. Joseph's Stockyard case, April 27, 1936. One was the New York Telephone case. Protests over the company's increase in rates in the winter of 1919 led to fifteen years at litigation. Mr. Justice Brandeis gives us a glimpse of the work involved:

> Before the commission there were, between 1920 and 1926, 189 days of hearings, 450 witnesses were examined orally. The evidence introduced fills, in the aggregate 26,332 pages; and there were, in addition, 1,035 elaborate exhibits, one alone being in 22 volumes. Hearings were also held from January 24, 1930. The opinions of the commission in these proceedings fill 396 pages. In the District Court the hearings

before the master occupied 710 days and extended over a period of four years; 609 witnesses being examined orally. They were recalled a total of 688 times. The evidence of that hearing fills 36,532 pages; and there were in addition 3,288 exhibits. The decree below was entered November 7, 1929. The company's counsel then labored two years in preparing a draft of the condensed narrative statement of the evidence required for the transcript of record on the appeal to this Court. On submitting this draft to counsel for the commission, the city, and the state, many errors were discovered. On 3,000 of the items counsel disagreed; months were devoted to composing the differences; and finally the items on which counsel could not agree were settled by the lower court. On November 14, 1933, more than four years after entry of the decree appealed from, the company filed here a record of 5,700 pages. On February 14, 1934, that appeal was dismissed.

No one need wonder why it is so hard to get a reduction in light, gas, heat or telephone rates.

The most amazing term of Court in this revolutionary period began in October, 1894. Our judicial Robespierres were ruthless, arbitrary, contemptuous of legal and constitutional precedents. By an interpretation of the commerce clause that would have shocked Marshall, the Court nullified the newly enacted anti-trust laws by holding that a trust controlling 98 per cent of the sugar manufactured in this country was engaged in "local" business and was not in restraint of trade. Though the Court has since receded from this extreme position in so far as anti-trust laws are concerned, the notorious Sugar Trust case is still part of our constitutional law, the forerunner of the NRA and Guffey decisions. At the same time the Court turned about to give federal power over interstate commerce an unprecedentedly broad interpretation in order to legalize Cleveland's action in breaking the Pullman strike and jailing Eugene Debs. This was the first case in which the Supreme Court gave its blessing to the labor injunction. It derived the process from the law of nuisances. Labor unions *were* a nuisance to the corporations the Court served. It prided itself on testimony showing that the Court had broken the strike and it advised workers to seek redress of wrongs, not by strikes, but "through the courts and at the ballot box." In the Sugar Trust case it was the dissenting minority that quoted Marshall. In the Debs case it was the triumphant majority that invoked his broad interpretation of the commerce clause. The contrast between the narrow view taken by the Court to protect the rights of great business combines and the broad view taken to destroy the rights of workers runs like an ugly thread through the subsequent history of our anti-trust laws.

Finally, at that term and at the following term of Court, in two decisions, the Supreme Court held federal income taxes unconstitutional. Federal income taxes had been imposed in 1861, 1862, 1863, 1864, 1865, 1866, 1867, and 1870, and upheld by the Supreme Court of the United States. Every commentator on American constitutional law, including such outstanding conservatives as James Kent, Joseph Story and Thomas Cooley, had upheld their constitutionality. The Court waved these precedents aside as "a century of error," saving millions of dollars to the wealthy; for it was not until 1913, seventeen years after its final decision, that the Income Tax Amendment was adopted. From the Pandora's box of this case came another evil. A federal law of 1867 forbade any court to enjoin the collection of a federal tax. But the Supreme Court permitted the now familiar "stockholder's suit" device by which, instead of directly enjoining collection of a tax, it gives a stockholder an injunction forbidding his corporation to pay the tax. The Court showed that henceforth it would do as it pleased with both law and Constitution.

The executive committee of the Minnesota Farmers Alliance was in session when the Third American Revolution began in 1890. The committee greeted the news of the Minnesota rate decision as "the subjection of the people and the states to the unlimited control of the railroad corporations of the country" and a resolution was adopted appealing "from this second Dred Scott decision to the people of the nation . . . with a request that they unite with us in an effort to amend the Constitution so as to abolish this new slavery." It was too late. The vast trusts which began to dominate our economic system between the 1870's and the 1890's had finally begun to dominate the Courts. On them now sat men who had been the servants of these trusts. The fabulous wealth that poured from the continent at the touch of these great combines (the Carnegie interests alone made $133,000,000 in profits between 1875 and 1890) represented an irresistible power, able to twist newspapers, legislators, lawyers and judges to its purposes.

The money power might meet temporary defeat at the polls, but the Court was its citadel.

22. Corporations Are Not Persons

Ralph Nader and Carl J. Mayer

Consumer advocate Ralph Nader is director of the Corporate Accountability Research Group, author of *Unsafe at Any Speed* (1965), and coauthor of *The Consumer and Corporate Responsibility* (1973), *The Menace of Atomic Energy* (1977), *Who's Poisoning America* (1981), and *The Big Boys: Power and Position in American Business* (1987).

Carl J. Mayer, professor of law at Hofstra University School of Law, is the author of "Personalizing the Impersonal: Corporations and the Bill of Rights," *Hastings Law Journal* (1990).

The following selection is reprinted by permission from the *New York Times*, 9 April 1988, 31. Copyright © 1988 by the New York Times Company.

Our constitutional rights were intended for real persons, not artificial creations. The Framers certainly knew about corporations but chose not to mention these contrived entities in the Constitution. For them, the document shielded *living* beings from arbitrary government and endowed them with the right to speak, assemble and petition.

Today, however, corporations enjoy virtually the same umbrella of constitutional protections as individuals do. They have become in effect artificial persons with infinitely greater power than humans. This constitutional equivalence must end.

Consider a few noxious developments during the last 10 years. A group of large Boston companies invoked the First Amendment in order to spend lavishly and thus successfully defeat a referendum that would have permitted the legislature to enact a progressive income tax that had no direct effect on the property and business of these companies. An Idaho electrical and plumbing corporation cited the Fourth Amendment and deterred a health and safety investigation. A textile supply company used Fifth Amendment protections and barred retrial in a criminal antitrust case in Texas.

The idea that the Constitution should apply to corporations as it applies to humans had its dubious origins in 1886. The Supreme Court said it did "not wish to hear argument" on whether corporations were "persons" protected by the 14th Amendment, a civil rights amendment designed to safeguard newly emancipated blacks from unfair government treatment. It simply decreed that corporations were persons.

Now *that* is judicial activism. A string of later dissents, by Justices Hugo Black and William O. Douglas, demonstrated that neither the history nor the language of the 14th Amendment was meant to protect corporations. But it was too late. The genie was out of the bottle and the corporate evolution into personhood was under way.

It was not until the 1970's that corporations began to throw their constitutional weight around. Recent court decisions suggest that the future may hold even more dramatic extensions of corporate protections.

In 1986, Dow Chemical, arguing before the Supreme Court, suggested that the Fourth Amendment's prohibition against unreasonable searches and seizures should prohibit the Environmental Protection Agency from flying planes over Dow's manufacturing facilities to monitor compliance with environmental laws. Although the Court permitted the flights on technical grounds, it appeared to endorse Dow's expansive view of the Constitution.

That year, corporations received the most sweeping enlargement of their free speech rights to date. In a 5–3 decision, the Court invalidated a California regulation ordering a public utility monopoly to enclose in its billing envelopes a communication from a nonprofit rate-payer advocacy group that financed the insert. The purpose of the regulation was to assist the Public Utility Commission in achieving its authorized goal of reasonable rates. Even so, the Court held that the enclosures violated a new corporate First Amendment right "not to speak." Associate Justice William H. Rehnquist wrote in a pro-consumer dissent that to "ascribe to such artificial entities an 'intellect' or 'mind' [for constitutional purposes] is to confuse metaphor with reality."

Today, corporations remain unsatisfied with their ascendant constitutional status. They want much more. At a 1987 judicial conference in Pennsylvania, lawyers counseled that corporations use the First Amendment to invalidate a range of Federal regulations, including Securities and Exchange Commission disclosure requirements that govern corporate takeovers, and rules affecting stock offerings.

Businesses angry at Congressional attempts to ban cigarette advertising—by that, we mean commercial carcinogenic speech—are alleging First Amendment violations.

The corporate drive for constitutional parity with real humans comes at a time when legislatures are awarding these artificial persons superhuman privileges. Besides perpetual life, corporations enjoy limited liability for industrial accidents such as nuclear power disasters, and the use of voluntary bankruptcy and other disappearing acts to dodge financial obligations while remaining in business.

The legal system is thus creating unaccountable Frankensteins that have human powers but are nonetheless constitutionally shielded from much actual and potential law enforcement as well as from accountability to real persons such as workers, consumers and taxpayers.

Of course individuals in these companies can always exercise their personal constitutional rights, but the drive for corporate rights is dangerously out of control.

Too frequently the extension of corporate constitutional rights is a zero-sum game that diminishes the rights and powers of real individuals. The corporate exercise of First Amendment rights frustrates the individual's right to participate more equally in democratic elections, to pay reasonable utility rates and to live in a toxin-free environment. Fourth Amendment rights applied to the corporation diminish the individual's right to live in an unpolluted world and to enjoy privacy.

Equality of constitutional rights plus an inequality of legislated and de facto powers leads inevitably to the supremacy of artificial over real persons. And now the ultimate irony. Corporate entities have the constitutional right, says the Supreme court to patent living beings such as genetically engineered cattle, pigs, chickens and, perhaps someday, humanoids.

This is not to say that corporations should have only the legal rights emanating from state charters that create them. What is required, however, is a constitutional presumption favoring the individual over the corporation.

To establish this presumption we need a constitutional amendment that declares that corporations are not persons and that they are only entitled to statutory protections conferred by legislatures and through referendums. Only then will the Constitution become the exclusive preserve of those whom the Framers sought to protect: real people.

23. The Second Reconstruction: Assessing the Civil Rights Movement

Manning Marable

Manning Marable, professor of political science and sociology at the University of Colorado at Boulder, is the author of *From the Grassroots: Social and Political Essays towards Afro-American Liberation* (1980), *Blackwater: Historical Studies in Race, Class Consciousness, and Revolution* (1981), *How Capitalism Underdeveloped Black America: Problems in Race, Political Economy, and Society* (1983), *Black American Politics*, volume 1: *Race, Politics, and Power* (1985), *W. E. B. Du Bois, Black Radical Democrat* (1986), *African and Caribbean Politics from Kwame Nkrumah to the Grenada Revolution* (1987), and other works.

The following selection is excerpted by permission from *Race, Reform, and Rebellion: The Second Reconstruction in Black America, 1945–1982* (Jackson: University Press of Mississippi, 1984), 208–12.

Was the Second Reconstruction a failure? Our judgment would be a resounding and unconditional 'no'. Legal Jim Crow is permanently dead. The American State is committed to equal opportunity under the law for all Americans. [W. E. B.] Du Bois' characterisation of the First Reconstruction as 'a splendid failure' does not seem to apply to the period 1945–82. The growth rate of black elected officials has declined since 1970, but the increase of black officeholders and administrators has continued. The black consumer market has grown dramatically in two decades, from $30 billion in 1960 to over $125 billion in 1980. Blacks currently occupy, as of this writing, positions as mayors in a number of major US cities: Los Angeles, New Orleans, Atlanta, Detroit, Birmingham, and Newark. Certainly, when the profile of the black élite is under consideration, the whole struggle for desegregation must be viewed as a dramatic success. It is in the tradition of

American policy-makers, politicians, and corporate executives to applaud the relative gains that Afro-Americans have made in the pursuit of equality: no person or class which has historically exploited another is likely to do otherwise. Similarly, the black élite now has an absolute material interest to defend the economic and political status quo. They may, upon occasion, offer a stinging rebuke to representatives of mass conservatism. For the black élite comprehends that its marginal influence upon public policy can be best maintained only when more liberal politicians of the centre dominate the State.

The ideological limitations impressed upon black thought and politics during the Cold War are still operative upon the current black leadership. The black élite will promulgate an economic programme which mirrors the right-wing tendencies of Social Democracy in most of the Western world's nations, but beyond that invisible boundary, they will go no further left. In short, the black élite calls for federal initiatives to provide employment for the poor, but will not advocate a clearly socialist agenda which would severely restrict the prerogatives of private capital. They denounce the growing trend of racist violence, but they will not see that such violence is a manifestation of a more profound crisis within the capitalist political economy. The élite has no viable solutions for the proliferating and permanent black reserve army of labour, or the deterioration of the inner cities. They are simply ready to administer the crisis, but are ill-prepared to resolve it.

Their failure, in brief, is one of vision. The Old Guard constantly manoeuvres, responding to minor political crises, but they are hopelessly inept in projecting a constructive programme to transform the large society. They react, rather than act; they imitate, rather than create; they plead, rather than demand. Theirs is a failure within a qualified and compromised success, and as the decade of the 1980s progresses, it has become obvious that the result of their limited vision has been the creation of a temporary yet quite real barrier between the immediate political agenda of the élite and the black majority. With DuBois, I must agree that many critical failures of both Reconstructions were the result of the blacks' leadership 'by the blind. We fell under the leadership of those who would compromise with truth in the past in order to make peace in the present and guide policy in the future.'[1] Such a judgment may be considered excessively harsh. Of course, as an Afro-American and a socialist, I cannot write this brief study without a clear and passionate belief in the central humanity of my people, without some degree of political commitment towards justice and a decent life for those on the edge of poverty and degradation, and without some sense of outrage for the many crimes that have been and still are being committed against blacks. 'But, too, as a student of science, I want to be fair, objective and judicial; to let no searing of the memory by intolerable insult and cruelty make me fail to sympathize with human frailties and contradiction, in the eternal paradox of good and evil.'[2] The story of the Second Reconstruction has no moral, other than the simple truth that an oppressed people will not remain oppressed forever. What have sustained black courage in the past are several basic ideals—democracy, equality and freedom—that have enabled millions of Americans to endure beatings, imprisonment, torture and harassments of every conceivable kind.

The prevailing attitude among most black leaders during the First and Second Reconstructions was a belief in the essential applicability of the American democratic system to the plight of the Afro-American. The US Constitution was viewed as being 'color-blind', despite the corpus of laws which validated black bondage for centuries. The majority of black activists fighting for desegregation desired the incorporation of the Negro into the existing system. It rarely occurred to them that a *biracial democracy* was impossible to create unless there was also a concomitant transition in the character of the capitalist economic system of the society. In 1945, DuBois suggested that any government which described itself as a democracy must have, as its guiding principles, the goals of 'the abolition of poverty, the education of the masses, protection from disease, and the scientific treatment of crime'. A democratic state should express in its public policies 'the right and the capacity' for peoples of colour to 'share in human progress' equally, without artificial barriers. It must outlaw any and all restrictions based on colour or gender. Using these criteria, a genuine democracy has never existed in the United States for a majority of the population.[3] DuBois was more frank in his assessment of the American State several years later, in a series of articles for the *National Guardian*. Democracy in the US was not 'obsolete'; it had never been tried because of racism and the powerful control of corporate capital over the lives of working-class people. Democracy for blacks and other oppressed minorities was dependent upon the socialisation of the economy, a massive reorganisation of wealth and power. If blacks chose to reject the economic patterns of private capital, and forged coalitions with the labouring and impoverished white classes, they would 'loose for future civilization the vast energy and potentialities of the mass of human beings now held in thrall by poverty, ignorance and disease'.[4] Given the evolution of capitalism, racism, and democracy in America, a truly anti-racist democratic state must of necessity also be a socialist democracy.

The goal of equality was certainly a part of the desegregation movement. But in the minds of many leaders, equality meant *parity*, or equal access, to the positions of political and economic affluence in America. Behind affirmative action is the notion that blacks were denied historically certain opportunities for advancement within the existing system solely on the basis of race. Technically, this still remains true. However, as a critical framework of analysis for black liberation, it reveals a limited vision of what remains to be done. The demand for racial parity within a state apparatus and economy which is based on institutional racism and capital accumulation at the expense of blacks and labour is fatally flawed from the outset. Racism and capitalist exploitation are logical and consistent by-products of the American system. Thus, as we review the modest successes of the black élite after 1970, we can observe that a racist/capitalist state can co-opt a small segment of the oppressed community, 'in the name of equal opportunity', and manipulate it against the material concerns and demands of the masses of black labour and the unemployed. Under Reaganism, a small number of blacks have been appointed within the administration to carry out essentially racist policies which are devastating to the great majority of blacks. The black movement must reorient itself to view the demand for equal opportunity as a necessary but only initial step in the pursuit of biracial democracy. Real equality, which I have defined previously in other works as the realisation of human fairness, connotes not the passage of laws, but the transferral of power from propertied élites to those who create all wealth, the working class. The problem of police brutality within American ghettoes will not be resolved simply by appointing additional numbers of black police officers, or by blacks controlling their municipal governments alone; it will cease only when black workers and the poor, along with other oppressed labourers, have the effective power to control their own neighbourhoods. Unemployment would not disappear with the passage of a [diluted full employment] Humphrey-Hawkins Bill; only the empowerment of workers at the point of production, and the general reallocation of wealth, will provide an effective barrier to the perpetual plight of black joblessness.[5]

In late twentieth-century America, capital is 'free' and labour is 'unfree'.

That is, there is a remarkable degree of freedom for the owners of corporations and factories to transfer their wealth into various forms, without regard
to the broader social impact that such transfers have upon the majority of the
American population. Failing corporations appeal to the Federal government
to provide loans or guarantees for their continued fiscal viability, yet profits
accrued from sales remain private. Plant closings in 1982 alone were responsible for the loss of almost 500,000 American jobs. As the perpetual bottom
of the labour market, blacks and Latinos are caught in a never-ending
economic vice—'the last hired' during an economic upturn, 'the first fired'
during cyclical recession. Freedom for black workers must connote the
assertion of a job as an absolute human right; the community's control over
factory closings or relocations; the freedom from the fear created by poor
medical facilities in inner cities and rural areas; the right to free public
education from pre-school levels through to the universities; the right to
decent housing. Such a definition of freedom is alien to the norms and
traditions of America's racist/capitalist state. Martin and Malcolm, DuBois
and Robeson, all in their own unique manner, came to this realisation.
There cannot be peaceful and productive race relations in the US, unless
there is economic justice; and without justice, there can be no peace. The
vision of a society freed from bigotry and hunger, freed from unemployment
and racial violence, will be realised only through a Third Reconstruction
which seeks the empowerment of the labouring classes, national minorities,
and all of the oppressed. The 'freedom' of capital must be restricted for the
common good.

A Third Reconstruction will arise in the not-too-distant future, to fulfil
the lost promises of the first and second social movements. Its vision is quite
clear. It is now only a question of power.

Notes

1. W. E. B. DuBois, *Black Reconstruction in America, 1860–1880* (New York:
   Atheneum, 1971), p. 727.
2. Ibid., p. 725.
3. W. E. B. DuBois, *Color and Democracy: Colonies and Peace* (New York:
   Harcourt, Brace, 1945), p. 17.
4. W. E. B. DuBois, 'There Must Come a Vast Social Change in the United
   States', *National Guardian* (11 July 1951); DuBois, 'The Choice That Confronts

America's Negroes, *National Guardian* (13 February 1952); DuBois, 'The Negro in America Today', five-part essay, *National Guardian* (16, 23, 30 January; 13 February; 5 March 1956).

5. DuBois makes the same point in 'Bound by the Color Line', *New Masses*, 58 (12 February 1946), 8, and 'Negroes and the Crisis of Capitalism in the United States', *Monthly Review*, 4 (April 1953), 478–85.

24. Freedom of Speech

David Kairys

David Kairys, a constitutional lawyer in Philadelphia and a local counsel to the National Emergency Civil Liberties Committee, is adjunct professor of sociology at the University of Pennsylvania and chair of the Theoretical Studies Committee of the National Lawyers Guild.

The following selection is excerpted, with emendations by the author for this edition, from "Freedom of Speech," in David Kairys, ed., *The Politics of Law: A Progressive Critique* (New York: Pantheon, 1982), 140–71. Compilation Copyright © 1982 by David Kairys. Reprinted by permission of Pantheon Books, a Division of Random House, Inc.

Free speech has always been a cornerstone of our society, a constitutional right guaranteed by our founding fathers. Right? Wrong. Free speech, as we know it, is a right won by working people trying to organize unions in the first three decades of this century.

Free speech law was basically transformed in the years between 1919 and 1940. Before that, one spoke on public property only at the discretion of local, and sometimes federal, authorities.

The Change in Legal Doctrine

Two Supreme Court cases 40 years apart illustrate how speech law was transformed. In 1894, the Reverend William F. Davis, an evangelist and longtime opponent of slavery, attempted to preach the gospel on Boston Common, a public park. On his first attempt, Davis was incarcerated for a few weeks in the Charles Street Jail; the second time, he was fined and appealed.

The Supreme Court of Massachusetts upheld Davis' conviction on the ground that a city ordinance prohibited "any public address" on public grounds without a permit from the mayor. Oliver Wendell Holmes—later a justice of the U.S. Supreme Court known for protecting freedom of speech —wrote the court's opinion. Like other state and lower federal court judges of his day, Holmes viewed the ordinance as a legitimate regulation of the use of the city's park, fully within the city's rights as property owner. "That such an ordinance is constitutional does not appear to us open to doubt," Holmes wrote. "For the Legislature absolutely or conditionally to forbid public speaking in a highway or public park is no more an infringement of the rights of a member of the public than for the owner of a private house to forbid it in his house."

The U.S. Supreme Court unanimously affirmed, quoting the private house analogy. In the only reference to it, the Court said the Constitution "does not have the effect of creating a particular and personal right in the citizen to use public property in defiance of the Constitution and laws of the state."

Forty years later, union organizers, like Rev. Davis, believed that public streets, sidewalks and parks should be open for public use. Before the '30s, labor organizers had regularly been denied freedom of speech, except in cities with reform or Socialist mayors. After Congress passed the National Labor Relations Act in 1935, the CIO sought to explain its provisions and the benefits of unions and collective bargaining to working people throughout the country. Nowhere was their reception more hostile than in Jersey City, N.J., the turf of political boss Frank Hague.

CIO plans to distribute literature on the streets and hold outdoor meetings in Jersey City were thwarted by Hague, who, in denying permits for these activities, declared: "I am the law."

But the CIO successfully brought suit against Hague. In its decision, the Supreme Court said: "Wherever the title of streets and parks may rest, they have immemorially been held in trust for the use of the public and, time out of mind, have been used for purposes of assembly, communicating thoughts between citizens and discussing public questions. Such use of the streets and public places has, from ancient times, been a part of the privileges, immunities, rights and liberties of citizens."

This established the basic concept of free speech we now take for granted, and was a direct repudiation of the theoretical basis and result in the *Davis* case. But the Court did not explicitly overrule *Davis* or discuss the lack of free speech prior to the 1930s. It did not even acknowledge that it had made a fundamental change in legal doctrine. The opinion was simply an exposition of a right to freedom of speech based on natural law, which, like all natural law principles, is timeless and without historical context.

The streets and parks in the *Hague* case appear, in the Court's words, "immemorially" to have been held for the people—used for speech "time out of mind." The right of free speech now stems "from ancient times," even though some 40 years earlier the same court had ruled the streets and parks to be city property—not that of the people—subject to whatever restrictions city officials wished to impose.

Before the Transformation

Davis was the only Supreme Court decision to address basic free-speech issues before this transformation began. But state and lower federal court decisions and practices throughout the country confirm that there was no tradition of protected free speech prior to the 1930s. There was often vigorous, sometimes vitriolic debate, and a tradition of speech—and struggle to obtain the right to speak—developed. But until the 1930s, speech was at the sufferance of local and national governments, which could and frequently did prohibit and punish anything that government officials, the business establishment or others who had influence did not want to hear.

• The Framers of the Constitution and the population generally in that period envisioned no substantial change from the English common law rules regarding speech. For example, criticism of the government or government officials, called seditious libel, could legally be and regularly was made criminal under English law. Every state had a seditious libel law when the Constitution was adopted, and the Founding Fathers in Congress initiated and passed the repressive Sedition Act (1798) within a decade of adoption of the First Amendment. The Federalists used this act to suppress their outspoken critics; when the Republicans gained the presidency in 1801, they also prosecuted their opponents, including a minister who criticized Thomas Jefferson in a Thanksgiving Day sermon. More than 2,000 people were prosecuted, and many served substantial prison terms. A laborer served two years for erecting a sign that criticized the tax laws and urged "peace and retirement to the President."

The Founding Fathers were an economic and political elite who were more interested in promoting commerce and restraining the democratic impulses of the public than in any new notions of free speech. Hamilton,

Madison, Washington, Franklin, even Jefferson and Paine—all supported criminalization of seditious libel. The first amendment—which by its language only limited Congress—probably was no more than a reservation of regulation of speech to the states.

The Sedition Act prosecutions were justified by two legal doctrines that would be repeatedly resurrected later: the "bad–tendency" doctrine, which allowed prosecution for words that could, in however remote or indirect a fashion, contribute to disorder or unlawful conduct in the future; and the "constructive–intent" doctrine, which ascribed to the speaker or writer the intent to cause such consequences. The Act and the prosecutions provoked a public outcry that constituted the beginning of popular demands for free speech along the lines we enjoy today.

• In 1837, in response to a series of petitions against slavery, Congress banned presentation of all such petitions so that "agitation of this subject should be finally arrested, for the purpose of restoring tranquility to the public mind."

• Writers and speakers opposed to slavery were regularly censored and suppressed with court approval or acquiescence. The "bad–tendency" doctrine was cited as legal justification on the ground that abolitionist speech could encourage slave rebellions.

• During the 1873–74 depression, police in New York attacked a group of demonstrating unemployed workers. The city had granted a permit, but revoked it minutes before the demonstration. Unaware of the revocation, demonstrators were clubbed by platoons of police who rushed into the crowd. Two meetings in a private hall called to protest the police action were also broken up by the police.

• In 1909 Emma Goldman was to deliver a lecture entitled "Henrik Ibsen as the Pioneer of Modern Drama" at Lexington Hall in New York City. When she mentioned "Ibsen," a police sergeant mounted the speaker's platform and said she was deviating from the topic. The crowd, at first amused by this absurdity, was roughly cleared from the hall.

• From 1909 to 1915, the Industrial Workers of the World (IWW) conducted a nationwide campaign to challenge denials of the right to speak on public streets, sidewalks and parks. Seeking mainly to reach migratory workers in the only places possible, the Wobblies saw themselves in a "struggle for the use of the streets for free speech and the right to organize."

This struggle—in which one Wobbly after another would mount a soapbox and begin a speech with the greeting, "Fellow workers and friends"—

became the focal point for employer attempts to stop IWW organizing. The four-word greeting ordinarily sufficed to cause arrest. As this process progressed, the jails soon filled. Then schools and other buildings were jammed with free speechers. This strategy regularly succeeded in winning *de facto* recognition of free speech.

• In the early 1900s, Margaret Sanger and Emma Goldman were frequently arrested and sometimes imprisoned for distributing leaflets about birth control. During several weeks in 1917, many women were arrested and imprisoned for picketing the White House in support of a constitutional amendment granting women the right to vote.

The Free-Speech Movement

While labor, religious groups and others denied freedom of expression usually viewed such denials as secondary to their substantive demands, they did raise the free-speech issue. But none of these early 1900s efforts was systematic or broadly based enough to command consistent national attention. The free-speech movement before World War I lacked a popular base, a national organization and effective organizers. After the war, it found all three in the labor movement, the National Civil Liberties Bureau [NCLB] (which became the American Civil Liberties Union in 1920) and Roger Baldwin.

In 1917 Baldwin and Crystal Eastman, a leader of the American Union Against Militarism (AUAM), convinced the board of AUAM to form an adjunct, the Civil Liberties Bureau, to oppose prosecution and harsh treatment of conscientious objectors during World War I. The bureau was greeted with hostility. The *New York Times* denounced it for "antagonizing the settled policies of our government."

The NCLB, soon separated from AUAM, took on the toughest civil liberties issues of the day: protection of conscientious objectors and the World War I Espionage Act prosecutions. The federal government responded by raiding the NCLB office and seizing all its files.

Many identified the NCLB with pacifism or even disloyalty. So it reorganized in 1920, renamed itself the American Civil Liberties Union and, according to a Baldwin memorandum, embarked on a "dramatic campaign of service to labor" with a leadership composed of labor leaders and sympathizers.

In an interview shortly before his death, Baldwin told me he viewed the free-speech issue as primarily political and only secondarily legal, and as inseparable from the rights of working people to organize and bargain collectively. "Organization was the basis of our service in the ACLU. As an organization we were powerless and therefore had to attach ourselves to the defense of movements that had power. If we had been a legal aid society helping people get their constitutional rights, as such agencies do their personal rights, we would have behaved quite differently. We would have stuck to constitutional lawyers and arguments in courts. But we did the opposite—we attached ourselves to the movements we defended. We identified ourselves with their demands [and] we depended on them for money and support."

Thus constituted and directed, in the '20s the ACLU proceeded to challenge and organize around anti-evolution statutes in the *Scopes* case, the Espionage Act prosecution of communist Benjamin Gitlow, the Sacco-Vanzetti prosecutions—and in 1937 the anti-labor and anti–free-speech actions of Boss Hague.

The Process of Change

The fundamental conflict between the *Davis* and *Hague* decisions explodes widely accepted myths about the decision-making process of the courts. The justices say their decisions are determined by legal precedent and analysis. If this were so—and if the law were separate from political and social forces, as it purports to be—there should be a coherent evolution of *legal* doctrine.

But in both these cases the Constitution, specifically the First and Fourteenth Amendments, was the source of law. It was identical in both cases, yet *Hague* held that the First Amendment—operating against the states through the Fourteenth Amendment—established an individual right to speak on public streets, sidewalks and parks, while *Davis* had held the exact opposite.

It might be argued that there was a legal barrier to enforcement of the First Amendment in the *Davis* case since it was decided before the Supreme Court's 1925 decision that the First Amendment also applied to the states. But this only begs the question; the constitutional provisions—in the Fourteenth Amendment—were in effect since the Civil War, and the Court could have chosen to apply the First Amendment at any time thereafter. In fact, the Court had discussed the issue before the *Davis* case.

Another possible explanation might be found in earlier decisions that interpreted the general language of the First Amendment. However, in both periods there were precedents and reasoning supporting each side.

Moreover, precedents and reasoning can be distinguished, modified or discarded. The law provides judges with a variety of stylized rationalizations from which they can pick and choose. Social and political judgments guide such choices, even when they are not explicit or conscious. There is no legally required rule or result, and despite endless attempts by judges and legal scholars to find transcendent legal principles, there simply are none.

However, one can make sense of these decisions by examining the social and political contexts in which they were made. Society underwent fundamental changes between *Davis* and *Hague*. Industrialization, World War I, the Depression, the New Deal and the growth of the labor movement led to basic shifts in consciousness and political relations.

These shifts affected judges as well as society generally. Some of the judges, though from the same strata of society as *Davis* era judges, came to see the justice of some left demands. Justice Holmes' reassessment of speech rights would seem to exemplify such change. His was not a change brought on by legal research but of his and society's altered state of consciousness.

Such a social change is transmitted to and affects individuals in various ways—through mass media, public and private associations, professional groups, peer pressures. The judges, like Holmes, who came to place considerable value on freedom of speech, did so not because they were more in touch with the Framers of the Constitution (who sponsored the Sedition Act) or were more competent judges, but because of historical and social events.

These judges generally express this new consciousness in legal terms, and many would honestly deny that their decisions stemmed form new social conditions.

Furthermore, the power of a movement like the CIO in the '30s also places judges in a bind. Though most were likely to be hostile or ambivalent toward labor and the left, the demand for free speech had clear historical roots and was popular. To deny this demand in the '30s, a judge would risk fomenting a major confrontation in a period of social turmoil. Moreover, it was becoming clear that if labor could not speak and organize legally, it would do so illegally, as the IWW did, often successfully, in its free-speech fights.

Some judges might have welcomed confrontation, but others may have found it preferable to bring labor's activities within and under the control of the system, as Congress did with the NLRA.

Finally, the power of the labor movement in the '30s and the precedents favoring local control over speech also raised institutional concerns. True, upholding the right of free speech required contradicting longstanding precedents and widespread practice. But to deny this demand—so long promised on paper and so widely supported—threatened to raise a public outcry, undermine the Court's authority, and even win support for Franklin D. Roosevelt's court-packing scheme announced in 1937.

The courts rely for their legitimacy on myths about the objectivity and nonpolitical nature of judicial decision-making. This, in turn, lends a broader legitimacy to social and power relations that are reflected, articulated and enforced by the legal system.

Within this context, institutional concerns present a choice between rejecting precedent and ruling against the mainstream of political thought. There was widespread controversy about the courts in the '30s, and the Court had recently moved in the direction of the mainstream in several related decisions.

The various factors discussed here do not necessarily operate intentionally or even consciously, nor do the justices necessarily see themselves as engaged in anything other than a legal analysis. They are accustomed to expressing social and political concerns and values as legal arguments and to implementing changes expressed in legal terms without understanding the nature of the changes they were making.

Thus, even as the law was being changed, the struggle for free speech, waged largely by leftists and finally realized by the labor and left movements, was being redefined as a set of natural rights whose essence and history are legal rather than political. A false pride in the legal system has displaced a source for genuine pride in the people, who fought business interests and the government—including the courts—to achieve recognition of free speech.

25. Women and the Constitution

Joan Hoff

Joan Hoff, professor of history at Indiana University and past executive secretary of the Organization of American Historians, is the author of *American Business and Foreign Policy, 1920–1933* (1971), *Ideology and Economics: United States Relations with the Soviet Union, 1918–1933* (1974), *Herbert Hoover: Forgotten Progressive* (1975), *Unequal before the Law: A Legal History of Women from the American Revolution to the Present* (1990), and *Nixon without Watergate* (forthcoming), coauthor of *Sexism and the Law* (1979), editor of *The Rights of Passage: The Past, Present, and Future of ERA* (1986), and coeditor of *Without Precedent: The Life and Career of Eleanor Roosevelt* (1984).

The following selection is excerpted by permission from "Women and the Constitution," APSA *News for Teachers* (Summer 1985): 10 and 12–14.

Since the drafting of the federal Constitution in 1787, the legal status of women in the United States has passed through four distinct phases and is on the brink of entering a fifth one. In this two-hundred-year period, there has been more change in the last twenty years than in the previous one hundred and eighty. Yet, a decade and a half ago scholarly classes about women and the Constitution could not be taught because too little primary research had been conducted in either the new social history with its subfield of women or the latest version of the new legal history with its subfield of sex discrimination.

Constitutional Neglect, 1787–1872

The first period, which lasted almost one hundred years from 1787 to 1872, can simply be called one of constitutional neglect because the Founding

Fathers did not have women's rights on their collective minds when they met in Philadelphia in 1787 to draft a new Constitution. Nor were the Federalists and Anti-Federalists thinking about women when the Bill of Rights later came into existence during the battle over ratification.

During the Colonial and Revolutionary periods women's complaints and issues certainly existed, especially in the form of formal petitions following the War for Independence.[1] None of these female concerns were discussed at the Constitutional Convention because they consisted of isolated individual complaints. There was little sustained or organized support by American women for an improvement in their societal or legal status. Unlike their later counterparts, the Republicans, during the French Revolution, American women did not organize to make their legal complaints collectively known to the men who gathered in Carpenters' Hall in 1787.

But there is even a more basic reason for the total neglect of women's issues at the Constitutional Convention; namely, the fact that both the Constitution of 1787 and the Bill of Rights were based on eighteenth-century common law concepts of liberty, justice, and equality which created an exclusively white, male system of law and order. The Founding Fathers were simply the patriarchal products of their time—nothing more and nothing less. For them to have considered granting political or other civil rights to women would have opened up possibilities which for even our enlightened Revolutionary leaders went beyond the pale of their western concepts of justice and politics.

We know this to be the case from one famous example: John Adams' response to his wife Abigail's rather mild-mannered request to limit the power husbands had over wives. To Abigail, John gave a supercilious answer, first comparing women to other dependent and disobedient "tribes" like Indians, children, apprentices, and blacks and then concluding that since women were the "more numerous and powerful" of all the "tribes," they really ruled their men from behind the scenes. To his friend and colleague James Sullivan, however, John Adams seriously addressed the dangers inherent in his wife's now famous desire that he and his Revolutionary colleagues "Remember the Ladies." According to Adams, to grant women voting rights would open up the possibility of propertyless adult men and young men demanding the same right,. thus upsetting the political hierarchy of the times.[2]

This period of constitutional neglect of women from 1787 to 1872 coincided with legislative neglect as well, with the exception of the passage of

Married Women's Property Acts. The same was not true for white males, however, whose legal, political, and economic powers were significantly expanded through post-Revolutionary state legislation, codification of the laws, and through judicial interpretation.

Morton J. Horwitz has noted that from 1780 to 1820 a new rationale for common law had to be worked out in the United States because the Revolution had undermined its legitimacy. American judges began to abandon the eighteenth-century, natural-law concept of law and to view it as an instrument to achieve policy goals. Horwitz argues that "an instrumental perspective on law did not simply emerge as a response to new economic forces in the nineteenth century. Rather, judges began to use law in order to encourage social change. . . ." At the same time, according to Peggy A. Rabkin, lawyers began to play a more important role than juries in private law-making through their influence over state legislatures and judicial decisions that "defeudalized social relations among men but left intergender social relations feudal."[3]

This legal reform of first private and then public law was considerably less liberalizing for female than for male citizens, especially in the area of contractual relationships. During the course of post-Revolutionary legal reforms, natural law was abandoned as a theoretical base for reforming American law. This increased the likelihood that women's legal rights would not be given much attention by post-Revolutionary lawyers or judges because only natural-law philosophical theories of the Englightenment, which had played such an important role in justifying rebellion against the Crown, had also allowed such writers as Condorcet and Mary Wollstonecraft to argue for equality of the sexes.

The codification process was both subtle and complex. There was a stage between the end of the Revolution and the beginning of codification in which private contract law in particular began to reflect the breakdown of customary law and conduct. At the same time there was a concerted effort to rid the United States of feudal vestiges of English law such as equity trusts to protect the property of married women. Most important, there was also increased commercialization and the beginning of industrialization in the United States during the period. As private law began to reflect a conscious tendency on the part of early United States federal judges and lawyers to use the law as a means of reform, it conveniently facilitated the needs of early American entrepreneurs.

Under Jacksonian democracy a popular antipathy developed toward both the legal profession and its manipulation of common law in the courts. This sentiment gave rise to the codification movement. Instead of democratizing American contract law or the legal system in general, all codification did was freeze or institutionalize the process where it was around 1850. While the power of judges and lawyers to influence private law through court decisions may have been reduced by the codification process, the result was that laws in the form of state statutes misleadingly appeared impartial and above petty political and economic interests. In fact, this public law simply institutionalized the existence of a legal and economic elite that had already been created by the early post-Revolutionary changes in private law. Rather than achieving a redistribution of wealth or even more proprietary rights for women, Jacksonian codificaton concretized existing inequalities between rich and poor men and between men and women in general.

Some of the original post-Revolutionary attempts to reform property law in New York, for example, actually made the laws governing the property of married women more complex and uncertain. Especially in the area of uses and trusts, equity procedures were restricted or eliminated without replacing them with other proprietary or contractual rights. When New York legal codifiers defeudalized and commercialized property in 1828 and again in 1836, with specific state laws governing transactions between white males, they inadvertently made inter-gender property relations more ambiguous than they had been under equity. The incompleteness of property reform, the virtual elimination of dower rights through court decisions, and the growing demand and concern of a number of men and women in a burgeoning industrial society for stable and clear-cut inheritance procedures led to the Married Women's Property Acts in various states both before and after (but not during) the American Civil War.

At no time in the course of the nineteenth century were Married Women's Property Acts liberally interpreted by the lower courts. The importance of these very legally limited and narrowly interpreted acts lies in the fact that reform of American law through state legislation was a major instrument whereby the legal status of women could be improved following independence from England. By 1900 this type of legislative reform constituted the most significant means of advance for women with respect to marital property rights.

We must remember that by the middle of the nineteenth century a debate over which of various traditional forms for achieving legal change should predominate had been in progress for some time. Besides state legislation, the other two basic instruments of such change since the colonial period were equity jurisprudence and legal fictions. The debate over these three means to legal reform intensified after 1800 as post-Revolutionary members of the legal profession began to influence private law and to codify the public laws of the new nation. By the end of the nineteenth century it was clear that for women and other disadvantaged groups, the dominant agents of law reform in the United States would be statutes passed by state legislatures, new amendments to the federal Constitution, and subsequent judicial interpretation of these state laws and of the Constitution. Later in the twentieth century, federal laws and presidential Executive Orders would also contribute to changing the legal status of those still seeking equal treatment under the law with white males.

Constitutional Discrimination, 1872–1908

Because women were left out of the 1787 Constitution and the Bill of Rights, it has taken until the last twenty years for them to begin to obtain the same treatment as men under the law. But as women entered what was to become the second period in their constitutional history—one I call "constitutional discrimination," lasting from 1872 until 1908—they were hopeful. Their hope stemmed in large measure from the fact that while they had not been specifically included in the language of the Constitution and Bill of Rights, they had not been specifically excluded from it either.

In fact, both documents were written in remarkably sex-neutral terms. Neither document specifically denied equal rights to women. By their frequent use of the term "persons," "people," and "electors," the Founding Fathers left open at least the possibility that women might be able to qualify to vote and to run for federal office at some time in the future. It was not until Supreme Court decisions following the Civil War specifically classified women as other than full citizens of the United States, that the hope they could obtain the same rights as men through state legislation and judicial interpretation faded.

Women who had become both advocates of abolition and women's rights before the Civil War were especially optimistic when the conflict ended because they expected to be rewarded for their war efforts and for shelving questions involving women's rights until after 1865. In particular, Susan B. Anthony and Elizabeth Cady Stanton believed that women should have been granted the right to vote when black males received that right under the

Fourteenth and Fifteenth Amendments following the Civil War. Consequently, Anthony and other women wasted no time testing both Amendments in court.

Unlike the War for Independence, during the Civil War Northern women had organized themselves into a variety of pro-Union groups which gave them greater political and legal expectations following the second conflict than following the first. During Reconstruction, the most vocal and politically active among them immediately tried to vote and enter certain all-male professions such as medicine and law. Between 1872 and 1900 the Supreme Court not only denied women the right to vote and to practice law under certain conditions,[4] but also more fundamentally questioned whether they were even "persons" under the law.

The most famous "persons" case in this country occurred in the 1890s when Belva A. Lockwood appealed to the Supreme Court because the state of Virginia refused to license her as an attorney. Lockwood's legal career had a stormy history long before her appeal to the Supreme Court in 1894. Admitted to the bar of the District of Columbia in 1873, three years later she was denied permission to practice before the Supreme Court of the United States. She overcame this obstacle by lobbying for federal legislation enabling all women lawyers the right to appear before the Supreme Court. In 1879 she became the first woman to benefit from the passage of this landmark statute. An avid suffragist, she ran for president of the United States as a candidate of the National Equal Rights Party in 1884 and 1888.

Against this formidable background reputation, the state of Virginia dared to deny her the right to practice law in 1894 although she had already been admitted to the bars of several other states, in addition to the District of Columbia. The state's bar admission act indicated that any "person" who had been licensed to practice in any other state or in the District of Columbia could practice in Virginia. In this instance the Supreme Court of Appeals of Virginia decided that "person" meant "male." The Supreme Court affirmed this position by refusing to order the state of Virginia to admit Lockwood to practice. The historical and legal importance of *In re Lockwood*, 154 U.S. 11 (1894), lies in the fact that the Supreme Court chose to allow states to confine their definition of a "person" to males only. From 1894 until *Reed v. Reed*, 404 U.S. 71 (1971) states could maintain that women were not legally "persons" by virtue of this single Supreme Court decision.

So by 1900 women had tried systematically to use the Fourteenth Amendment to improve their legal and political status—initially through the privileges and immunities clause, then through the due process clause, and finally through the equal protection clause. Failing in almost every instance, they turned to political action, focusing primarily on suffrage. In fact, to the degree the courts discouraged improvement of female legal status in the late nineteenth century, women took compensatory political action. A similar, but less obvious, relationship exists today, especially since the defeat of the Equal Rights Amendment in 1982.

Thus, the second period in the development of the legal status of U.S. women ended on a discouraging note, but with one principle well established which would reemerge in the third and fourth periods; namely that women should have equal rights with men under the Constitution.

Constitutional Protection, 1908–1964

The third period in the development of the legal status of women, unlike the first period of constitutional neglect in which women's rights were largely ignored and the second period of constitutional discrimination in which the courts actively discriminated against women's professional, political, and civil aspirations, was characterized by a variety of Supreme Court decisions and state legislation aimed at protecting women, especially those in lower socio-economic strata, based on what are considered today to be very questionable stereotypical views of women.

The dates of this third period are 1908 to 1964, but the groundwork for protective legislation and Supreme Court decisions placing limits on hours and types of work in which women could engage were laid in the late nineteenth century in response to the human wreckage created by industrialization. This third period is very important because it also is the one in which a fifty-year battle line was drawn between those female reformers who thought certain groups of women needed protection and those who thought that all women would be better off if they simply obtained equal rights with men.

The most famous of the Supreme Court decisions symbolizing the protective approach to women's rights was *Muller v. Oregon*, 208 U.S. 412 (1908). There is more gender-related constitutional scholarship on this single decision than on any other Supreme Court decision affecting women before *Roe v. Wade*, 410 U.S. 113 (1973). Yet until the recent work of Nancy S. Erickson, Jennifer Friesen and Ronald K. L. Collins, doctrinal analysis and evaluation of the long-range legal impact of the *Muller* decision have not been very sophisticated.[5] Although the much heralded "Brandeis brief" did set a precedent for the use of economic, sociological and statistical data in arguing future cases, it was essentially ignored in the unanimous opinion written by Justice David J. Brewer, a known opponent of both labor and the Progressive Movement in the early twentieth century. While supporting equal political rights for women, Brewer did not believe that women were or should be considered equal in the workplace.

Erickson finally pointed out the obvious, but largely ignored, fact that the decision would have been the same with or without the Brandeis "authorities." The Justices relegated the famed brief's data of 113 pages to one extensive footnote, choosing to base their opinion on standard sex stereotyping of, and paternalistic protectionism toward, women as "bearers of the race." This sexist assumption had been a long-standing feature of American law in both the first and second stages in the constitutional development of women. When faced with the economic reality of the same, applying this "common knowledge" about the special nature of women to minimum wages (Muller only involved minimum hours) in Adkins v. Children's Hospital, 261 U.S. 525 (1923), and related state wage cases, the courts readily distinguished between the unconstitutionality of having women work long hours because it would inhibit their ability to produce healthy children, and the unconstitutionality of forcing employers to pay a minimum wage to insure the continued health of mothers and their offspring. In Muller women had to pay an economic price for future generations; in Adkins employers did not. And neither decision was based on scientific data about working women, even though Felix Frankfurter appended 1,138 pages of statistical and other data to Adkins, outdoing by tenfold the Brandeis tradition set in Muller.

Ironically, the modern-sounding aspects of Muller v. Oregon are found today only in the brief of Curt Muller's attorney William D. Fenton. He argued on behalf of the employer (not the female employee who had worked longer hours than the state of Oregon allowed), pointing out that some women absolutely had to work to support themselves or their families. Thus, Fenton directly challenged the prevailing chivalrous notion that half of the members of the human race remained "sheltered in happy homes free from the exacting demands . . . [of pursuing] a living." Relying exclusively on Lochner v. New York, 198 U.S. 45 (1905), he insisted that female workers did not need the "protecting arm of the legislature" any more than male workers when contracting with employers for their labor. Fenton anticipated that "protecting" women by limiting their working hours might turn into general restriction of women in the work place rather than general protection of them (as indeed happened over the next half century). He also futilely made a contemporary racial analogy by arguing:

> if the statute had forbidden employment for more than ten hours, of all persons of white color, the statute would have had application to all of that class, . . . no one would contend that the classification was reasonable or one that could be sustained.[6]

In 1908, isolated women's groups agreed with Fenton by describing the potential dangers ahead in the application of the sex-stereotyped defense of protective legislation in the Brewer opinion. However, they could not prevail against the avalanche of positive publicity in the decision received from the press and such prominent women advocates of protective legislation as Florence Kelley and Jane Addams.

It is easy to denigrate the long-term deleterious impact of *Muller* in particular, and of protective legislation in general, on job opportunities and advancement for women. We know now that protective labor legislation as a concept and as a body of statutes strengthened sexual segregation and stratification patterns in the labor market, for such laws were based on the assumption that women would always be cheap, temporary, unskilled labor. Protective laws helped define patterns of discrimination against female wage-earners, limited women's economic opportunities, and reinforced stereotypic notions of women as frail, passive, and dependent. Similarly, we know that those who supported protective legislation also stressed the reproductive and nurturing characteristics of women to the exclusion of other characteristics. This bolstered a highly traditional and restrictive definition of woman's role in society generally as well as in the work place.

There is, nonetheless, something positive about the position of those well-educated and often well-to-do women in the Progressive Movement who supported protective legislation for working women (and men). Theirs was a social or group approach to reform, albeit they limited this collective protection, by and large, to lower-class women and did not apply it to themselves. Their advocacy of this modern collective justice should not be forgotten because it is so easy to criticize the long-term negative consequences of protective legislation.

Progressive women's ideology and goals are also difficult to appreciate today because they seem contradictory and ambiguous. On the one hand, Progressive women explicitly committed themselves to women's rights—the right to equal political participation and to the opportunity for meaningful, productive, and well-paid work. On the other hand, the very same women successfully established legal constraints on women's rights in the work place. Such women as Jane Addams, Florence Kelley, Julia Lathrop, and Margaret Dreier Robins, established highly visible public careers, taught themselves to lobby, speak, and organize, learned the ins and outs of political power and the workings of the political process. Unfortunately, they declared their devotion to what seems today an idealized and dangerously romantic vision of maternity, home, and family. These female reformers simultaneously insisted that some women were autonomous individuals and others had to be protected because they could not take care of themselves.

Despite all their shortcomings, the middle- and upper-class Progressive women who supported protective legislation spoke in Victorian terminology about morality, maternity, feminine sensibilities, and virtue that struck a cord in all women. Their language clearly indicates that they were trying to preserve a female haven—rooted in social and biological feminine behavior—a haven from male culture and male institutions. This peculiarly effective female form of communication was lost in the 1920s, according to Carroll Smith-Rosenberg,[7] and it has only been since the 1970s that attempts to create a similarly unifying language and to preserve the best of female socialized behavior has come back into vogue in certain feminist circles. Historians and lawyers alike contribute to this effort when they question whether the contemporary single-minded pursuit of individualistic equal rights with men is not ultimately as restrictive and debilitating as was the equally single-minded pursuit of protective legislation for women in the early twentieth century.

Before the collective, rather than individualistic, pursuit of justice for all women (not only those designated as disadvantaged) could be fully appreciated, however, the supporters of protective legislation and equal rights divided into two irreconcilable camps which fought each other to a standstill from the 1920s down to the early 1970s—thus destroying the First Women's Movement and delaying the start of the Second Women's Movement. Until the third and fourth periods in women's constitutional development played out, feminist reformers could not think about going beyond the boundaries of liberal legalism to improve their constitutional status by obtaining equal justice for themselves on other than male standards of individualism.

Prior to experiencing this debilitating division, however, women remained united enough to obtain their major constitutional goal in this third period; namely, the Nineteenth Amendment. When women finally achieved the right to vote in 1920, little else of significance had been done to improve their constitutional status. Questions of full citizenship, property and fiduciary rights, personhood, credit, wages, domicile, divorce settlements, child custody—even the right of married women to a birth name—all remained largely neglected or subject to legislation which varied drastically from state to state. Not until the late 1960s did a Second Women's Movement emerge to raise these matters in litigation.

By 1920, U.S. women had more political, legal, educational, and economic opportunities than they had had in 1865. But they still had not achieved constitutional equality before the law with men. Between the 1920s and the 1960s, there was no congressional legislation that made gender a central issue; the Nineteenth Amendment remains the only successful attempt to include women by gender in the Constitution. During the same decades, aside from cases involving protective legislation, there were few significant Supreme Court decisions which focused on gender and those that did usually limited a wide variety of female activities such as the right to tend bar and to serve on juries.[8]

Under the influence of the New Deal legislation, the Supreme Court reversed itself and finally granted minimum wages to both men and women, but some of that same federal legislation discriminated against married working women and encouraged wage differentials between male and female workers.[9] In addition, from 1894 until 1971 state courts often maintained that women were not legally "persons" for contractual and professional purposes because that term had come to be legally synonymous with "male."

Constitutional Equality, 1964–1984

In the last twenty years, there has been a juridical metamorphosis in recent case law from protection to equality. This transformation is far from complete, primarily because the equal protection clause of the Fourteenth Amendment has been subjected to several levels of interpretation with respect to women beginning with *Reed v. Reed*, 404 U.S. 71 (1971).

Just as the First Women's Movement arose out of female dissatisfaction with former male abolitionists following the Civil War, the Second Women's Movement arose, in part, out of a not so dissimilar female dissatisfaction with the male-dominated civil rights and antiwar organizations of the late 1960s. Both represented the ongoing struggle of American women to achieve equality under the law with American men. Although women had tried for two centuries to obtain legal equality with men, their most dramatic successes have all occurred since the 1960s. *Except for the right to vote, U.S. women have experienced more improvement in their legal status in the last twenty years than in the last two hundred.*

Beginning in the 1960s, therefore, a series of congressional acts, executive orders, and guidelines issued by government agencies created to enforce affirmative action, marked a quantum leap in the legal status of American women. The breakthrough began with the Equal Pay Act in 1963, Title VII of the 1964 Civil Rights Act, and two executive orders in 1965 and 1967 (nos. 11246 and 11375) prohibiting certain kinds of discrimination by federal contractors. It continued in Congress with Title IX of the 1972 Educational Amendments and a 1978 amendment to Title VII requiring employers to provide employee benefits for pregnancy-related disabilities. In 1981 Congress passed legislation allowing state courts to divide military pensions equally when long-term marriages ended in divorce, and in 1984 it approved legislation facilitating the enforcement of child support payments and the collection of pension payments for women. All of these actions have greatly aided women in their battle against sex discrimination in the workplace, in educational institutions, and in their roles as wives and mothers.

Supportive Supreme Court decisions began to appear in the 1970s, but the record of the justices has not been as consistently favorable to the cause of women's legal equality with men as have actions taken by Congress (some of which have overturned Supreme Court decisions), most recent presidents, and government agencies. The multi-tiered way in which the Supreme Court has applied the equal protection clause to women since 1971 forces an evaluation of how much constitutional progress they have made from the point of view of both traditional liberal legalism and newly emerging concepts about feminist jurisprudence.

In 1971 the U.S. Supreme Court struck down an Idaho statute which automatically preferred men over women of the same entitlement class as administrators of estates. Borrowing from a 1920s' case the justices said in *Reed v. Reed* that when a statute accorded different treatment on the basis of sex alone, it "establishes a classification subject to scrutiny under the equal protection clause," thus creating a "middle tier" or intermediate level of scrutiny for women, instead of the strict scrutiny or suspect classification traditionally applied in cases of racial discrimination.

Although gender would appear to be similarly qualified for suspect categorization, only a plurality of Supreme Court justices have ever held this and then only once in *Frontiero v. Richardson*, 411 U.S. 677 (1973). Three years later with *Craig v. Boren*, 492 U.S. 190 (1976), the Supreme Court did establish a "heightened" sense of scrutiny by requiring that "classification by gender must serve important governmental objectives and must be substantially related to the achievement of these objectives." The combined effect of *Reed* and *Craig* would appear to be that in a number of cases the justices have abandoned the traditional view of women as homemakers operating primarily within a private sphere. This change is most evident in decisions involving military, social security, welfare and worker's compensation benefits.[10] This use of "heightened" scrutiny is all because it indicates that the courts have finally recognized the demographic facts of life in the last quarter of the twentieth century; namely, that women are not only wage earners, but often the sole breadwinners as the single heads of families.

The limitations of this break through judicial interpretation became almost immediately evident, however. Not all the cases decided since 1971 fit neatly into this new, liberal image of women. Old stereotypic views of women still abound, such as those found in the 1981 decisions upholding a California statutory rape law and the all male draft.[11] Moreover, there are a whole series of "reverse discrimination" cases brought by white males objecting to affirmative action programs by minorities and women, and another series in which the justices have endorsed "benign" sex discrimination.[12] Granted, this latter set of rulings have often been aimed at redressing economic or other societal disadvantages that have historically confronted U.S. women. They remain rooted in paternalistic notions about "protecting" females.[13] Still other decisions categorically denied statutes having a disparate adverse impact on women as a group are unconstitutional (such as the 1979 decision upholding veterans' preferences in civil service jobs) on the grounds that although their results may be discriminatory, their intent was not.[14]

Certain Supreme Court decisions such as those on pregnancy benefits for women have had to be overruled by Congress legislation which has some disturbing "protective" implications,[15] and many abortion decisions since *Roe v. Wade*, 410 U.S. 113 (1973), have narrowed the chances of poor women obtaining funding for legal abortions and restricted conditions under which they can be obtained. Moreover, even *Roe* was not based on the right of women to control their own bodies but on the right of privacy between doctors and their female patients seeking abortions. Latest decisions continue to reflect a mixed constitutional bag for women with one striking at the heart of Title IX which has yet to be overturned by Congress.[16]

Even this cursory summary analysis of court decisions affecting women since 1971 indicates that it is time for women to begin to think carefully about whether they prefer *equal treatment as unequal individuals (based on male standards), or special treatment as a protected (and thus implicitly) inferior group.* Faced with these equally unattractive interpretations, the long sought after strict scrutiny or suspect classification under the Fourteenth Amendment or ultimate passage of an Equal Rights Amendment may prove a mixed blessing for contemporary women.

It may well be that neither option will have to be faced. After all, there is no reason to believe an ERA will be ratified in the near future. At the same time, the very "otherness" and lingering sex-stereotyped notions about women's nature may indefinitely prevent the Supreme Court from granting them suspect classification because women implicitly and explicitly challenge liberal (and largely male) legal standards of "self" more than other groups now receiving strict constitutional scrutiny.

In the wake of the ERA's defeat, we are prone to forget that this amendment, like the Fourteenth before it and all previous Civil Rights Acts, was not designed to change values but to modify behavior of mainstream citizens by changing the constitutional status of a particular group. The ERA's purpose was (and is) to provide equality of opportunity through the Constitution and legal system for those women who want to realize full personal and professional expectations within mainstream America.

Had the ERA been ratified, it would have been absolutely noncoercive when it came to individual lifestyles because its enforcement powers were directed only against state and federal agencies or public officials, not private citizens. It would also not have automatically changed public policy based on remaining sexist assumptions about women. Nonetheless, the passage of the ERA in 1982 would have gradually promoted legal uniformity in the treatment of females in state and federal statutes in a way that no previous acts of Congress, executive orders, or Supreme Court decisions could.

Ultimately, the ERA may be more important in defeat than in victory as a symbol of how far women still have to go to obtain true constitutional equality with men in American society. Its defeat has forced advocates of civil rights for women to seek creative legislative and judicial solutions in their continuing struggle for full and equal legal status with men. It has already resulted in a greater questioning of public policy that continues to inconvenience women, such as the lack of comparable pay scales and the incompatability of the working hours of private and public institutions such as schools, banks, and post offices, with the typical nine-to-five shift of many working mothers.

Rather than being lulled into complacency, as many of those in the First Women's Movement were with the passage of the Nineteenth Amendment, it is possible that the failure of the Twenty-Seventh will inspire those in the Second Women's Movement to continue not only to strive for legal rights but also for public policy changes which will positively affect the everyday lives of women and begin to restructure society to meet their needs.

Notes

1. Linda K. Kerber, *Women of the Republic: Intellect and Ideology in Revolutionary America* (Chapel Hill: University of North Carolina Press, 1980), 41, 85, 93–94, 99, 112, 162, 287.

2. Alice S. Rossi, ed., *The Feminist Papers: From Adams to de Beauvoir* (New York: Columbia University Press, 1973; reprint Bantam edition, 1974), 10–15.

3. Morton J. Horwitz, *Transformation of American Law* (Cambridge: Harvard University Press, 1977), 4; Peggy A. Rabkin, *Fathers to Daughters: The Legal Foundations of Female Emancipation* (Westport, Connecticut: Greenwood Press, 1980), 69. Following discussion in this section is based on Albie Sachs and Joan Hoff-Wilson, *Sexism and the Law: A Study in Male Beliefs and Legal Bias in Britain and the United States* (New York: The Free Press, 1979), 75–80; and Richard H. Chused, "Married Women's Property Law: 1800–1850," *The Georgetown Law Journal* 71 (1983): 1359–1425.

4. For details about such voting and law practice cases as *United States v. Anthony*, 24 F Cas. 892 (C.C.N.D.N.Y. 1873); *Bradwell v. Illinois*, 83 U.S. (16 Wall.) 130 (1873); and *Minor v. Happersett*, 88 U.S. 162 (1875), see Sachs and Wilson, *Sexism and the Law*, 85–106.

5. The following discussion of *Muller* is from Nancy S. Erickson, "Historical Background of 'Protective' Labor Legislation: *Muller v. Oregon*," in D. Kelly Weisberg, *Women and the Law: A Social Historical Perspective* (Cambridge: Schenkman Publishing Company, Inc., 1982), 2: 155–186; Jennifer Friesen and Ronald K. L. Collins, "Looking Back on *Muller v. Oregon*," *American Bar Association Journal* 69 (March and April 1983): 294–98, 472–77; and Sachs and Wilson, *Sexism and the Law*, 113–16.

6. Muller's brief, 24. Erickson notes that this analogy was very similar to one used by Mathew Carpenter in defending Myra Bradwell's right to practice law in *Bradwell v. Illinois* 83 U.S. 130, 134 (1873).

7. Carroll Smith-Rosenberg, *Disorderly Conduct: Visions of Gender in Victorian America* (New York: A. A. Knopf, 1985), 252–305, 358 (ftnt 127).

8. *Goesaert et al. v. Cleary et al., Members of the Liquor Control Commission of*

Michigan, 335 U.S. 464 (1948). *Goesaert* was not overruled until *Sail'er Inn, Inc. v. Kirby*, 5 Cal. 3d 1. 20 585 P. 2d 329 (1971). *Hoyt v. Florida*, 368 U.S. 57 (1961). *Hoyt* was not overruled until *Taylor v. Lousiana* 419 U.S. 522 (1975).

9. *West Coast Hotel v. Parrish*, 300 U.S. 379 (1937); Sachs and Wilson, *Sexism and the Law*, 114–16; Lois Scharf, "ER and Feminism," in Joan Hoff-Wilson and Marjorie Lightman, eds., *Without Precedent: The Life and Career of Eleanor Roosevelt* (Bloomington, Indiana: Indiana University Press, 1984), 234–36; idem, *Female Employment, Feminism, and the Great Depression* (Westport, Connecticut: Greenwood Press, 1980), 86–138.

10. For example, see: *Frontiero v. Richardson*, 411 U.S. 677 (1973); *Califano v. Goldfarb*, 430 U.S. 199 (1977); *Califano v. Westcott*, 433 U.S. 76 (1979); *Wengler v. Druggists Mutual Insurance Co.*, 446 U.S. 142 (1980).

11. *Michael M. v. Superior Court*, 450 U.S. 464 (1981); *Rostker v. Goldberg*, 453 U.S. 57 (1981).

12. The most famous of the "reverse discrimination" cases remains, *Regents of University of California v. Bakke*, 438 U.S. 265 (1978), even though this decision did not decide the issue because the Justices chose to argue on narrow statutory grounds that UC Davis had to admit Bakke to medical school because it had violated Title VI of the 1964 Civil Rights Acts, while also maintaining that race "may" be a factor in affirmative action programs at educational institutions. Most "reverse discrimination" cases have involved union seniority questions or voluntary affirmative action programs undertaken by cities or industries.

13. For example, see: *Kahn v. Shevin*, 416 351 (1974); *Schlesinger v. Ballard*, 419 U.S. 498 (1975); and *Califano v. Webster*, 97 S. Ct. 1192.

14. *Personnel Administration of Massachusetts v. Feeney*, 442 U.S. 256 (1979).

15. See Ann Scales, "Towards a Feminist Jurisprudence," *Indiana Law Journal*, 56, 3 (1981): 375–444 for a detailed discussion of Supreme Court cases on pregnancy; and Wendy W. Williams, "The Equality Crisis: Some Reflections on Culture, Courts, and Feminism," *Women's Rights Law Reporter*, 7, 3 (1982): 175–200 for ways the Pregnancy Discrimination Act (PDA) has been used not to treat women equally, but to give them special treatment.

16. In 1984, for example, the Supreme Court ordered the U.S. Jaycees to admit women and said that law firms may not discriminate on the basis of sex which lawyers to promote as partners. See: *Roberts, et al. v. United States Jaycees*, 82 L. Ed. 2nd 462 (1984), and *Hishon v. King and Spaulding*, 81 L. Ed. 2nd 59 (1984). At the same time in *Grove City College v. Bell*, 79 L., Ed. 2nd 516 (1984). It gutted Title IX by deciding that individual units of educational institutions could discriminate and not endanger the federal aid received by other units, saying receipt of Basic Educational Opportunity Grants by some students did not require institution wide coverage under Title IX. Attempts last year to override this decision with provisions in a Civil Rights Restoration Act failed in Congress.

26. On the Bicentennial of the Constitution: A Marxist View

Herbert Aptheker

Historian Herbert Aptheker is a member of the national committee of the Communist Party, USA. He is the author of *American Negro Slave Revolts* (1943), *The Colonial Era* (1959), *The American Revolution* (1960), *Afro-American History: The Modern Era* (1971), *Early Years of the Republic* (1973), *Abolitionism: A Revolutionary Movement* (1989), and other writings and the editor of *A Documentary History of the Negro People in the United States*, 3 vols. (1951–1974), *The Published Writings of W. E. B. Du Bois*, 40 vols. (1973–1986), and other works.

The following selection is reprinted from "On the Bicentennial of the Constitution: A Marxist View," *Nature, Society, and Thought*, no. 2 (1988): 277–90. By permission of Nature, Society, and Thought, 116 Church St. S. E., Minneapolis, Minn. 55455.

Keynote Address, 1987 Marxist Scholars Conference, 12–15 November 1987, University of California, Berkeley

In 1913 Charles A. Beard's *Economic Interpretation of the Constitution* gave precise expression and documentation to the view, advanced previously by historians as well as political leaders, that the Constitution at the moment of its framing was in essence the victory of ultraconservatism, reflecting contempt for democratic rights and devoted to the sanctification and protection of the rich minority. Eminently conservative historians, like John W. Burgess, went so far as to refer to the adoption of the Constitution as a *coup d'état*, while publicists of the schools of progressivism during the first decades of this century, like J. Allen Smith and Herbert Croly, held a similar view. Early socialist books—economic determinist rather than Marxist—did not differ basically on this point, as the writings of A. M. Simons, Gustavus Myers, and Allan Benson attest, the last named entitling his work *Our Dishonest Constitution* (1913).

In view of the near unanimity, it may well be asked why Beard's book caused so much furor, with President Nicholas Murray Butler of Columbia University denouncing it as little short of obscene. The full answer does not lie in a *misreading* of the author's intent as one denunciatory of the Constitution. What was new in Beard's work and what disturbed the conservatives and reactionaries was not his assessment of the Constitution as a victory for reaction but rather his detailed demonstration that the document represented not eternal verities but the class needs of its framers. It was this exposure (partial and one-sided though it was) of the class nature of the law and the state—unquestionably, a contribution at that time to realistic, critical thinking about American history—that was obnoxious to reactionaries.

Is it true that the Constitution was the product of counterrevolution?

We may begin by considering an argument often cited to uphold that view, namely the absence from the Constitutional Convention of such Revolutionary leaders as Thomas Jefferson, Samuel Adams, John Hancock, and Thomas Paine, with the inference that they were in basic opposition to the Constitution. Like the conservative John Adams, at the time minister to Great Britain, Thomas Jefferson was away as minister to France; like Adams, he supported the document, albeit with serious reservations. John Hancock was the presiding officer in the Massachusetts Convention of 1788 which ratified the Constitution, with his support; and Samuel Adams was a member of that same convention, and he, too, approved ratification. Paine was abroad at the time, but he approved, like Jefferson, with reservations; as he wrote Washington in 1796: "I would have voted for it myself, had I been in America, or even for worse, rather than have none. . . ." It is true that these revolutionists would have preferred a founding document which gave fuller expression to the democratic rights of the people, and their reservations therefore were mainly concerned with the failure to include the Bill of Rights. But they did not oppose ratification of a Constitution they considered the most enlightened of the age.

Meanwhile, in Europe, promonarchical writers had been describing anarchy in the republican United States, and reporting refugees by the thousands fleeing to Canada. These penmen dismissed the idea of republican unity for the United States as "the idlest and most visionary of notions." On the other hand, the Constitution and its ratification were hailed by "Scottish

Burgh reformer, Irish patriot, British radical" as a "thorn in the flesh" of tyrants, monarchs, and their lackeys.

To treat as an ultraconservative triumph this document hailed by radicals and revolutionists in Europe, its ratification supported by Sam Adams, Hancock, Paine, and Jefferson, is, to say the least, paradoxical. It is, in effect, to misinterpret the Constitution, to view it mechanically, divorced from time and place. It is, today, to give the Constitution to reaction which now seeks to destroy it.

The Constitution was framed as a bourgeois-democratic document for the governing of a republic which still retained precapitalist features, notably slavery. However, rather than a renunciation of the American Revolution, it represents a consolidation of that revolution by the classes which led it.

The very idea of a written constitution wherein the powers of government are enumerated is a logical consummation of that revolution. The theoretical essence of the constitutional democratic movement was, with Locke and against Hobbes, the inherent evil of government, of regulation, of control. The heart of liberty, in its bourgeois, antifeudal connotation, is the absence of restraint; it is not the wherewithal to accomplish desired objectives. Therefore, where there is tyranny—in the eighteenth century this meant absolute monarchy—there would be and could be no written constitution, since enumerating the powers of the omnipotent is an impossible, and useless, task.

This is why to the archconservative of the epoch, Edmund Burke, a written constitution appeared hateful and seditious, *per se*, while to a Thomas Paine it was "to liberty, what a grammar is to language." For, to him, the presence of a written constitution connoted the opposite of tyranny, i.e., popular sovereignty, and therefore, he held, "a government without a constitution is power without right."

The feudal emphasis upon tenure and authority makes status the basic aim of society; the bourgeois emphasis upon fluidity, progress, and reason makes property the basic aim of society. Amongst the delegates at the Constitutional Convention there is almost unanimity on this point. This property is to be secured by freedom—i.e., freedom from the old restraints, delimiting laws, regulatory provisions, and status-enshrined privileges. Property so secured and so freed will therefore be enhanced. Accumulation is the hallmark of freedom, and the varied and unequal distribution of that accumulated property is the result, as it is the essence, of liberty. Madison, leading theoretician of the Constitution, repeatedly makes that point. Writing to Jefferson (October 24, 1787), he insisted that what he called "natural distinctions"—by which he meant property distinctions as contrasted with "artificial" ones based on religion or politics—"result from the very protection which a free Government gives to unequal faculties of acquiring it."

Liberty, then, was defined in the only way the bourgeoisie can define it and can understand it, i.e., liberty to accumulate property. Of course this liberty entails inequality and helps produce its own negation. Despite the limitations, this is a kind of freedom, compared to the system it supplanted, that is progressive and liberating. This property definition of liberty is made by an eighteenth-century bourgeoisie, young and virile, competitive and progressive. Its enunciation and incorporation in the Constitution do not violate the spirit of the Revolution, but rather make that document the logical expression of the Revolution. The enunciation by that bourgeoisie at that time and place and under those circumstances of the sacredness of property rights and the freedom to accumulate capital and to protect what comes into being cannot be equated with verbally similar protestations of devotion to "free enterprise" by a late twentieth-century, monopolistic, thoroughly reactionary, historically obsolete capitalism.

Beard concludes his chapter evaluating the contents of the Constitution with these words: "It was an economic document drawn with superb skill by men whose property interests were immediately at stake, and as such it appealed directly and unerringly to identical interests in the country at large."

This statement is characteristic of the oversimplification that marks Beard's very influential view. The Constitution was not simply an economic document. It was a constitution—that is, a political document reflecting the new bourgeois order (in which, however, chattel slavery existed). Of course, a considerable part of it dealt with the regulation of certain economic aspects of that order. Since it was a bourgeois order, it was drawn up by propertied men—in fact, only by propertied *white* (overwhelmingly *Anglo-Saxon*) men, and this reflects the chauvinist and male supremacist nature of the bourgeois order, even in its youth.

But this does not make the document reactionary, for it must be seen in terms of its time and place. Nor does it make the document counterrevolutionary, for the economics expressed in the Constitution reflects the economics basic to the Revolution, and to the national economic tasks of the period. Of course, the Constitution appealed to planters, merchants, bankers, creditors, budding manufacturers, and their professional servitors, since these together ruled and without their approval the Constitution would neither have been drafted nor adopted. But, in the first place, the appeal was by no means confined to these individuals and was by no means unanimous among them, or equally great among them. And, in the second place, once again, these groups and classes are of the eighteenth century in a newly emancipated colony seeking national unification, not at the close of the twentieth century in an advanced imperialist country.

The goal of national unity, central to the bourgeois revolution of the time, is seen in the economic provisions of the Constitution itself in terms of money, debts, tariffs, treaties, contracts, police power, and political centralization—creating a single and expandable national market upon which the bourgeoisie might feed, and in turn develop. All this, basic to the Constitution, is not sinister or vulgar or reactionary. On the contrary, it is the material fundament, in legal form, of a nascent bourgeois order.

Was there, then, no general political trend in the United States shown by a comparison of the Declaration of Independence with the Constitution? Granted, one was a manifesto justifying revolution and the other was an instrument for the governing of a nation, and, therefore, the two documents are not strictly comparable. Still, do they not symbolize some drift, and is not this towards the right?

I think that question requires an affirmative answer, but not by characterizing one as a counterrevolutionary victory compared with the other. The Declaration of Independence came at the high point of revolutionary struggle and bore the strong imprint of the left in the revolutionary coalition. The other is the legal embodiment and crystallization of the fundamental content of that revolution, particularly as seen by the well-to-do—national self-determination, the breaking of imperial fetters upon the development of the home market and the means of production and resources of the country, and the enhancement of the democratic and humanist content of life in the new country. It comes after the fighting, after the highpoint of enthusiasm, after the bourgeois elements find the nation independent and set out to reap, as fully as possible, the enormous benefits of that independence. The mass—and therefore left, democratic—component of the revolutionary coalition is less needed now than in 1776; and the sober second thoughts and exploitative drives of the bourgeoisie and the planters are coming to the fore. Now their ever-present fears of the masses are intensified—especially as those masses display continued militancy—and what they want is Law and Order, Stability and Calm.

Jefferson put the matter extremely well in a remarkably prophetic letter written in 1780, as the war was coming to a close: "It can never to be too often repeated, that the time for fixing every essential right on a legal basis is while our rulers are honest, and ourselves united. From the conclusion of this war we shall be going down hill. It will not then be necessary to resort every moment to the people for support. They will be forgotten therefore and their rights disregarded."

The center and especially the right of the revolutionary coalition—men like the Morrises and Hamilton—moved by these considerations and opportunities, sought the means whereby to combine the urge for stronger unity, which is very much broader than their own circles, with their special preoccupation with the dangers from the masses, from what they called agrarian, leveling, and anarchistic threats. They seized above all upon the debtor protest movement led by Captain Daniel Shays, perhaps even stimulated some of its excesses and, certainly, distorted its aims and grossly exaggerated the danger that it represented for the bourgeois order.

It is not alone these elements of the revolutionary coalition, however, which are interested in the achievement of "a more perfect Union." The dream of a powerful, lasting, secure, and happy United States filled the minds of farmers and yeomen, mechanics and artisans, and they were dreams expressive of a more noble patriotism than the rich, in any period, can know. And there were dangers from the extreme right in American life—very serious dangers, which played as significant a role as did Shays' Rebellion in arousing a desire for "the hooping of the barrel's thirteen states," to quote the words Thomas Paine used in recalling his early desire for firm unity.

In the early 1780's the demand for closer federation was quite general. Leaders of the most varied political alignments and philosophies, from Washington to Madison to Mason to R. H. Lee, to Jefferson and Hancock were promoting the idea. The multiplicity of tariffs, the trade wars, the varied currencies, the dumping by England, the sharply unfavorable balance of trade, the rise in the cost of finished products, the concomitant fall in the selling price of crops, and the disappearance of specie did not trouble only the merchant and planter; these hurt the hired farm hand, the seaman and the artisan. The contempt with which the United States was treated in the capitals of Europe and especially in London, the world's capital, provoked a national resentment and a desire for stronger unity among the people.

Above all, there was the most serious threat to the continued existence of the American Republic coming not from "levelers" and Shaysites, who represented no such threat at all, but from the Tories and their agents and sympathizers, from monarchists, from real reactionaries and true subversives, and from the rulers of Great Britain, who actively sought to dismember that republic whose very existence was an affront. Proposals and projects looking towards a monarch, a dictator, the splitting of the country into two, three, or more confederacies came from and were seriously considered by the highest figures in the army, in state government, and in the Continental Congress. The Constitutional Convention itself found it necessary to assure that the public that "we never once thought of a king." The necessity for that assurance came not only from the reality of such dangers but also from the fierce opposition among the American masses to monarchy, to tyranny, to anything smacking of real counterrevolution.

There was unanimity among the members of the Constitutional Convention regarding the fundamentals of their bourgeois order—the sacredness of private property, the sanctity of contract, the inevitability of rich and poor, and their existence as reflecting immutable qualities of human society. Economic differences were confined to conflicts arising from different kinds of propertied interests—land, slaves, ships, banks, etc.—with the delegates agreeing that the most consequential difference was that between North and South, i.e., economies based on slave labor and (largely) free labor. These problems were subjected to ingenious compromises, the details of which have been described many times and need not detain us here.

But this was a bourgeois society at the beginning of its career, and the delegates were representatives of propertied groups which had just led a war of national liberation. Moreover, they were keenly aware of the freedom-loving masses who but recently, arms in hand, had done the fighting in that war and whose spirit of restiveness and independence they had frequently displayed—sometimes in dramatic form—since the war. Because of all these reasons, the propertied delegates themselves in drafting a constitution had to keep in mind the popular liberties so far as they were then comprehended. And the records of their convention are filled with such evidence—with explicit recognition of the fact that, unless this or that popular provision is included or this and that antidemocratic provision is omitted or modified, the people, that "iron flail" as Milton called them, would simply not tolerate the result. Certainly, most of them were looking for the absolute minimum, for no more than what they thought they had to give, making the mistake of omitting a Bill of Rights.

Concretely, in terms of the provisions of the original Constitution, how are these positive, progressive influences manifested?

The Constitution provides for complete separation of church and state, including the forbidding of any religious requirements or qualifications for both electors and elected—provisions in advance of anything then in existence either in Europe or in the state constitutions.

The Constitution forbids all titles of nobility or the acceptance of such titles if offered by other sovereignties—a provision of considerable consequence in a still largely monarchical world with serious royalist tendencies in the United States. It forbids bills of attainder and *ex post facto* laws, both frequently employed devices of tyranny. It guarantees the write of habeas corpus against suspension except in times of rebellion or critical emergency. It provides for jury trial in all criminal cases. It subordinates the military to the civil power and provides that no military appropriation is to be made for a period greater than two years. It provides for the popular election of the House of Representatives. It provides that only Congress shall declare a state of war.

Despite urgent arguments in its favor, the Constitution sets up no property qualification, either for the electors or for the legislators and other officeholders, quite unlike existing provisions in England, or in the states. It provides stated salaries for all officials; this was done quite consciously as a rejection of the common practice of making such service voluntary and thus possible only for the rich. Moreover, except in the case of the president, who must be native-born, no disability or penalty or invidious distinction of any kind is indicated as between native and naturalized citizens, although again heated demands were made in favor of such nationalistic proposals.

The Constitution's definition of treason is strict and, as a safeguard against tyrannical persecution, was far in advance of any other government of its time. Strong opposition was voiced by such members as Gouverneur Morris of New York and John Rutledge of South Carolina to this provision and they sought alterations which would broaden its definition and make conviction easier. But the Constitution defines treason only as levying war against the United States or adhering to its enemies, the latter clause made more precise and restrictive by defining it as "giving aid or comfort." And treason is not to be constructive, nor is it to consist in ideas or words, for its proof requires two eyewitnesses "to the same *overt* act." The last words were added particularly at the urging of Benjamin Franklin, who said he "wished this amendment to take place. Prosecutions for treason were generally virulent; and perjury too easily made use of against innocence."

Provision for the admission of new states, with those states to be equal in all respects with the original ones, was also won only over strong opposition, especially from eastern members.

The limited and stated terms of office for all officials—with the notable exception of judges—was a blow to the monarchical and aristocratic factions.

The possibility of amending the Constitution is also amongst its most farsighted provisions. While the process of amendment is very cumbersome, some process is present. This is reflective of the principle of popular sovereignty and of the idea—repeatedly stressed by Jefferson—that only the living should bind the living and that provisions for change and improvement must exist in any popular organic law.

The whole republican framework of the Constitution was a blow to the friends of absolutism. Contrary to those who see in the idea of a republic something contrasting with or opposed to democracy, a republic was conceived of in the Constitution as the device necessary in a large and populous country where what Madison called "pure democracy" (i.e., direct, personal participation by every citizen) was impossible in order to make possible and effective the majority's will. This not only included the sovereignty of the people but also included the idea that necessarily flows from that sovereignty —i.e., the right to alter, change or abolish—to revolutionize—the form of government. This point, found in the writings of Jefferson, Madison and many of their leading contemporaries (including Hamilton), is stated with particular clarity by James Wilson, a delegate from Pennsylvania to the Convention and later an Associate Justice of the Supreme Court: "A revolution principle certainly is, and certainly should be taught as a principle of the U.S. and of every State in the Union. This revolution principle that the sovereign power residing in the people, they may change their constitution of government whenever they please, is not a principle of discord, rancor or war; it is a principle of melioration, contentment, and peace."

The Constitution *guaranteed* a republican form of government to every state and this, at a time when separation and monarchical ideas and plots were widespread, was momentous. *That is, no other form of government was permitted.*

Of course, in saying the Constitution was bourgeois-democratic we have indicated not only its positive features but also its severely limited nature. The "democracy" of the bourgeoisie, since it is the democracy of an exploiting, oppressing class, is inevitably limited and hesitant. And the "democracy" of this bourgeois-democratic republic at its founding was severely limited in a most consequential additional sense—within it, held in chattel slavery, were about 750,000 people, or a full 20 percent of the total population, as well as about 200,000 indentured servants. Characteristic, too, of such a society was the complete political enslavement of that half of the "free" population made up of women. The Native American peoples were ignored.

The disabilities of the women, while commented upon by some amongst them, went completely unnoticed by the Founding Fathers and are present, in the Constitution, as natural and assumed. The disabilities of the unfree, indentured servants, and slaves, while frequently in the minds of the Fathers —as employers and slaveowners facing the far from passive dispossessed— nowhere are remedied in the Constitution. On the contrary, the document assumes their existence, provides for their policing and contains some severe "compromises" relative to apportionment, to the slave trade, and to the return of fugitive slaves—though, be it noted, the word "slave" was deliberately omitted.

The central limitation of the Constitution is organic to a bourgeois document, i.e., it labors to safeguard an exploitative economic order. It is the contradiction between the interests of the owners and of the laboring masses that is the central difficulty, though it is rarely explicitly mentioned.

Madison, however, touches it when he poses the problem that faces the exploiters in a republican society where the will of the majority (the exploited) is supposed to be sovereign. It is to get around this that the complex and extensive federal system is hailed by him and made basic to the structure of the new government. The Fathers see the multiplicity of local and state governments as so many restraining walls before the "hasty," "unthinking" masses. They see the complex processes of electing senators and the president, the permanent tenure of the judges, the great powers of the judiciary, the veto power of the president, the extremely complex process of amendment, as invaluable bulwarks between their property interests and the democratic process.

They wanted politics to be confined to struggles among varied propertied groups, not between the propertied and the propertyless, and they created a federal constitution to mirror this aim, in order to obscure fundamental class antagonisms and to give the appearance of a balance wheel—impartial, accurate, and just. At the same time that the political grants made to the people serve as important mediums for struggle, they also serve to deflect the target of the struggle into channels picked by the political representatives of the propertied groups.

As previously indicated, various elements on the right, for their own really reactionary reasons, opposed the Constitution. This is a story neglected in the literature, but time forbids its full telling here. The most consequential opposition, however, came from the masses, who feared the document was not sufficiently democratic, and therefore demanded the inclusion of a Bill of Rights, specifically to guarantee as inviolable the freedoms most important to the people—freedom of speech, press, and assembly, religious liberty, trial by jury, protection against unreasonable searches and seizures, and other provisions against persecution, such as the right not to bear witness against oneself.

This struggle, led by Mason, Henry, Lamb of New York, Sam Adams, and Jefferson, was organized and, for fear of reactionary duplicity and persecution, even conducted secretly, with codes and intermediate addresses.

The extent of the mass pressure will be indicated when it is noted that Massachusetts, South Carolina, New Hampshire, Virginia, and New York, in ratifying the Constitution, simultaneously urged in the strongest possible terms that a Bill of Rights be added, which (to quote the New Hampshire document) "would remove the fears and quiet the apprehensions of many of the good people of this State." North Carolina, in announcing its decision neither to reject nor ratify the Constitution, said that it wanted a Bill of Rights passed by Congress "previous to the Ratification," and when Congress passed the Bill of Rights, in September 1789, North Carolina ratified in November.

The Congress, in passing the first ten amendments (under the leadership of Madison) specifically declared that, since the demand for them was so general "and as extending the ground of public confidence in the Government, will best ensure the beneficent ends of its institution," therefore they were submitted to the states for adoption. Finally, Rhode Island, ratifying in May 1790, referring to the Bill of Rights, remarked that the rights enumerated therein "cannot be abridged or violated," and found that they "are consistent with the said Constitution" and so announced its ratification.

The Bill of Rights is, indeed, "consistent with the Constitution," in the sense that it extends and specifies the democratic rights only partially or inadequately expressed in that document.

The evidence establishes, I think, that the Constitution of the United States represents a consolidation, not a repudiation, of the American Revolution. While, on balance, it does represent a rightward trend from the highpoint of the Revolution, it nevertheless comprises the essence of that Revolution— national independence and unity, the unfettering of the nascent U.S. bourgeoisie, the renunciation of tyrannical and monarchical government, the political sovereignty of the people, the establishment of republican rule as the form *par excellence* of bourgeois democracy. In its most glaring failing— the recognition, though camouflaged, of chattel slavery—it reflects the greatest failing of the Revolution—the maintenance of that slavery.

Taking it overall and viewing it historically—that is, in relation to its time and place—the author of the Declaration of Independence was correct when he said of the Constitution that it "is unquestionably the wisest ever presented to man"—and that was his opinion even before the Bill of Rights had been added. Certainly with those ten amendments, which were and are of the essence of the Constitution, the Constitution was what Jefferson said it was. Madison, let it be added, thought of the First Amendment as absolute and subject to no exceptions whatsoever. "A supposed freedom," he wrote, "which admits of exceptions, alleged to be licentious, is not freedom at all."

The Constitution is one of the great milestones in the forward march of humanity. Indeed, the U.S. ruling class today, seeking to turn back that march, is driven to undermine and to violate the American Constitution. It is for those who resist war and reaction to defend that Constitution in the process of defending peace and freedom in the best interests of the people of the United States.

There is then good reason *for us* to celebrate the bicentennial of the Constitution. That document, when created, was the most advanced charter of government in the world.

The Constitution's Preamble—which is, of course, an integral part of the document as a whole—affirmed the revolutionary theory of popular sovereignty, as opposed to inherited sovereignty; that was something new and startling for the world of the eighteenth century. No wonder European states made possession of a copy of the U.S. Constitution a criminal offense, well into the nineteenth century!

With all its positive features, including the popularly demanded Bill of Rights, the Constitution, however, *was* an eighteenth-century document, drafted and confirmed by states dominated by private-property owners, including especially slaveowners. The result was not only the document's main weakness—recognizing slavery (albeit ashamed to use the word); it also meant limiting the concept of freedom—for others—to *political* only and even there very incompletely, especially as concerns the Native American peoples, people without significant property ownership, and all women.

Recognizing the positive features of the Constitution, *for its time*, and underlining the limitations of the document, *even for its time*, it is necessary also to insist, in tune with the forward-looking essence of the Constitution, that the twentieth century and the twenty-first that looms just over the horizon demand a very great extension of the concept of freedom. This must mean now, in the first place, the full consideration of all the people, including the vast majority of the people, that is to say, all women, all minorities, and working people as a whole.

This must mean also the expansion of the definition of freedom, which to the bourgeoisie was concerned only with matters political and even there meant freedom *from*, not freedom *to*, meant what government might *not* do, and not what government *could* do and *must* do to make life really full and decent and creative for the entire population. This means specifically in our day the expansion of the concept of freedom so that it includes all the traditional freedoms—so nobly described in our Bill of Rights—but also includes basic socioeconomic rights; the right to a life of sufficient economic and material requirements and a life free of indignities and insults. Freedom is a mockery when it is freedom to be hungry, to be unemployed, to be illiterate, to be ill-housed, to live in fear of illness, to live in fear of insecurity when elderly, to live with the burden of others being "free" to hurl racial and national and religious insults and to practice racist or chauvinist acts. Such "freedom" always was unjust, but in this day and age, with its knowledge, its capacities, its experiences, to permit such conditions to exist is not to be an adherent of freedom but rather to be a sustainer of inhumanity and atrocious cruelty.

Our Constitution includes the right of revolution, our Constitution is itself a capstone of revolution. The amending process of our Constitution endured through the Second American Revolution, highlighted by the XIII and XIV Amendments, which in the first place abolished without compensation billions of dollars worth of previously recognized private property, and, which secondly sustained such confiscation—without due process, by the way—in that provision of the XIV Amendment which refused to hear suits by former slaveowners—including those who had been loyal to the Union —seeking compensation for property in slaves taken from them.

If our Constitution made possible through amendment the abolition of property in slaves because it was found to be anachronistic, socially harmful and economically regressive, might it not be possible for later generations to come to similar conclusions about other property held in private ownership for reasons of individual enrichment? If such generations do come to such conclusions, they might act with regard to such property as our ancestors did with regard to property in slaves. Let us hope that if that comes to pass it may reach implementation with less bloodshed than was required to put the XIIIth Amendment into our Constitution!

Indeed, let us not only hope for such a goal; let us so *act* today on the social, economic, political—and individual—fronts as to hasten the moment when popular sovereignty includes control over the resources of this country. That being achieved, it will be possible to eliminate such abominations as poverty, unemployment, indecent housing, inadequate healthcare, racism, and male chauvinism. This accomplished, humanity will have confined warmaking to museum exhibits.

With that, the prehuman stage of history will be transcended and men and women—fully equal men and women—fully free women and men— will create a heaven on earth.

27. Some Truths Are Not Self-Evident

Howard Zinn

Historian and playwright Howard Zinn is the author of A *People's History of the United States*, excerpted in chapter 1 of this volume.

The following selection is reprinted from "Some Truths Are Not Self-Evident," *The Nation* magazine, 1–8 August 1987, 87–88. By permission of The Nation Company, Inc. © 1987.

This year Americans are talking about the Constitution but asking the wrong questions, such as, Could the Founding Fathers have done better? That concern is pointless, 200 years after the fact. Or, Does the Constitution provide the framework for a just and democratic society today? That question is also misplaced, because the Constitution, whatever its language and however interpreted by the Supreme Court, does not determine the degree of justice, liberty or democracy in our society.

The proper question, I believe, is not how good a document is or was the Constitution but, What effect does it have on the quality of our lives? And the answer to that, it seems to me, is, Very little. The Constitution makes promises it cannot by itself keep, and therefore deludes us into complacency about the rights we have. It is conspicuously silent on certain other rights that all human beings deserve. And it pretends to set limits on governmental powers, when in fact those limits are easily ignored.

I am not arguing that the Constitution has no importance; words have moral power and principles can be useful even when ambiguous. But, like other historic documents, the Constitution is of minor importance compared with the actions that citizens take, especially when those actions are joined in social movements. Such movements have worked, historically, to secure the rights our human sensibilities tell us are self-evidently ours, whether or not those rights are "granted" by the Constitution.

Let me illustrate my point with five issues of liberty and justice:

• First is the matter of racial equality. When slavery was abolished, it was not by constitutional fiat but by the joining of military necessity with the moral force of a great antislavery movement, acting outside the Constitution and often against the law. The Thirteenth, Fourteenth and Fifteenth Amendments wrote into the Constitution rights that extralegal action had already won. But the Fourteenth and Fifteenth Amendments were ignored for almost a hundred years. The right to equal protection of the law and the right to vote, even the Supreme Court decision in *Brown v. Board of Education* in 1954 underlining the meaning of the equal protection clause, did not become operative until blacks, in the fifteen years following the Montgomery bus boycott, shook up the nation by tumultuous actions inside and outside the law.

The Constitution played a helpful but marginal role in all that. Black people, in the political context of the 1960s, would have demanded equality whether or not the Constitution called for it, just as the antislavery movement demanded abolition even in the absence of constitutional support.

• What about the most vaunted of constitutional rights, free speech? Historically, the Supreme Court has given the right to free speech only shaky support, seesawing erratically by sometimes affirming and sometimes overriding restrictions. Whatever a distant Court decided, the real right of citizens to free expression has been determined by the immediate power of the local police on the street, by the employer in the workplace and by the financial limits on the ability to use the mass media.

The existence of a First Amendment has been inspirational but its protection elusive. Its reality has depended on the willingness of citizens, whether labor organizers, socialists or Jehovah's Witnesses, to insist on their right to speak and write. Liberties have not been given; they have been taken. And whether in the future we have a right to say what we want, or air what we say, will be determined not by the existence of the First Amendment or the latest Supreme Court decision but by whether we are courageous enough to speak up at the risk of being jailed or fired, organized enough to defend our speech against official interference and can command resources enough to get our ideas before a reasonably large public.

• What of economic justice? The Constitution is silent on the right to earn a moderate income, silent on the rights to medical care and decent housing as legitimate claims of every human being from infancy to old age. Whatever degree of economic justice has been attained in this country (impressive compared with others, shameful compared with our resources) cannot be attributed to something in the Constitution. It is the result of the concerted action of laborers and farmers over the centuries, using strikes, boycotts and minor rebellions of all sorts, to get redress of grievances directly from employers and indirectly from legislators. In the future, as in the past, the Constitution will sleep as citizens battle over the distribution of the nation's wealth, and will be awakened only to mark the score.

• On sexual equality the Constitution is also silent. What women have achieved thus far is the result of their own determination, in the feminist upsurge of the nineteenth and early twentieth centuries, and the more recent women's liberation movement. Women have accomplished this outside the Constitution, by raising female and male consciousness and inducing courts and legislators to recognize what the Constitution ignores.

• Finally, in an age in which war approaches genocide, the irrelevance of the Constitution is especially striking. Long, ravaging conflicts in Korea and Vietnam were waged without following Constitutional procedures, and if there is a nuclear exchange, the decision to launch U.S. missiles will be made, as it was in those cases, by the President and a few advisers. The public will be shut out of the process and deliberately kept uninformed by an intricate web of secrecy and deceit. The current Iran/*contra* scandal hearings before Congressional select committees should be understood as exposing not an aberration but a steady state of foreign policy.

It was not constitutional checks and balances but an aroused populace that prodded Lyndon Johnson and then Richard Nixon into deciding to extricate the United States from Vietnam. In the immediate future, our lives will depend not on the existence of the Constitution but on the power of an aroused citizenry demanding that we not go to war, and on Americans refusing, as did so many G.I.s and civilians in the Vietnam era, to cooperate in the conduct of a war.

The Constitution, like the Bible, has some good words. It is also, like the Bible, easily manipulated, distorted, ignored and used to make us feel comfortable and protected. But we risk the loss of our lives and liberties if we depend on a mere document to defend them. A constitution is a fine adornment for a democratic society, but it is no substitute for the energy, boldness and concerted action of the citizens.

IV. TOWARD A MORE ADEQUATE THEORY OF THE U.S. CONSTITUTION

28. Law and Constitutionalism in Capitalist Society

Excerpts from the Writings of Karl Marx and Friedrich Engels

Karl Marx (1818–1883) and Friedrich Engels (1820–1895) were not among the Founders, and neither ever held elective office in the United States. Marx was European correspondent for the *New York Tribune* from 1852 to 1862, and Engels paid one short visit to the United States in 1888. The following selections are from assorted writings.

Marx and Engels, from *The German Ideology*

The ideas of the ruling class are in every epoch the ruling ideas: i.e., the class which is the ruling *material* force of society is at the same time its ruling *intellectual force*. The class which has the means of material production at its disposal, consequently also controls the means of mental production, so that the ideas of those who lack the means of mental production are on the whole subject to it. The ruling ideas are nothing more than the ideal expression of the dominant material relations, the dominant material relations grasped as ideas; hence of the relations which make the one class the ruling one, therefore, the ideas of its dominance. The individuals composing the ruling class possess among other things consciousness, and therefore think. Insofar, therefore, as they rule as a class and determine the extent and compass of an historical epoch, it is self-evident that they do this in its whole range, hence among other things rule also as thinkers, as producers of ideas, and regulate the production and distribution of the ideas of their age: thus their ideas are the ruling ideas of the epoch. For instance, in an age and in a country where royal power, aristocracy and bourgeoisie are contending for domination and where, therefore, domination is shared, the doctrine of the separation of powers proves to be the dominant idea and is expressed as an "eternal law".

Collected Works (London: Lawrence and Wishart, 1976), 5: 59

Marx and Engels, from *The German Ideology*

In actual history those theoreticians who regard *might* as the basis of right were in direct contradiction to those who looked on *will* as the basis of right. . . . If power is taken as the basis of right, as Hobbes, etc., do, then right, law, etc. are merely the symptom, the expression of *other* relations upon which state power rests. The material life of individuals, which by no means depends merely on their "will", their mode of production and form of intercourse, which mutually determine each other—this is the real basis of the state and remains so at all the stages at which the division of labour and private property are still necessary, quite independently of the *will* of individuals. These actual relations are in no way created by the state power; on the contrary they are the power creating it. The individuals who rule in these conditions—leaving aside the fact that their power must assume the form of the *state*—have to give their will, which is determined by these definite conditions, a universal expression as the will of the state, as law, an expression whose content is always determined by the relations of this class, as the civil and criminal law demonstrates in the clearest possible way. Just as the weight of their bodies does not depend on their idealistic will or on their arbitrary decision, so also the fact that they enforce their own will in the form of law, and at the same time make it independent of the personal arbitrariness of each individual among them, does not depend on their idealistic will. Their personal rule must at the same time assume the form of average rule. Their personal power is based on conditions of life which as they develop are common to many individuals, and the continuance of which they, as ruling individuals, have to maintain against others and, at the same time, to maintain that they hold good for everybody. The expression of this will, which is determined by their common interests, is the law.

Collected Works, 5: 329–30

Engels, from *Ludwig Feuerbach and the End of Classical German Philosophy*

If the state and public law are determined by economic relations, so, too, of course is private law, which indeed in essence only sanctions the existing economic relations between individuals which are normal in the given circumstances. The form in which this happens can, however, vary considerably. It is possible, as happened in England, in harmony with the whole national development, to retain in the main the forms of the old feudal laws while giving them a bourgeois content; in fact, directly reading a bourgeois meaning into the feudal name. But, also, as happened in western continental Europe, Roman Law, the first world law of a commodity-producing society, with its unsurpassably fine elaboration of all the essential legal relations of simple commodity owners (of buyers and sellers, debtors and creditors, contracts, obligations, etc.), can be taken as the foundation. In which case, for the benefit of a still petty-bourgeois and semi-feudal society, it can either be reduced to the level of such a society simply through judicial practice (common law) or with the help of allegedly enlightened, moralising jurists; it can be worked into a special code of law to correspond with such social level —a code which in these circumstances will be a bad one also from the legal standpoint (for instance, Prussian *Landrecht*). In which case, however, after a great bourgeois revolution, it is also possible for such a classic law code of bourgeois society as the French *Code Civil* to be worked out upon the basis of this same Roman Law. If, therefore, bourgeois legal rules merely express the economic life conditions of society in legal form, then they can do so well or ill according to circumstances.

Selected Works (Moscow: Progress Publishers, 1970), 3: 371–72

Engels, from *The State of Germany*

The middle classes being powerful by money only, cannot acquire political power but by making money the only qualification for the legislative capacity of an individual. They must merge all feudalistic privileges, all political monopolies of past ages, in the one great privilege and monopoly of *money*. The political dominion of the middle classes is, therefore, of an essentially *liberal* appearance. They destroy all the old differences of several estates co-existing in a country, all arbitrary privileges and exemptions; they are obliged to make the elective principle the foundation of government—to recognise equality in principle, to free the press from the shackles of monarchical censorship, to introduce the jury, in order to get rid of a separate class of judges, forming a state in the state. So far they appear thorough democrats. But they introduce all the improvements so far only, as thereby all former individual and hereditary privileges are replaced by the privilege of *money*.

Thus the principle of election is, by property qualifications for the right of electing and being elected, retained for their own class. Equality is set aside again by restraining it to a mere "equality before the law", which means equality in spite of the inequality of rich and poor—equality within the limits of the chief inequality existing—which means, in short, nothing else but giving *inequality* the name of equality. Thus the liberty of the press is, of itself, a middle-class privilege, because printing requires *money*, and buyers for the printed productions, which buyers must have the money again. Thus the jury is a middle-class privilege, as proper care is taken to bring none but "respectables" into the jury-box.

Collected Works, 6: 28–29

Marx, from *The Eighteenth Brumaire of Louis Bonaparte*

The inevitable general staff of the liberties of 1848, personal liberty, liberty of the press, of speech, of association, of assembly, of education and religion, etc., received a constitutional uniform, which made them invulnerable. For each of these liberties is proclaimed as the *absolute* right of the French *citoyen* but always with the marginal note that it is unlimited so far as it is not limited by the *"equal rights of others* and the *public safety"* or by "laws" which are intended to mediate just this harmony of the individual liberties with one another and with the public safety. For example: "The citizens have the right of association, of peaceful and unarmed assembly, of petition and of expressing their opinions, whether in the press or in any other way. *The enjoyment of these rights has no limit save the equal rights of others and the public safety."* (Chapter II of the French Constitution, 8.)—"Education is free. Freedom of education shall be *enjoyed* under the conditions fixed by law and under the supreme control of the state." (*Ibidem*, 9.)—"The home of every citizen is inviolable *except* in the forms prescribed by law." (Chapter II, 3.) Etc., etc. —The Constitution, therefore, constantly refers to future *organic* laws which are to put into effect those marginal notes and regulate the enjoyment of these unrestricted liberties in such manner that they will collide neither with one another nor with the public safety. And later, these organic laws were brought into being by the friends of order and all those liberties regulated in such manner that the bourgeoisie in its enjoyment of them finds itself unhindered by the equal rights of the other classes. Where it forbids these liberties entirely to "the others" or permits enjoyment of them under conditions that are just so many police traps, this always happens solely in the interest of *"public safety,"* that is, the safety of the bourgeoisie, as the Constitution prescribes. In the sequel, both sides accordingly appeal with complete justice to the Constitution: the friends of order, who abrogated all these liberties, as well as the democrats, who demanded all of them. For each paragraph of the Constitution contains its own antithesis, its own Upper and Lower House, namely, liberty in the general phrase, abrogation of liberty in the marginal note. Thus, so long as the name of freedom was respected and only its actual realisation prevented, of course in a legal way, the constitutional existence of liberty remained intact, inviolate, however mortal the blows dealt to its existence *in actual life.*

Selected Works (Moscow: Progress Publishers, 1969), 1: 408–9

Engels, Letter to Franz Mehring, July 14, 1895

Ideology is a process accomplished by the so-called thinker consciously, indeed, but with a false consciousness. The real motives impelling him remain unknown to him, otherwise it would not be an ideological process at all. Hence he imagines false or apparent motives. Because it is a process of thought he derives both its form and its content from pure thought, either his own or that of his predecessors. He works with mere thought material which he accepts without examination as the product of thought, he does not investigate further for a more remote process independent of thought; indeed its origin seems obvious to him, because as all action is produced through the medium of thought it also appears to him to be ultimately based upon thought. The ideologist who deals with history (history is here simply meant to comprise all the spheres—political, juridical, philosophical, theological—belonging to society and not only to nature), the ideologist dealing with history then possesses in every sphere of science material which has formed itself independently out of the thought of previous generations and has gone through an independent series of developments in the brains of these successive generations. True, external facts belonging to its own or other spheres may have exercised a co-determining influence on this development, but the tacit pre-supposition is that these facts themselves are also only the fruits of a process of thought, and so we still remain within the realm of pure thought which has successfully digested the hardest facts.

It is above all this appearance of an independent history of state constitutions, of systems of law, of ideological conceptions in every separate domain, which dazzles most people. If Luther and Calvin "overcome" the official

Catholic religion, or Hegel "overcomes" Fichte and Kant, or if the constitutional Montesquieu is indirectly "overcome" by Rousseau with his "Social Contract," each of these events remains within the sphere of theology, philosophy or political science, represents a stage in the history of these particular spheres of thought and never passes outside the sphere of thought. And since the bourgeois illusion of eternity and the finality of capitalist production has been added as well, even the victory of the physiocrats and Adam Smith over the mercantilists is accounted as a sheer victory of thought; not as the reflection in thought of changed economic facts but as the finally achieved correct understanding of actual conditions subsisting always and everywhere—in fact if Richard Coeur-de-Lion and Philip Augustus had introduced free trade instead of getting mixed up in the crusades we should have been spared five hundred years of misery and stupidity.

This side of the matter, which I can only indicate here, we have all, I think, neglected more than it deserves. It is the old story: form is always neglected at first for content. As I say, I have done that too, and the mistake has always only struck me later. So I am not only far from reproaching you with this in any way, but as the older of the guilty parties I have no right to do so, on the contrary; but I would like all the same to draw your attention to this point for the future. Hanging together with this too is the fatuous notion of the ideologists that because we deny an independent historical development to the various ideological spheres which play a part in history we also deny them any effect upon history. The basis of this is the common undialectical conception of cause and effect as rigidly opposite poles, the total disregarding of interaction; these gentlemen often almost deliberately forget that once an historic element has been brought into the world by other elements, ultimately by economic facts, it also reacts in its turn and may react on its environment and even on its own causes.

Selected Correspondence (Moscow: Progress Publishers, 1975), 434–35

29. Theses on the Capitalist State

Bertell Ollman

Bertell Ollman, professor of politics at New York University, is the author of *Alienation: Marx's Conception of Man in Capitalist Society* (1971; rev. ed. 1976), *Social and Sexual Revolution: Essays on Marx and Reich* (1979), and *Class Struggle Is the Name of the Game* (1983) and coeditor of *Studies in Socialist Pedagogy* (1978) and *The Left Academy: Marxist Scholarship on American Campuses*, 3 vols. (1982, 1984, and 1986).

The following selection is a reprint of "Theses on the Capitalist State," *Monthly Review* 34 (December 1982): 41–46. Copyright © 1982 by Monthly Review Inc. Reprinted by permission of Monthly Review Foundation.

1. One major aim of Marx's analysis of capitalism is to explain how people can make their own history and be made by it at the same time, how we are both free and conditioned, and how the future is both open and necessary.

2. In Marx's theory of politics, the capitalist state is conceived of as a complex social relation of many different aspects, the main ones being political processes and institutions (including the Constitution), the ruling class, an objective structure of political/economic functions, and an arena for class struggle.

3. These aspects also offer ways into the study of the state as a whole (perspectives from which to view and piece together its constituent elements).

4. Viewed from one aspect, or one side, the state appears as a one-sided relation—not partial (because in most cases the various parts are all represented) but one-sided (because the parts are structured in function of where one begins, which also affects the attention given to each one).

5. The main interpretations of Marx's theory of the state—that it is an instrument of the capitalist class (Lenin and Ralph Miliband), an objective

structure of political functions interlocked with capitalist economic functions (early Poulantzas), an arena of class struggle (late Poulantzas), the illusory community arising out of alienated social relations (early Ollman), and the hegemonic political ideology (Gramsci)—are such one-sided relations.

6. None of these interpretations denies the possibility that the institutions of the state at a particular time and place are in the hands of a faction or fragment of the capitalist class (or a coalition of such) who use them to promote their own special interests. Indeed, this is usually the case. Such inner-class political conflict constitutes the subject matter of most political science. The ways in which the state simultaneously represents the interests of the whole capitalist class in opposition to the working class, the former ruling class, other dominated classes, and fragments of the capitalist class itself (including the one which has temporarily come out on top in the inner-class conflict), on the one hand, constitutes the subject matter of a Marxist theory of politics.

7. Each of these one-sided interpretations of the state (see no. 5) brings out something important about the capitalist state—about its appearance, structure, functioning (including contradictory functioning), ties to the rest of capitalism and potential for change—just as it hides and distorts much else. And in so far as each of these interpretations integrates politics with economic and social processes, they all carry us outside the boundaries of relevance drawn by orthodox political science.

8. Some problems are better studied inside one rather than another of these interpretations. How the state protects the *status quo*, for example, is most usefully approached within the framework supplied by the view of the state as the instrument of the capitalist class. But it is the view of the state as a set of objective structures interlocked with capitalist economic processes that provides the most relevant framework in which to examine how the state contributes to the reproduction of capitalist conditions of existence. The requirements of tomorrow's capitalism and how they exert influence today emerge most clearly within this framework. The same political develop-ments, when viewed inside these two different interpretations, will often exhibit a dual role: they defend existing capitalist relations while simulta-neously laying down a necessary condition for what they are becoming.

9. These different Marxist interpretations of the state are dependent to some degree (in when they are formulated, which ones get stressed, etc.) on the conditions and events in the lives of the people who hold them. Allowing for many exceptions, we can say in general that the structural view of the

state (the state as a set of objective structures) is most popular in "quiet" periods; the Gramscian view of the state as the hegemonic political ideology, which stresses the capitalists' near perfect control over the workers' thinking, emerges in periods of political reaction; while the views of the state as the instrument of the ruling class and as an arena of class struggle come to the fore in periods of rapid social change.

10. Some of the interpretations of the state mentioned seem to contradict one another. For example, the view of the state as an instrument of the capitalist class (which suggests that the capitalists are in direct control of the state and consciously use its institutions to promote their interests) appears to contradict the view of the state as a set of objective structures tied to capitalist economic processes whose requirements it must satisfy (which suggests that the actions of whichever group controls the state are determined by forces outside its control, given that it does not want to overturn the entire capitalist system).

11. These apparently contradictory views of the state are equally true—if not equally important (this is determined by research)—representing as they do different tendencies inside the state relation. Dialectical truth does not fit together like the pieces of a puzzle, but allows for the kind of multiple one-sidedness and apparent contradictoriness that results from studying any subject from perspectives associated with its different aspects. (Perhaps the best known example of this phenomenon in Marxism is the claim that capitalists are an "embodiment of capital" which stands in apparent contradiction to the claim that capital functions as it does because it is in the control of capitalists who use it to further their profit-maximizing interests.)

12. Particular political developments may also have apparently contradictory meanings when viewed within different Marxist interpretations of the state. For example, a political reform that favors the working class, when viewed within the framework of the capitalist state as an arena of class struggle, appears as a victory for the workers, perhaps one which helps set limits to the exercise of capitalist power. On the other hand, viewing the same reform within the framework of the state as the instrument of the capitalist class leads to the conclusion that the capitalists have adopted a more sophisticated way of controlling or cooling out the workers, that it is a higher order victory for the capitalists. These different conclusions do not balance out, and a compromise makes no sense. Rather, both conclusions are true, depending as they do on the interpretation of the state in which the event in question is placed.

13. As regards the future, the apparently contradictory versions of the present which emerge from analyzing the same event within different interpretations of the state indicate the variety of real possibilities which make up the future. In the case of a political reform which seems to favor the workers, it could strengthen their hand in the class struggle; it could also—in quite different ways—weaken them. These alternative futures are part of the present; they don't begin tomorrow. It is only by studying present political developments within different interpretations of the state that we can capture the full potential for change, and change in different directions, which constitutes an essential part of the present moment—and maximize our chances for influencing them.

14. The widespread debate among Marxists over the relative autonomy of the state usually goes on at cross purposes because the people involved do not sufficiently distinguish between these different Marxist interpretations of the state, and hence whether (under certain circumstances) the state is relatively autonomous from the ruling capitalist class, or from the economic requirements of capitalism, or from other alienated social relations, etc. As a matter of fact, there is a case to be made for relative autonomy within each of these perspectives on the state. What is important is to avoid the confusion that results from thinking there is only one debate when there are really several.

15. Note for further research. The model for constructing the relations between the different views of the state arising out of approaches rooted in its different aspects is the complex set of "identities" Marx uncovers between production, distribution, exchange, and consumption in his unfinished Introduction to the *Grundrisse*.

16. These complementary yet quite distinct Marxist views of the state have somewhat different consequences for the development of political consciousness and revolutionary will. For most people, their eyes are first opened politically when they grasp the state as an instrument of the ruling class; the society-wide dimensions of the problem only come into view when the state is also grasped as an objective structure tied in with capitalist economic structures. Their understanding is deepened—and the problems of organizing against capitalism better appreciated—when they also see the state as the illusory community and the hegemonic political ideology. But only when/if the state is also grasped as an arena of class struggle does Marxism become not only a way of understanding the world but a means for changing it through political activity.

17. The narrow focus that political science imposes on the study of politics (whether in American Government, Comparative Government, International Relations, or Public Administration), especially when combined with its ahistorical approach, radically falsifies both the degree of freedom and the degree of necessity that characterizes our political lives. In the absence of any inquiry into the state as an instrument of the capitalist class, political science seriously exaggerates the citizen's freedom to use the state to achieve his/her ends. Ignoring the state's character as an objective set of political structures tied in with capitalist economic processes, political science also underestimates the objective constraints under which any party in power acts, given a desire to retain even some capitalist relations (the classic dilemma of social democracy). However, should such a party decide to do away with capitalism entirely, the same view of the state accords to people greater freedom of action than most political scientists think they have (or could have). Likewise, on the level of individual effectiveness, viewing the state as an arena of class struggle means that people actually have more freedom to determine their lives (because it is only through class struggle that major change occurs) than they do in more traditional political-science views of the state which exalt the role of personal freedom while denying or ignoring class struggle.

18. The interpretations of the state which contribute most to the development of revolutionary will are those which give a prominent place to the capitalist class, which is to say the view of the state as an instrument or ruling committee of this class and the view of the state as an arena of class struggle. To build up a full head of steam in and for the struggle, to maximize rational hostility as a politically motivating factor, most people require opponents in human form, other people who embody the oppressive functions of the system. It is as hard to hate abstract enemies as it is to love abstract friends. It is true that an analysis of the state as a set of objective structures (and, to a lesser extent, as the illusory community) is necessary to fully grasp the origins of existing oppression, how it works and for whom, the weak points in the armor of oppression, who are one's potential allies, and even how the oppressors themselves may be suffering from the system that carries their name. But it is also true that only by directing the struggle against actual, living capitalists can people be sufficiently motivated to engage in revolutionary struggle. To ignore the structural dimension of the analysis is to increase the danger that revolutionary politics will degenerate into reformism, directed toward removing the worst politicians. Without the class dimension, the

danger is that revolutionary politics—lacking "fire in the belly"—will degenerate into scholasticism.

19. By studying the state from the perspectives associated with its different aspects, Marxism is able to show how in politics people make their own history and are made by it at the same time, how we are both free and conditioned, and how the future is both open and necessary.

30. The Development of Legal Ideology

Michael Tigar with Madeleine R. Levy

Michael Tigar, professor of law at the University of Texas School of Law at Austin, is chair of the Section of Litigation of the American Bar Association and a frequent contributor to law journals. Tigar has worked in South Africa doing trial advocacy training with black activists, and his book, *Law and the Rise of Capitalism* (1978) has been studied by the Nelson Mandela Defense Committee. His writings include "The Right of Property and the Law of Theft," *Texas Law Review* 62 (1984), and "Crime Talk, Rights Talk, and Double-Talk: Thoughts on Reading *Encyclopedia of Crime and Justice*," *Texas Law Review* 65 (1986).

The following selection is excerpted from Tigar's book, written with the assistance of Madeleine R. Levy, *Law and the Rise of Capitalism* (New York: Monthly Review, 1978), 277–89. Reprinted by permission of Monthly Review Foundation. Copyright © 1977 by Michael E. Tigar.

In all cases of system-building, the legal rules and principles are justified by resort to sources that are accepted because of their reputed age and authenticity and to principles of social theory that are believed to be self-evidently valid but that in fact merely express the aspirations of the group which has for the moment achieved dominance. Thus, systems of legal rules expressed as legal ideology were not only predictions as to how state power—that is to say, organized violence—would be used in the future: they carried within them justifications of the legitimacy of the exercise of that power.

Because a legal ideology thus created is separate from the system of social relations which it regulates, it seems—both to those to whom it is promulgated and, in time, to those who made it up—to take on a life of its own. The practical consequences of this are soon evident. Warring factions are invited, indeed commanded, to subdue their rivalry and are drawn instead to the interpretation of rules and laws to determine how they shall be applied in particular cases. The warfare moves off the streets to the tribunals. This aspect of legal ideology was described by Engels in *The Origin of the Family, Private Property and the State:*

> In possession of the public power and the right of taxation, the officials now present themselves as organs of society standing *above* society. The free, willing respect accorded to the organs of the gentile constitution is not enough for them, even if they could have it. Representatives of a power which estranges them from society, they have to be given prestige by means of special decrees which invest them with a peculiar sanctity and inviolability. The lowest police officer of the civilized state has more "authority" than all the organs of gentile society put together. But the mightiest prince and the greatest statesman or general of civilization might envy the humblest of the gentile chiefs, the unforced and unquestioned respect accorded to him. The one stands in the midst of society, the other is forced to pose as something outside and above it.

The claim that state legal ideology stands outside and above the social classes that it governs is characteristic of all successful aspirants to state power in the period we have been studying. Legal ideology took the form of detailed and increasingly—as the bourgeoisie gained in strength—comprehensive and highly structured systems of positive law. These systems were counterposed to the "anarchy" of feudal law, which was either actively hostile to commerce or was simply too incomplete and chaotic to permit predictable reliance upon it. Even the laissez-faire idealism of the young American nation was only a superideology, within which the highly refined, centuries-old customary law merchant was received and attentively applied.

Legal Ideology, Jurisprudence, and Insurgency: Some Definitions

We cannot clearly set out our theory that social struggle motivates changes in legal structure, nor contrast it with alternative ways of looking at law, unless we define our terms.

A legal ideology is a statement, in terms of a system of rules of law, of the aspirations, goals, and values of a social group.

It is not, however, the property solely of the group possessing effective control. To the contrary, as we have seen, groups that aspire to state power have formulated their attack in terms of systems of legal rules and principles. But when a group does possess state power—defined as effective control over a particular territory—its legal ideology is "the law." The question of how much territory or control is necessary need not detain us, for it is answered in each historical period by the effective units of production, exchange, and political viability: it may be a city in one historical period, a nation-state in another.

A legal ideology may consist of a number of different kinds of explicit and implicit statements. It may include "rules of recognition," which define the competence of certain persons to exercise legislative and judicial functions. The term may include such general ideological assertions as "the law-making body of the city should represent all the citizens." The ideology may encompass both individually and generally addressed commands, to adopt a distinction commonly used in the writings of legal positivists. The former are, in John Austin's words, "occasional or particular," in the sense that they "oblige . . . to a specific act or forbearance, or to acts or forbearances which it determines specifically and individually," such as judicial judgments. The latter are legislative commands, which speak in general terms and are addressed to unnamed persons at large. A legal ideology may be expressed as volumes of laws, rules, and judgments; or, as was the case in the earliest urban communes, it may consist of a few simple precepts and then the all-important provision of *who* is competent to make rules and issue orders.

The distinction between types of commands does not, in the development of bourgeois law, necessarily follow the line between legislative and judicial branches so familiar to modern bourgeois democratic theory. Decisions in individual cases, leading to individually addressed commands to pay money, restore certain property, or suffer a certain punishment, developed into a system of generally addressed "legislative" rules. This type of customary law is not based on ancient usage (usually fictitious), but on decisions made within living memory and having the force of precedent. The bourgeoisie, in all the regions we have examined, was unremitting in the cultivation and elaboration of legal ideology in this form.

We use the term "jurisprudence" to describe the process by which legal ideology is created and elaborated. The term "jurisprudence of insurgency" describes a certain kind of jurisprudential activity, in which a group challenging the prevailing system of social relations no longer seeks to reform it but rather to overthrow it and replace it with another.

. . . [W]hen the merchant traders of the 1000s and 1100s wished to put their activity on a firm legal basis, they embodied their demands and later their victories in the form of charters and treaties, in effect creating for themselves a place in the feudal legal order. The task of the lawyers for this upstart group was to find texts that would appear authoritative to even the most recalcitrant lord or reactionary prelate and use them as justification for the existence and operation of artisanal and merchant activity.

The merchants sought only a small place within the feudal system, however, and few if any realized the corrosive effects that would ultimately result from granting them this place. This was not a jurisprudence of insurgency, a fact that is reflected in the life histories of merchant families across several generations: the bourgeois aspirations to noble status acknowledged that the system of nobility was dominant, and the large number of merchants who took vows of poverty and ended their days in monasteries demonstrated the grip that the ideology of the organized Church still had upon them.

Because an ideology is a time-bound system of words and phrases crystallized out of human conflict, and because the legal ideology of a group holding state power is (as we have said) designed to subdue rivalries and turn the people's attention to interpreting the "system" of rules, there will always be room for interpreting the rules in different ways. As time goes on, more and more contradictions may develop between the prevailing system of social relations and the content of the formal rules that purport to govern it, and one early task of a dissident group is to explore the limits of the dominant legal ideology in order to see how much can be accomplished within those limits.

In every movement we can thus see the stage at which it accepts the dominant assumptions of the governing class and seeks to use them to its own advantage. The richly varied and highly developed legal ideology of the West, after the rediscovery—or reimportation—of Roman law, permitted and encouraged such an approach.

If the ideology has the relatively unstructured character of much European feudalism between 1000 and about 1350, the process is easy—if at times entailing some disorder. Open, ill-defined systems of authority, with emphasis upon the person entitled to make rules and binding judgments rather than upon the content of the rules themselves, leave more space for changes which do not appear to depart from the basic norms of the existing ideology.

This is not, however, a "jurisprudence of insurgency" as we have defined it, but in making this distinction we do not mean to deny the effect on the dominant legal ideology of jurisprudence sponsored by groups that are not opposed to the existing regime and that do not wish to achieve state power. It will remain to consider how to distinguish dissident groups which are insurgent from those which are not.

Legal Ideology and Economic Interest

Throughout this book we have tried to show the relationship between legal ideology and the system of social relations from which it springs. We have provided some evidence for the view, set forth in the writings of Marx and Engels, that the state imposes itself as the agent of one class in dominating the other classes in a society, and that the maintenance and regulation of relations of production in the interest of the dominant class is the primary goal of legal ideology in the hands of the holders of state power.

Why, then, if the root of legal ideology is economic self-interest, put so much stress upon the content and development of the ideology itself? Our concern is due in part to the central role played by legal ideology in the justification for the sovereigns' exercise of state power and for their challengers' resort to arms. Legal ideology was the popular justification for controlling the daily lives of men and women and for the official violence visited upon them. Calls for social change were phrased as legal ideologies.

However, to assert that the origin and eventual justification of legal ideology is in economic self-interest does not mean that there is a direct and immediate relationship between each element of legal ideology—or even each individually addressed command—and the economic self-interest of a particular group. To the contrary, it is precisely the contradictions between ideology and self-interest that permit insurgent groups to win partial and temporary victories within the parameters of existing law.

These contradictions may arise from several sources.

As legal ideology takes on a life of its own, it becomes subject to interpretation and application, and the decisions of those applying it must bear at least some relationship to the ideology as initially stated, regardless of their particular interests. The possibility of contradictions between official jurisprudence and class interest is increased if the task of formulating individually and generally addressed commands is handed over to a specially trained class of jurisprudents who are accustomed to think in terms of the ideology itself, rather than in terms of the class interest.

Another source of contradiction lies in the fact that legal ideology is formulated at a given moment, while the underlying social relations are constantly changing. The result is that the ideology tends to become an empty form—which is what happened to the democratic features of the early city charters. Further, a rising class may seize an old ideology and turn it against its perpetrators, which is exactly what occurred when the European bourgeoisie used the Roman law—already semisanctified by the Church— to batter down legal barriers to commerce. In the same way, the dominant class, confronted by displeasing elements of its own ideology, may cast them aside and rely instead upon sheer class interest.

Legal ideologies may also contain gaps, or uncertainties, that are filled in and clarified to suit the insistent demands of powerful forces. We observed this suppleness in feudal customary law, which was not based on any detailed set of written customs and was largely administered personally by the lord. The same kind of exploitation of open spaces in the law occurred in England: when the semifeudal town charters proved too restrictive to permit introduction of new technology and larger units of production by the new entrepreneurs, the latter simply bought up land outside the cities and obtained favorable legislative treatment to begin building their enterprises.

31. The Rule of Law

E. P. Thompson

British historian E. P. Thompson is the author of *The Making of the English Working Class* (1963), *The Poverty of Theory* (1978), *Writing by Candlelight* (1981), and *Beyond the Cold War* (1982), coauthor of *Albion's Fatal Tree: Crime and Society in Eighteenth-Century England* (1975), and is the coeditor of *Protest and Survive* (1981). He is currently active in Britain with the Campaign for Nuclear Disarmament (CND) and the Committee for European Nuclear Disarmament (END).

The following selection is excerpted from *Whigs and Hunters: The Origin of the Black Act* (New York: Pantheon, 1975; London: Penguin Books, 1977), 258–66. Copyright © 1975, 1977 by E. P. Thompson. Reprinted by permission of Pantheon Books, a Division of Random House, Inc. and Penguin Books, Ltd.

We might be wise to end here. But since readers of this study may be provoked to some general reflections upon the law and upon British traditions, perhaps we may allow ourselves the same indulgence.

From a certain traditional middle ground of national historiography the interest of this theme (the Black Act and its evolution) may be evident. [The Black Act, passed by the British Parliament in 1723, created fifty new capital offenses, all concerning threats to property. —EDS.] But this middle ground is now being eroded, from at least two directions. On one hand the perspective within which British political and social historians have been accustomed to view their own history is, quite properly, coming under challenge. As the last imperial illusions of the twentieth century fade, so preoccupation with the history and culture of a small island off the coast of Europe becomes open to the charge of narcissism. The culture of constitutionalism which flowered here, under favoured conditions, is an episode too exceptional to carry any universal significance. If we judge it in terms of its own self-sufficient values we are imprisoned within its own parochialism.

Alternative perspectives must diminish the complacency of national historical preoccupation. If we see Britain within the perspective of the expansion of European capitalism, then the contest over interior rights and laws will be dwarfed when set beside the exterior record of slave-trading, of the East India Company, of commercial and military imperialism. Or, to take up a bright new conservative perspective, the story of a few lost common rights and of a few deer-stealers strung from the gallows is a paltry affair when set beside the accounts of mass repression of almost any day in the day-book of the twentieth century. Did a few foresters get a rough handling from partisan laws? What is that beside the norms of the Third Reich? Did the villagers of Winkfield lose access to the peat within Swinley Rails? What is that beside the liquidation of the *kulaks?* What is remarkable (we are reminded) is not that the laws were bent but the fact that there was, anywhere in the eighteenth century, a rule of law at all. To ask for greater justice than that is to display mere sentimentalism. In any event, we should adjust our sense of proportion; against the handfuls carried off on the cart to Tyburn (and smaller handfuls than have been carried off in Tudor times) we must see whole legions carried off by plague or dearth.

From these perspectives concern with the rights and wrongs at law of a few men in 1723 is concern with trivia. And the same conclusion may be reached through a different adjustment of perspective, which may coexist with some of the same arguments. This flourishes in the form of a sophisticated, but (ultimately) highly schematic Marxism which, to our surprise, seems to spring up in the footsteps of those of us in an older Marxist tradition. From this standpoint the law is, perhaps more clearly than any other cultural or institutional artifact, by definition a part of a 'superstructure' adapting itself to the necessities of an infrastructure of productive forces and productive relations. As such, it is clearly an instrument of the *de facto* ruling class: it both defines and defends these rulers' claims upon resources and labour-power—it says what shall be property and what shall be crime—and it mediates class relations with a set of appropriate rules and sanctions, all of which, ultimately, confirm and consolidate existing class power. Hence the rule of law is only another mask for the rule of a class. The revolutionary can have no interest in law, unless as a phenomenon of ruling-class power and hypocrisy; it should be his aim simply to overthrow it. And so, once again, to express surprise at the Black Act or at partial judges is—unless as confirmation and illustration of theories which might easily be demonstrated without all this labour—simply to expose one's own naivety.

So the old middle ground of historiography is crumbling on both sides. I stand on a very narrow ledge, watching the tides come up. Or, to be more explicit, I sit here in my study, at the age of fifty, the desk and the floor piled high with five years of notes, xeroxes, rejected drafts, the clock once again moving into the small hours, and see myself, in a lucid instant, as an anachronism. Why have I spent these years trying to find out what could, in its essential structures, have been known without any investigation at all? And does it matter a damn who gave Parson Power his instructions; which forms brought 'Vulcan' Gates to the gallows; or how an obscure Richmond publican managed to evade a death sentence already determined upon by the Law Officers, the First Minister and the King?

I am disposed to think that it does matter; I have a vested interest (in five years of labour) to think it may. But to show this must involve evacuating received assumptions—that narrowing ledge of traditional middle ground— and moving out onto an even narrower theoretical ledge. This would accept, as it must, some part of the Marxist-structural critique; indeed, some parts of this study have confirmed the class-bound and mystifying functions of the law. But it would reject its ulterior reductionism and would modify its typology of superior and inferior (but determining) structures.

First, analysis of the eighteenth century (and perhaps of other centuries) calls in question the validity of separating off the law as a whole and placing it in some typological superstructure. The law when considered as institution (the courts, with their class theatre and class procedures) or as personnel (the judges, the lawyers, the Justices of the Peace) may very easily be assimilated to those of the ruling class. But all that is entailed in 'the law' is not subsumed in these institutions. The law may also be seen as ideology, or as particular rules and sanctions which stand in a definite and active relationship (often a field of conflict) to social norms; and, finally, it may be seen simply in terms of its own logic, rules and procedures—that is, simply *as law*. And it is not possible to conceive of any complex society without law.

We must labour this point, since some theorists today are unable to see the law except in terms of 'the fuzz' setting about inoffensive demonstrators or cannabis-smokers. I am no authority on the twentieth century, but in the eighteenth century matters were more complex than that. To be sure I have tried to show, in the evolution of the Black Act, an expression of the ascendancy of a Whig oligarchy, which created new laws and bent old legal forms in order to legitimize its own property and status; this oligarchy employed the law, both instrumentally and ideologically, very much as a modern structural Marxist should expect it to do. But this is not the same thing as to say that the rulers had need of law, in order to oppress the ruled, while those who were ruled had need of none. What was often at issue was not property, supported by law, against no-property; it was alternative definitions of property-rights: for the landowner, enclosure—for the cottager, common rights; for the forest officialdom, 'preserved grounds' for the deer; for the foresters, the right to take turfs. For as long as it remained possible, the ruled —if they could find a purse and a lawyer—would actually fight for their rights by means of law; occasionally the copyholders, resting upon the precedents of sixteenth-century law, could actually win a case. When it ceased to be possible to continue the fight at law, men still felt a sense of legal wrong: the propertied had obtained their power by illegitimate means.

Moreover, if we look closely into such an agrarian context, the distinction between law, on the one hand, conceived of as an element of 'superstructure', and the actualities of productive forces and relations on the other hand, becomes more and more untenable. For law was often a definition of actual agrarian *practice*, as it had been pursued 'time out of mind'. How can we distinguish between the activity of farming or of quarrying and the rights to this strip of land or to that quarry? The farmer or forester in his daily occupation was moving within visible or invisible structures of law: this merestone which marked the division between strips; that ancient oak— visited by processional on each Rogation Day—which marked the limits of the parish grazing; those other invisible (but potent and sometimes legally enforceable) memories as to which parishes had the right to take turfs in this waste and which parishes had not; this written or unwritten customal which decided how many stints on the common land and for whom—for copyholders and freeholders only, or for all inhabitants?

Hence 'law' was deeply imbricated within the very basis of productive relations, which would have been inoperable without this law. And, in the second place, this law, as definition or as rules (imperfectly enforceable through institutional legal forms), was endorsed by norms, tenaciously transmitted through the community. There were alternative norms; that is a matter of course; this was a place, not of consensus, but of conflict. But we cannot, then, simply separate off all law as ideology, and assimilate this also to the state apparatus of a ruling class. On the contrary, the norms of foresters might reveal themselves as passionately supported values, impelling them upon a course of action which would lead them into bitter conflict—with 'the law'.

So we are back, once again, with *that* law: the institutionalized procedures of the ruling class. This, no doubt, is worth no more of our theoretical attention; we can see it as an instrument of class power *tout court*. But we must take even this formulation, and see whether its crystalline clarity will survive immersion in scepticism. To be sure, we can stand no longer on that traditional ground of liberal academicism, which offers the eighteenth century as a society of consensus, ruled within the parameters of paternalism and deference, and governed by a 'rule of law' which attained (however imperfectly) towards impartiality. That is not the society which we have been examining; we have not observed a society of consensus; and we have seen the law being devised and employed, directly and instrumentally, in the imposition of class power. Nor can we accept a sociological refinement of the old view, which stresses the imperfections and partiality of the law, and its subordination to the functional requirements of socio-economic interest groups. For what we have observed is something more than the law as a pliant medium to be twisted this way and that by whichever interests already possess effective power. Eighteenth-century law was more substantial than that. Over and above its pliant, instrumental functions it existed in its own right, as ideology; as an ideology which not only served, in most respects, but which also legitimized class power. The hegemony of the eighteenth-century gentry and aristocracy was expressed, above all, not in military force, not in the mystifications of a priesthood or of the press, not even in economic coercion, but in the rituals of the study of the Justices of the Peace, in the quarter-sessions, in the pomp of Assizes and in the theatre of Tyburn.

Thus the law (we agree) may be seen instrumentally as mediating and reinforcing existent class relations and, ideologically, as offering to these a legitimation. But we must press our definitions a little further. For if we say that existent class relations were mediated by the law, this is not the same thing as saying that the law was no more than those relations translated into other terms, which masked or mystified the reality. This may, quite often, be true but it is not the whole truth. For class relations were expressed, not in any way one likes, but *through the forms of law*; and the law, like other institutions which from time to time can be seen as mediating (and masking) existing class relations (such as the Church or the media of communication), has its own characteristics, its own independent history and logic of evolution.

Moreover, people are not as stupid as some structuralist philosophers suppose them to be. They will not be mystified by the first man who puts on a wig. It is inherent in the especial character of law, as a body of rules and procedures, that it shall apply logical criteria with reference to standards of universality and equity. It is true that certain categories of person may be excluded from this logic (as children or slaves), that other categories may be debarred from access to parts of the logic (as women or, for many forms of eighteenth-century law, those without certain kinds of property), and that the poor may often be excluded, through penury, from the law's costly procedures. All this, and more, is true. But if too much of this is true, then the consequences are plainly counterproductive. Most men have a strong sense of justice, at least with regard to their own interests. If the law is evidently partial and unjust, then it will mask nothing, legitimize nothing, contribute nothing to any class's hegemony. The essential precondition for the effectiveness of law, in its function as ideology, is that it shall display an independence from gross manipulation and shall seem to be just. It cannot seem to be so without upholding its own logic and criteria of equity; indeed, on occasion, by actually *being* just. And furthermore it is not often the case that a ruling ideology can be dismissed as a mere hypocrisy; even rulers find a need to legitimize their power, to moralize their functions, to feel themselves to be useful and just. In the case of an ancient historical formation like the law, a discipline which requires years of exacting study to master, there will always be some men who actively believe in their own procedures and in the logic of justice. The law may be rhetoric, but it need not be empty rhetoric. Blackstone's *Commentaries* represent an intellectual exercise far more rigorous than could have come from an apologist's pen.

I do not know what transcultural validity these reflections may have. But they are certainly applicable to England in the eighteenth century. Douglas Hay, in a significant essay in *Albion's Fatal Tree*, has argued that the law assumed unusual pre-eminence in that century, as the central legitimizing ideology, displacing the religious authority and sanctions of previous centuries. It gave way, in its turn, to economic sanctions and to the ideology of the free market and of political liberalism in the nineteenth. Turn where you will, the rhetoric of eighteenth-century England is saturated with the notion of law. Royal absolutism was placed behind a high hedge of law; landed estates were tied together with entails and marriage settlements made up of elaborate tissues of law; authority and property punctuated their power by regular 'examples' made upon the public gallows. More than this, immense efforts were made (and Hay has explored the forms of these) to project the image of a ruling class which was itself subject to the rule of law, and whose legitimacy rested upon the equity and universality of those legal forms. And the rulers were, in serious senses, whether willingly or unwillingly, the prisoners of their own rhetoric; they played the games of power according to rules which suited them, but they could not break those rules or the whole game would be thrown away. And, finally, so far from the ruled shrugging off this rhetoric as a hypocrisy, some part of it at least was taken over as part of the rhetoric of the plebeian crowd, of the 'free-born Englishman' with his inviolable privacy, his *habeas corpus*, his equality before the law. If this rhetoric was a mask, it was a mask which John Wilkes was to borrow, at the head of ten thousand masked supporters.

So that in this island and in that century above all one must resist any slide into structural reductionism. What this overlooks, among other things, is the immense capital of human struggle over the previous two centuries against royal absolutism, inherited, in the forms and traditions of the law, by the eighteenth-century gentry. For in the sixteenth and seventeenth centuries the law had been less an instrument of class power than a central arena of conflict. In the course of conflict the law itself had been changed; inherited by the eighteenth-century gentry, this changed law was, literally, central to their whole purchase upon power and upon the means of life. Take law away, and the royal prerogative, or the presumption of the aristocracy, might flood back upon their properties and lives; take law away and the string which tied together their lands and marriages would fall apart. But it was inherent in the very nature of the medium which they had selected for their own self-defence that it could not be reserved for the exclusive use only of their own class. The law, in its forms and traditions, entailed principles of equity and universality which, perforce, had to be extended to all sorts and degrees of men. And since this was of necessity so, ideology could turn necessity to advantage. What had been devised by men of property as a defence against arbitrary power could be turned into service as an apologia for property in the face of the propertyless. And the apologia was serviceable up to a point: for these 'propertyless', as we have seen, comprised multitudes of men and women who themselves enjoyed, in fact, petty property rights or agrarian use-rights whose definition was inconceivable without the forms of law. Hence the ideology of the great struck root in a soil, however shallow, of

292 E. P. THOMPSON

actuality. And the courts gave substance to the ideology by the scrupulous care with which, on occasion, they adjudged petty rights, and, on all occasions, preserved proprieties and forms.

We reach, then, not a simple conclusion (law = class power) but a complex and contradictory one. On the one hand, it is true that the law did mediate existent class relations to the advantage of the rulers; not only is this so, but as the century advanced the law became a superb instrument by which these rulers were able to impose new definitions of property to their even greater advantage, as in the extinction by law of indefinite agrarian use-rights and in the furtherance of enclosure. On the other hand, the law mediated these class relations through legal forms, which imposed, again and again, inhibitions upon the actions of the rulers. For there is a very large difference, which twentieth-century experience ought to have made clear even to the most exalted thinker, between arbitrary extra-legal power and the rule of law. And not only were the rulers (indeed, the ruling class as a whole) inhibited by their own rules of law against the exercise of direct unmediated force (arbitrary imprisonment, the employment of troops against the crowd, torture, and those other conveniences of power with which we are all conversant), but they also believed enough in these rules, and in their accompanying ideological rhetoric, to allow, in certain limited areas, the law itself to be a genuine forum within which certain kinds of class conflict were fought out. There were even occasions (one recalls John Wilkes and several of the trials of the 1790s) when the Government itself retired form the courts defeated. Such occasions served, paradoxically, to consolidate power, to enhance its legitimacy, and to inhibit revolutionary movements. But, to turn the paradox around, these same occasions served to bring power even further within constitutional controls.

The rhetoric and the rules of a society are something a great deal more than sham. In the same movement they may modify, in profound ways, the behaviour of the powerful, and mystify the powerless. They may disguise the true realities of power, but, at the same time, they may curb that power and check its intrusions. And it is often from within that very rhetoric that a radical critique of the practice of the society is developed: the reformers of the 1790s appeared, first of all, clothed in the rhetoric of Locke and of Blackstone.

These reflections lead me on to conclusions which may be different from those which some readers expect. I have shown in this study a political oligarchy inventing callous and oppressive laws to serve its own interests. I have shown judges who, no less than bishops, were subject to political influence, whose sense of justice was humbug, and whose interpretation of the laws served only to enlarge their inherent class bias. Indeed, I think that this study has shown that for many of England's governing élite the rules of law were a nuisance, to be manipulated and bent in what ways they could; and that the allegiance of such men as Walpole, Hardwicke or Paxton to the rhetoric of law was largely humbug. But I do not conclude from this that the rule of law itself was humbug. On the contrary, the inhibitions upon power imposed by law seem to me a legacy as substantial as any handed down from the struggles of the seventeenth century to the eighteenth, and a true and important cultural achievement of the agrarian and mercantile bourgeoisie, and of their supporting yeomen and artisans.

More than this, the notion of the regulation and reconciliation of conflicts through the rule of law—and the elaboration of rules and procedures which, on occasion, made some approximate approach towards the ideal—seems to me a cultural achievement of universal significance. I do not lay any claim as to the abstract, extra-historical impartiality of these rules. In a context of gross class inequalities, the equity of the law must always be in some part sham. Transplanted as it was to even more inequitable contexts, this law could become an instrument of imperialism. For this law has found its way to a good many parts of the globe. But even here the rules and the rhetoric have imposed some inhibitions upon the imperial power. If the rhetoric was a mask, it was a mask which Gandhi and Nehru were to borrow, at the head of a million masked supporters.

I am not starry-eyed about this at all. . . . I am insisting only upon the obvious point, which some modern Marxists have overlooked, that there is a difference between arbitrary power and the rule of law. We ought to expose the shams and inequities which may be concealed beneath this law. But the rule of law itself, the imposing of effective inhibitions upon power and the defence of the citizen from power's all-intrusive claims, seems to me to be an unqualified human good. To deny or belittle this good is, in this danger-ous century when the resources and pretensions of power continue to en-large, a desperate error of intellectual abstraction. More than this, it is a self-fulfilling error, which encourages us to give up the struggle against bad laws and class-bound procedures, and to disarm ourselves before power. It is to throw away a whole inheritance of struggle *about* law, and within the forms of law, whose continuity can never be fractured without bringing men and women into immediate danger.

V. APPENDICES

APPENDICES

A. Ruling Class Intent

Woodrow Wilson

Woodrow Wilson (1856–1924), prior to becoming the twenty-eighth president of the United States, was professor of jurisprudence and political economy at Princeton University. His writings include *Congressional Government* (1885), *George Washington* (1896), and *Constitutional Government in the United States* (1908).

The following selection is excerpted from *Division and Reunion* (New York: Longmans, Green, 1906), 12–13.

The federal government was not by intention a democratic government. In plan and structure it had been meant to check the sweep and power of popular majorities. The Senate, it was believed, would be a stronghold of conservatism, if not of aristocracy and wealth. The President, it was expected, would be the choice of representative men acting in the electoral college, and not of the people. The federal Judiciary was looked to, with its virtually permanent membership, to hold the entire structure of national politics in nice balance against all disturbing influences, whether of popular impulse or of official overbearance. Only in the House of Representatives were the people to be accorded an immediate audience and a direct means of making their will effective in affairs. The government had, in fact, been originated and organized upon the initiative and primarily in the interest of the mercantile and wealthy classes. Originally conceived in an effort to accommodate commercial disputes between the States, it had been urged to adoption by a minority, under the concerted and aggressive leadership of able men representing a ruling class. The Federalists not only had on their side the power of convincing argument, but also the pressure of a strong and intelligent class possessed of unity and informed by a conscious solidarity of material interest.

B. Economic Bill of Rights

Franklin D. Roosevelt

Franklin D. Roosevelt (1882–1945) was the thirty-second president of the United States.

The following selection, Roosevelt's suggestion for an Economic Bill of Rights, is excerpted from his 1944 State of the Union address.

This Republic had its beginning, and grew to its present strength, under the protection of certain inalienable political rights—among them the right of free speech, free press, free worship, trial by jury, freedom from unreasonable searches and seizures. They were our rights to life and liberty.

As our Nation has grown in size and stature, however—as our industrial economy expanded—these political rights proved inadequate to assure us equality in the pursuit of happiness.

We have come to a clear realization of the fact that true individual freedom cannot exist without economic security and independence. "Necessitous men are not freemen." People who are hungry and out of a job are the stuff of which dictatorships are made.

In our day these economic truths have become accepted as self-evident. We have accepted, so to speak, a second Bill of Rights under which a new basis of security and prosperity can be established for all—regardless of station, race, or creed.

Among these are—

The right to a useful and remunerative job in the industries, or shops or farms or mines of the Nation;

The right to earn enough to provide adequate food and clothing and recreation;

The right of every farmer to raise and sell his products at a return which will give him and his family a decent living;

The right of every businessman, large and small, to trade in an atmosphere of freedom from unfair competition and domination by monopolies at home or abroad;

The right of every family to a decent home;

The right to adequate medical care and the opportunity to achieve and enjoy good health;

The right to adequate protection from the economic fears of old age, sickness, accident, and unemployment;

The right to a good education.

All of these rights spell security. And after this war is won we must be prepared to move forward, in the implementation of these rights, to new goals of human happiness and well-being.

C. A Bicentennial View from the Supreme Court

Thurgood Marshall

Thurgood Marshall has been an Associate Justice of the U.S. Supreme Court since 1967.

The following article is reprinted from a speech presented at the annual seminar of the San Francisco Patent and Trademark Law Association in Maui, Hawaii, on 6 May 1987.

1987 marks the 200th anniversary of the United States Constitution. A Commission has been established to coordinate the celebration. The official meetings, essay contests, and festivities have begun.

The planned commemoration will span three years, and I am told 1987 is "dedicated to the memory of the Founders and the document they drafted in Philadelphia."[1] We are to "recall the achievements of our Founders and the knowledge and experience that inspired them, the nature of the government they established, its origins, its character, and its ends, and the rights and privileges of citizenship, as well as its attendant responsibilities."[2]

Like many anniversary celebrations, the plan for 1987 takes particular events and holds them up as the source of all the very best that has followed. Patriotic feelings will surely swell, prompting proud proclamations of the wisdom, foresight, and sense of justice shared by the Framers and reflected in a written document now yellowed with age. This is unfortunate—not the patriotism itself, but the tendency for the celebration to oversimplify, and overlook the many other events that have been instrumental to our achievements as a nation. The focus of this celebration invites a complacent belief that the vision of those who debated and compromised in Philadelphia yielded the "more perfect Union" it is said we now enjoy.

I cannot accept this invitation, for I do not believe that the meaning of the Constitution was forever "fixed" at the Philadelphia Convention. Nor do I find the wisdom, foresight, and sense of justice exhibited by the Framers particularly profound. To the contrary, the government they devised was defective from the start, requiring several amendments, a civil war, a momentous social transformation to attain the system of constitutional government, and its respect for the individual freedoms and human rights, we hold as fundamental today. When contemporary Americans cite "The Constitution," they invoke a concept that is vastly different from what the Framers barely began to construct two centuries ago.

For a sense of the evolving nature of the Constitution we need look no further than the first three words of the document's preamble: "We the People." When the Founding Fathers used this phrase in 1787, they did not have in mind the majority of America's citizens. "We the People" included, in the words of the Framers, "the whole Number of free Persons."[3] On a matter so basic as the right to vote, for example, Negro slaves were excluded, although they were counted for representational purposes—at three-fifths each. Women did not gain the right to vote for over a hundred and thirty years.[4]

These omissions were intentional. The record of the Framers' debates on the slave question is especially clear: the Southern States acceded to the demands of the New England States for giving Congress broad power to regulate commerce, in exchange for the right to continue the slave trade. The economic interests of the regions coalesced: New Englanders engaged in the "carrying trade" would profit from transporting slaves from Africa as well as goods produced in America by slave labor. The perpetuation of slavery ensured the primary source of wealth in the Southern States.

Despite this clear understanding of the role slavery would play in the new republic, use of the words "slaves" and "slavery" was carefully avoided in the original document. Political representation in the lower House of Congress was to be based on the population of "free Persons" in each State, plus three-fifths of all "other Persons."[5] Moral principles against slavery, for those who had them, were compromised, with no explanation of the conflicting principles for which the American Revolutionary War had ostensibly been fought: the self-evident truths "that all men are created equal, that they are endowed by their Creator with certain unalienable Rights, that among these are Life, Liberty and the pursuit of Happiness."[6]

It was not the first such compromise. Even these ringing phrases from the

Declaration of Independence are filled with irony, for an early draft of what became that Declaration assailed the King of England for suppressing legislative attempts to end the slave trade and for encouraging slave rebellions.[7] The final draft adopted in 1776 did not contain this criticism. And so again at the Constitutional Convention eloquent objections to the institution of slavery went unheeded, and its opponents eventually consented to a document which laid a foundation for the tragic events that were to follow.

Pennsylvania's Gouverneur Morris provides an example. He opposed slavery and the counting of slaves in determining the basis for representation in Congress. At the Convention he objected that

the inhabitant of Georgia [or] South Carolina who goes to the coast of Africa, and in defiance of the most sacred laws of humanity tears away his fellow creatures from their dearest connections and damns them to the most cruel bondages, shall have more votes in a Government instituted for protection of the rights of mankind, than the Citizen of Pennsylvania or New Jersey who views with a laudable horror, so nefarious a practice.[8]

And yet Gouverneur Morris eventually accepted the three-fifths accommodation. In fact, he wrote the final draft of the Constitution, the very document the bicentennial will commemorate.

As a result of compromise, the right of the Southern States to continue importing slaves was extended, officially, at least until 1808. We know that it actually lasted a good deal longer, as the Framers possessed no monopoly on the ability to trade moral principles for self-interest. But they nevertheless set an unfortunate example. Slaves could be imported, if the commercial interests of the North were protected. To make the compromise even more palatable, customs duties would be imposed at up to ten dollars per slave as a means of raising public revenues.[9]

No doubt it will be said, when the unpleasant truth of the history of slavery in America is mentioned during this bicentennial year, that the Constitution was a product of its times, and embodied a compromise which, under other circumstances, would not have been made. But the effects of the Framers' compromise have remained for generations. They arose from the contradiction between guaranteeing liberty and justice to all, and denying both to Negroes.

The original intent of the phrase, "We the People," was far too clear for any ameliorating construction. Writing for the Supreme Court in 1857, Chief Justice Taney penned the following passage in the *Dred Scott* case,[10] on the issue whether, in the eyes of the Framers, slaves were "constituent members of the sovereignty," and were to be included among "We the People":

We think they are not, and that they are not included, and were not intended to be included. . . . They had for more than a century before been regarded as beings of an inferior order, and altogether unfit to associate with the white race. . . ; and so far inferior, that they had no rights which the white man was bound to respect; and that the negro might justly and lawfully be reduced to slavery for his benefit. . . . [A]ccordingly, a negro of the African race was regarded . . . as an article of property, and held, and bought and sold as such. . . . [N]o one seems to have doubted the correctness of the prevailing opinion of the time.

And so, nearly seven decades after the Constitutional Convention, the Supreme Court reaffirmed the prevailing opinion of the Framers regarding the rights of Negroes in America. It took a bloody civil war before the 13th Amendment could be adopted to abolish slavery, though not the consequences slavery would have for future Americans.

While the Union survived the Civil War, the Constitution did not. In its place arose a new, more promising basis for justice and equality, the 14th Amendment, ensuring protection of the life, liberty, and property of *all* persons against deprivations without due process, and guaranteeing equal protection of the laws. And yet almost another century would pass before any significant recognition was obtained of the rights of black Americans to share equally even in such basic opportunities as education, housing, and employment, and to have their votes counted, and counted equally. In the meantime, blacks joined America's military to fight its wars and invested untold hours working in its factories and on its farms, contributing to the development of this country's magnificent wealth and waiting to share in its prosperity.

What is striking is the role legal principles have played throughout America's history in determining the condition of Negroes. They were enslaved by law, emancipated by law, disenfranchised and segregated by law; and, finally, they have begun to win equality by law. Along the way, new constitutional principles have emerged to meet the challenges of a changing society. The progress has been dramatic, and it will continue.

The men who gathered in Philadelphia in 1787 could not have envisioned these changes. They could not have imagined, nor would they have accepted, that the document they were drafting would one day be construed by a Supreme Court to which had been appointed a woman and the descendent of an African slave. "We the People" no longer enslave, but the credit does not belong to the Framers. It belongs to those who refused to acquiesce in outdated notions of "liberty," "justice," and "equality," and who strived to better them.

And so we must be careful, when focusing on the events which took place in Philadelphia two centuries ago, that we not overlook the momentous events which followed, and thereby lose our proper sense of perspective. Otherwise, the odds are that for many Americans the bicentennial celebration will be little more than a blind pilgrimage to the shrine of the original document now stored in a vault in the National Archives. If we seek, instead, a sensitive understanding of the Constitution's inherent defects, and its promising evolution through 200 years of history, the celebration of the "Miracle at Philadelphia"[11] will, in my view, be a far more meaningful and humbling experience. We will see that the true miracle was not the birth of the Constitution, but its life, a life nurtured through two turbulent centuries of our own making, and a life embodying much good fortune that was not.

Thus, in this bicentennial year, we may not all participate in the festivities with flag-waving fervor. Some may more quietly commemorate the suffering, struggle, and sacrifice that has triumphed over much of what was wrong with the original document, and observe the anniversary with hopes not realized and promises not fulfilled. I plan to celebrate the bicentennial of the Constitution as a living document, including the Bill of Rights and the other amendments protecting individual freedoms and human rights.

Notes

1. Commission on the Bicentennial of the United States Constitution, *First Full Year's Report*, at 7 (September 1986).
2. Commission on the Bicentennial of the United States Constitution, *First Report*, at 6 (September 17, 1985).
3. United States Constitution, Art. 1, §2 (Sept. 17, 1787).
4. The 19th Amendment (ratified in 1920).
5. United States Constitution, Art. 1, §2 (Sept. 17, 1787).
6. "Declaration of Independence" (July 4, 1776).
7. See Carl Becker, *The Declaration of Independence: A Study in the History of Political Ideas* 147 (New York: Knopf, 1942).

8. Max Farrand, ed., *The Records of the Federal Convention of 1787*, vol. II, 222 (New Haven: Yale University Press, 1911).

9. United States Constitution, Art. 1, §9 (Sept. 17, 1787).

10. *Dred Scott v. Sandford*, 60 U.S. (19 How.) 393, 405, 407–408 (1857).

11. Catherine Drinker Bowen, *Miracle at Philadelphia: The Story of the Constitutional Convention, May to September 1787* (Boston: Little Brown, 1966).

D. Constitution of the United States of America and Amendments

Preamble

We the people of the United States, in order to form a more perfect union, establish justice, insure domestic tranquillity, provide for the common defense, promote the general welfare, and secure the blessings of liberty to ourselves and our posterity, do ordain and establish this Constitution for the United States of America.

Article I

Section 1   All legislative powers herein granted shall be vested in a Congress of the United States, which shall consist of a Senate and a House of Representatives.

Section 2   The House of Representatives shall be composed of members chosen every second year by the people of the several States, and the electors in each State shall have the qualifications requisite for electors of the most numerous branch of the State Legislature.

No person shall be a Representative who shall not have attained to the age of twenty-five years, and been seven years a citizen of the United States, and who shall not, when elected, be an inhabitant of that State in which he shall be chosen.

Representatives and direct taxes shall be apportioned among the several States which may be included within this Union, according to their respective numbers, *which shall be determined by adding to the whole number of free persons, including those bound to service for a term of years and excluding Indians not taxed, three-fifths of all other persons.* The actual enumeration shall be made within three years after the first meeting of the Congress of the United States, and within every subsequent term of ten years, in such manner as they shall by law direct. The number of Representatives shall not

Passages no longer in effect are printed in italic type.

306

exceed one for every thirty thousand, but each State shall have at least one Representative; *and until such enumeration shall be made, the State of New Hampshire shall be entitled to choose three, Massachusetts eight, Rhode Island and Providence Plantations one, Connecticut five, New York six, New Jersey four, Pennsylvania eight, Delaware one, Maryland six, Virginia ten, North Carolina five, South Carolina five, and Georgia three.*

When vacancies happen in the representation from any State, the Executive authority thereof shall issue writs of election to fill such vacancies.

The House of Representatives shall choose their Speaker and other officers; and shall have the sole power of impeachment.

Section 3 The Senate of the United States shall be composed of two Senators from each State, *chosen by the legislature thereof,* for six years; and each Senator shall have one vote.

Immediately after they shall be assembled in consequence of the first election, they shall be divided as equally as may be into three classes. The seats of the Senators of the first class shall be vacated at the expiration of the second year, of the second class at the expiration of the fourth year, and of the third class at the expiration of the sixth year, so that one-third may be chosen every second year; *and if vacancies happen by resignation or otherwise, during the recess of the legislature of any State, the Executive thereof may make temporary appointments until the next meeting of the legislature, which shall then fill such vacancies.*

No person shall be a Senator who shall not have attained to the age of thirty years, and been nine years a citizen of the United States, and who shall not, when elected, be an inhabitant of that State for which he shall be chosen.

The Vice-President of the United States shall be President of the Senate, but shall have no vote, unless they be equally divided.

The Senate shall choose their other officers, and also a President pro tempore, in the absence of the Vice-President, or when he shall exercise the office of President of the United States.

The Senate shall have the sole power to try all impeachments. When sitting for that purpose, they shall be on oath or affirmation. When the President of the United States is tried, the Chief Justice shall preside: and no person shall be convicted without the concurrence of two-thirds of the members present.

Judgment in cases of impeachment shall not extend further than to removal from the office, and disqualification to hold and enjoy any office of honor, trust or profit under the United States: but the party convicted shall nevertheless be liable and subject to indictment, trial, judgment and punishment, according to law.

Section 4 The times, places and manner of holding elections for Senators and Representatives shall be prescribed in each State by the legislature thereof; but the Congress may at any time by law make or alter such regulations, except as to the places of choosing Senators.

The Congress shall assemble at least once in every year, and such meeting *shall be on the first Monday in December, unless they shall by law appoint a different day.*

Section 5 Each house shall be the judge of the elections, returns and qualifications of its own members, and a majority of each shall constitute a quorum to do business; but a smaller number may adjourn from day to day, and may be authorized to compel the attendance of absent members, in such manner, and under such penalties, as each house may provide.

Each house may determine the rules of its proceedings, punish its members for disorderly behavior, and with the concurrence of two-thirds, expel a member.

Each house shall keep a journal of its proceedings, and from time to time publish the same, excepting such parts as may in their judgment require secrecy; and the yeas and nays of the members of either house on any question shall, at the desire of one-fifth of those present, be entered on the journal.

Neither house, during the session of Congress, shall, without the consent of the other, adjourn for more than three days, nor to any other place than that in which the two houses shall be sitting.

Section 6 The Senators and Representatives shall receive a compensation for their services, to be ascertained by law and paid out of the treasury of the United States. They shall in all cases except treason, felony and breach of the peace, be privileged from arrest during their attendance at the session of their respective houses, and in going to and returning from the same; and for any speech or debate in either house, they shall not be questioned in any other place.

No Senator or Representative shall, during the time for which he was elected, be appointed to any civil office under the authority of the United States, which shall have been created, or the emoluments whereof shall have been increased, during such time; and no person holding any office under the United States shall be a member of either house during his continuance in office.

Section 7   All bills for raising revenue shall originate in the House of Representatives; but the Senate may propose or concur with amendments as on other bills.

Every bill which shall have passed the House of Representatives and the Senate, shall, before it becomes law, be presented to the President of the United States; if he approve he shall sign it, but if not he shall return it with objections to that house in which it originated, who shall enter at large on their journal, and proceed to reconsider it. If after such reconsideration two-thirds of that house shall agree to pass the bill, it shall be sent, together with the objections, to the other house, by which it shall likewise be reconsidered, and, if approved by two-thirds of that house, it shall become a law. But in all such cases the votes of both houses shall be determined by yeas and nays, and the names of the persons voting for and against the bill shall be entered on the journal of each house respectively. If any bill shall not be returned by the President within ten days (Sundays excepted) after it shall have been presented to him, the same shall be a law, in like manner as if he had signed it, unless the Congress by their adjournment prevent its return, in which case it shall not be a law.

Every order, resolution, or vote to which the concurrence of the Senate and House of Representatives may be necessary (except on a question of adjournment) shall be presented to the President of the United States; and before the same shall take effect, shall be approved by him, or being disapproved by him, shall be repassed by two-thirds of the Senate and House of Representatives, according to the rules and limitations prescribed in the case of a bill.

Section 8   The Congress shall have power
To lay and collect taxes, duties, imposts, and excises, to pay the debts and provide for the common defense and general welfare of the United States; but all duties, imposts and excises shall be uniform throughout the United States;
To borrow money on the credit of the United States;

To regulate commerce with foreign nations, and among the several States, and with the Indian tribes;

To establish an uniform rule of naturalization, and uniform laws on the subject of bankruptcies throughout the United States;

To coin money, regulate the value thereof, and of foreign coin, and fix the standard of weights and measures;

To provide for the punishment of counterfeiting the securities and current coin of the United States;

To establish post offices and post roads;

To promote the progress of science and useful arts by securing for limited times to authors and inventors the exclusive right to their respective writings and discoveries;

To constitute tribunals inferior to the Supreme Court;

To define and punish piracies and felonies committed on the high seas and offenses against the law of nations;

To declare war, grant letters of marque and reprisal, and make rules concerning captures on land and water;

To raise and support armies, but no appropriation of money to that use shall be for a longer term than two years;

To provide and maintain a navy;

To make rules for the government and regulation of the land and naval forces;

To provide for calling forth the militia to execute the laws of the Union, suppress insurrections, and repel invasions;

To provide for organizing, arming, and disciplining the militia, and for governing such part of them as may be employed in the service of the United States, reserving to the States respectively the appointment of the officers, and the authority of training the militia according to the discipline prescribed by Congress;

To exercise legislation in all cases whatsoever, over such district (not exceeding ten miles square) as may, by cession of particular States, and the acceptance of Congress, become the seat of government of the United States, and to exercise like authority over all places purchased by the consent of the legislature of the State, in which the same shall be, for erection of forts, magazines, arsenals, dock-yards, and other needful buildings;—and

To make all laws which shall be necessary and proper for carrying into execution the foregoing powers, and all other powers vested by this Constitution in the government of the United States, or in any department or officer thereof.

Section 9   The migration or importation of such persons as any of the States now existing shall think proper to admit shall not be prohibited by the Congress prior to the year 1808; but a tax or duty may be imposed on such importation, not exceeding $10 for each person.

The privilege of the writ of habeas corpus shall not be suspended, unless when in cases of rebellion or invasion the public safety may require it.

No bill of attainder or ex post facto law shall be passed.

No capitation, or other direct, tax shall be laid, unless in proportion to the census or enumeration herein before directed to be taken.

No tax or duty shall be laid on articles exported from any State.

No preference shall be given by any regulation of commerce or revenue to the ports of one State over those of another; nor shall vessels bound to, or from, one State, be obliged to enter, clear, or pay duties in another.

No money shall be drawn from the treasury, but in consequence of appropriations made by law; and a regular statement and account of the receipts and expenditures of all public money shall be published from time to time.

No title of nobility shall be granted by the United States: and no person holding any office of profit or trust under them, shall, without the consent of the Congress, accept of any present, emolument, office, or title, of any kind whatever, from any king, prince, or foreign state.

Section 10   No State shall enter into any treaty, alliance, or confederation; grant letters of marque and reprisal; coin money; emit bills of credit; make anything but gold and silver coin a tender in payment of debts; pass any bill of attainder, ex post facto law, or law impairing the obligation of contracts, or grant any title of nobility.

No State shall, without the consent of Congress, lay any imposts or duties on imports or exports, except what may be absolutely necessary for executing its inspection laws: and the net produce of all duties and imposts, laid by any State on imports or exports, shall be for the use of the treasury of the United States; and all such laws shall be subject to the revision and control of the Congress.

No State shall, without the consent of Congress, lay any duty of tonnage, keep troops or ships of war in time of peace, enter into any agreement or compact with another State, or with a foreign power, or engage in war, unless actually invaded, or in such imminent danger as will not admit of delay.

Article II

Section 1   The executive power shall be vested in a President of the United States of America. He shall hold his office during the term of four years, and, together with the Vice-President, chosen for the same term, be elected as follows:

Each State shall appoint, in such manner as the legislature thereof may direct, a number of electors, equal to the whole number of Senators and Representatives to which the State may be entitled in the Congress; but no Senator or Representative, or person holding an office of trust or profit under the United States, shall be appointed an elector.

The electors shall meet in their respective States, and vote by ballot for two persons, of whom one at least shall not be an inhabitant of the same State with themselves. And they shall make a list of all the persons voted for, and of the number of votes for each; which list they shall sign and certify, and transmit sealed to the seat of government of the United States, directed to the President of the Senate. The President of the Senate shall, in the presence of the Senate and House of Representatives, open all the certificates, and the votes shall then be counted. The person having the greatest number of votes shall be the President, if such number be a majority of the whole number of electors appointed; and if there be more than one who have such majority, and have an equal number of votes, then the House of Representatives shall immediately choose by ballot one of them for President; and if no person have a majority, then from the five highest on the list said house shall in like manner choose the President. But in choosing the President the votes shall be taken by States, the representation from each State having one vote; a quorum for this purpose shall consist of a member or members from two-thirds of the States, and a majority of all the States shall be necessary to a choice. In every case, after the choice of the President, the person having the greatest number of votes of the electors shall be the Vice-President. But if there should remain two or more who have equal votes, the Senate shall choose from them by ballot the Vice-President.

The Congress may determine the time of choosing the electors and the day on which they shall give their votes; which day shall be the same throughout the United States.

No person except a natural-born citizen, *or a citizen of the United States at the time of the adoption of this Constitution*, shall be eligible to the office of President; neither shall any person be eligible to that office who shall not have attained to the age of thirty-five years, and been fourteen years a resident within the United States.

In case of the removal of the President from office or of his death, resignation, or inability to discharge the powers and duties of the said office, the same shall devolve on the Vice-President, and the Congress may by law provide for the case of removal, death, resignation, or inability, both of the President and Vice-President, declaring what officer shall then act as President, and such officer shall act accordingly, until the disability be removed, or a President shall be elected.

The President shall, at stated times, receive for his services a compensation, which shall neither be increased nor diminished during the period for which he shall have been elected, and he shall not receive within that period any other emolument from the United States, or any of them.

Before he enter on the execution of his office, he shall take the following oath or affirmation: — "I do solemnly swear (or affirm) that I will faithfully execute the office of the President of the United States, and will to the best of my ability preserve, protect and defend the Constitution of the United States."

Section 2 The President shall be commander in chief of the army and navy of the United States, and of the militia of the several States, when called into the actual service of the United States; he may require the opinion, in writing, of the principal officer in each of the executive departments, upon any subject relating to the duties of their respective offices, and he shall have power to grant reprieves and pardons for offenses against the United States, except in cases of impeachment.

He shall have power, by and with the advice and consent of the Senate, to make treaties, provided two-thirds of the Senators present concur; and he shall nominate, and by and with the advice and consent of the Senate, shall appoint ambassadors, other public ministers and consuls, judges of the Supreme Court, and all other officers of the United States, whose appointments are not herein otherwise provided for, and which shall be established by law: but Congress may by law vest the appointment of such inferior officers, as they think proper, in the President alone, in the courts of law, or in the heads of departments.

The President shall have power to fill up all vacancies that may happen during the recess of the Senate, by granting commissions which shall expire at the end of their next session.

Section 3   He shall from time to time give to the Congress information of the state of the Union, and recommend to their consideration such measures as he shall judge necessary and expedient; he may, on extraordinary occasions, convene both houses, or either of them, and in case of disagreement between them, with respect to the time of adjournment, he may adjourn them to such time as he shall think proper; he shall receive ambassadors and other public ministers; he shall take care that the laws be faithfully executed, and shall commission all the officers of the United States.

Section 4   The President, Vice-President and all civil officers of the United States shall be removed from office on impeachment for, and on conviction of, treason, bribery, or other high crimes and misdemeanors.

Article III

Section 1   The judicial power of the United States shall be vested in one Supreme Court, and in such inferior courts as the Congress may from time to time ordain and establish. The judges, both of the Supreme and inferior courts, shall hold their offices during good behavior, and shall, at stated times, receive for their services a compensation which shall not be diminished during their continuance in office.

Section 2   The judicial power shall extend to all cases, in law and equity, arising under this Constitution, the laws of the United States, and treaties made, or which shall be made, under their authority;—to all cases affecting ambassadors, other public ministers and consuls;—to all cases of admiralty and maritime jurisdiction;—to controversies to which the United States shall be a party;—to controversies between two or more States;—*between a State and citizens of another State*;—between citizens of different States;—between citizens of the same State claiming lands under grants of different States, and between a State, or the citizens thereof, and foreign states, citizens or subjects.

In all cases affecting ambassadors, other public ministers and consuls, and those in which a State shall be party, the Supreme Court shall have original jurisdiction. In all the other cases before mentioned, the Supreme Court shall have appellate jurisdiction, both as to law and fact, with such exceptions, and under such regulations, as the Congress shall make.

The trial of all crimes, except in cases of impeachment, shall be by jury; and such trial shall be held in the State where said crimes shall have been committed; but when not committed within any State, the trial shall be at such place or places as the Congress may by law have directed.

Section 3   Treason against the United States shall consist only in levying war against them, or in adhering to their enemies, giving them aid and comfort. No person shall be convicted of treason unless on the testimony of two witnesses to the same overt act, or on confession in open court.

The Congress shall have power to declare the punishment of treason, but no attainder of treason shall work corruption of blood, or forfeiture except during the life of the person attainted.

Article IV

Section 1   Full faith and credit shall be given in each State to the public acts, records, and judicial proceedings of every other State. And the Congress may by general laws prescribe the manner in which such acts, records, and proceedings shall be proved, and the effect thereof.

Section 2   The citizens of each State shall be entitled to all privileges and immunities of citizens in the several States.

A person charged in any State with treason, felony, or other crime, who shall flee from justice, and be found in another State, shall on demand of the executive authority of the State from which he fled, be delivered up, to be removed to the State having jurisdiction of the crime.

No person held to service or labor in one State, under the laws thereof, escaping into another, shall, in consequence of any law or regulation therein, be discharged from such service or labor, but shall be delivered up on claim of the party to whom such service or labor may be due.

Section 3   New States may be admitted by the Congress into this Union; but no new State shall be formed or erected within the jurisdiction of any other

State; nor any State be formed by the junction of two or more States, or parts of States, without the consent of the legislatures of the States concerned as well as of the Congress.

The Congress shall have power to dispose of and make all needful rules and regulations respecting the territory or other property belonging to the United States; and nothing in this Constitution shall be so constructed as to prejudice any claims of the United States, or of any particular State.

Section 4   The United States shall guarantee to every State in this Union a republican form of government, and shall protect each of them against invasion; and on application of the legislature, or of the executive (when the legislature cannot be convened), against domestic violence.

Article V

The Congress, whenever two-thirds of both houses shall deem it necessary, shall propose amendments to this Constitution, or, on the application of the legislatures of two-thirds of the several States, shall call a convention for proposing amendments, which, in either case, shall be valid to all intents and purposes, as part of this Constitution, when ratified by the legislatures of three-fourths of the several States, or by conventions in three-fourths thereof, as the one or the other mode of ratification may be proposed by the Congress; provided *that no amendments which may be made prior to the year one thousand eight hundred and eight shall in any manner affect the first and fourth clauses in the ninth section of the first article;* and that no State, without its consent, shall be deprived of its equal suffrage in the Senate.

Article VI

All debts contracted and engagements entered into, before the adoption of this Constitution, shall be as valid against the United States under this Constitution, as under the Confederation.

This Constitution, and the laws of the United States which shall be made in pursuance thereof; and all treaties made, or which shall be made, under the authority of the United States, shall be the supreme law of the land; and the judges in every State shall be bound thereby, anything in the Constitution or laws of any State to the contrary notwithstanding.

The Senators and Representatives before mentioned, and the members of the several State legislatures, and all executive and judicial officers, both of the United States and of the several States, shall be bound by oath or affirmation to support this Constitution, but no religious test shall ever be required as a qualification to any office or public trust under the United States.

Article VII

The ratification of the conventions of nine States shall be sufficient for the establishment of this Constitution between the States so ratifying the same.

Done in Convention by the unanimous consent of the States present, the seventeenth day of September in the year of our Lord one thousand seven hundred and eighty-seven and of the Independence of the United States of America the twelfth. In witness whereof we have hereunto subscribed our names.

GEORGE WASHINGTON
and thirty-seven others

Amendment I

Congress shall make no law respecting an establishment of religion, or prohibiting the free exercise thereof; or abridging the freedom of speech, or of the press; or the right of the people peaceably to assemble, and to petition the government for a redress of grievances.

Amendment II

A well-regulated militia being necessary to the security of a free State, the right of the people to keep and bear arms shall not be infringed.

Amendment III

No soldier shall, in time of peace, be quartered in any house without the consent of the owner, nor in time of war, but in a manner to be prescribed by law.

The first ten Amendments (the Bill of Rights) were adopted in 1791.

Amendment IV

The right of the people to be secure in their persons, houses, papers, and effects, against unreasonable searches and seizures, shall not be violated, and no warrants shall issue but upon probable cause, supported by oath or affirmation, and particularly describing the place to be searched, and the persons or things to be seized.

Amendment V

No person shall be held to answer for a capital, or otherwise infamous crime, unless on a presentment or indictment of a grand jury, except in cases arising in the land or naval forces, or in the militia, when in actual service in time of war or public danger; nor shall any person be subject for the same offense to be twice put in jeopardy of life or limb; nor shall be compelled in any criminal case to be a witness against himself, nor be deprived of life, liberty, or property, without due process of law; nor shall private property be taken for public use without just compensation.

Amendment VI

In all criminal prosecutions, the accused shall enjoy the right to a speedy and public trial, by an impartial jury of the State and district wherein the crime shall have been committed, which district shall have been previously ascertained by law, and to be informed of the nature and cause of the accusation; to be confronted with the witnesses against him; to have compulsory process for obtaining witnesses in his favor, and to have the assistance of counsel for his defense.

Amendment VII

In suits at common law, where the value in controversy shall exceed twenty dollars, the right of trial by jury shall be preserved, and no fact tried by a jury shall be otherwise reexamined in any court of the United States, than according to the rules of the common law.

Amendment VIII

Excessive bail shall not be required, nor excessive fines imposed, nor cruel and unusual punishments inflicted.

Amendment IX

The enumeration in the Constitution, of certain rights, shall not be construed to deny or disparage others retained by the people.

Amendment X

The powers not delegated to the United States by the Constitution, nor prohibited by it to the States, are reserved to the States respectively, or to the people.

Amendment XI [Adopted 1798]

The judicial power of the United States shall not be construed to extend to any suit in law or equity, commenced or prosecuted against one of the United States by citizens of another State, or by citizens or subjects of any foreign state.

Amendment XII [Adopted 1804]

The electors shall meet in their respective States, and vote by ballot for President and Vice-President, one of whom, at least, shall not be an inhabitant of the same State with themselves; they shall name in their ballots the person voted for as President, and in distinct ballots the person voted for as Vice-President, and they shall make distinct lists of all persons voted for as President, and of all persons voted for as Vice-President, and of the number of votes for each, which lists they shall sign and certify, and transmit sealed to the seat of government of the United States, directed to the President of the Senate;—the President of the Senate shall, in the presence of the Senate and House of Representatives, open all the certificates and the votes shall then be counted;—the person having the greatest number of votes for President shall be the President, if such number be a majority of the whole number of electors appointed; and if no person have such majority, then from the persons having the highest numbers not exceeding three on the list of those voted for as President, the House of Representatives shall choose immediately, by ballot, the President. But in choosing the President, the votes shall be taken by States, the representation from each State having one vote; a quorum for this purpose shall consist of a member or members from two-thirds of the States, and a majority of all the States shall be necessary to a choice. And if the House of Representatives shall not choose a President whenever the right of choice shall devolve upon them, before *the fourth day of March* next following, then the Vice-President shall act as President, as in the case of the death or other constitutional disability of the President.

The person having the greatest number of votes as Vice-President shall be the Vice-President, if such number be a majority of the whole number of electors appointed; and if no person have a majority, then from the two highest numbers on the list the Senate shall choose the Vice-President; a quorum for the purpose shall consist of two-thirds of the whole number of Senators, and a majority of the whole number shall be necessary to a choice. But no person constitutionally ineligible to the office of President shall be eligible to that of Vice-President of the United States.

Amendment XIII [Adopted 1865]

Section 1   Neither slavery nor involuntary servitude, except as a punishment for crime whereof the party shall have been duly convicted, shall exist within the United States, or any place subject to their jurisdiction.

Section 2   Congress shall have power to enforce this article by appropriate legislation.

Amendment XIV [Adopted 1868]

Section 1   All persons born or naturalized in the United States, and subject to the jurisdiction thereof, are citizens of the United States and of the State wherein they reside. No State shall make or enforce any law which shall abridge the privileges or immunities of citizens of the United States; nor shall any State deprive any person of life, liberty, or property, without due process of law; nor deny to any person within its jurisdiction the equal protection of the laws.

Section 2   Representatives shall be apportioned among the several States according to their respective numbers, counting the whole number of persons in each State, excluding Indians not taxed. But when the right to vote at any election for the choice of Electors for President and Vice-President of the United States, Representatives in Congress, the executive and judicial officers of a State, or the members of the legislature thereof, is denied to any of the male inhabitants of such State, being twenty-one years of age and citizens of the United States, or in any way abridged, except for participation in rebellion, or other crime, the basis of representation therein shall be reduced in the proportion which the number of such male citizens shall bear to the whole number of male citizens twenty-one years of age in such State.

Section 3   No person shall be a Senator or Representative in Congress, or Elector of President and Vice-President, or hold any office, civil or military, under the United States, or under any State, who, having previously taken an oath, as a member of Congress, or as an officer of the United States, or as a member of any State legislature, or as an executive or judicial officer of any State, to support the Constitution of the United States, shall have engaged in insurrection or rebellion against the same, or given aid or comfort to the enemies thereof. Congress may, by a vote of two-thirds of each house, remove such disability.

Section 4   The validity of the public debt of the United States, authorized by law, including debts incurred for payment of pensions and bounties for services in suppressing insurrection or rebellion, shall not be questioned. But neither the United States nor any State shall assume or pay any debt or obligation incurred in aid of insurrection or rebellion against the United States, or any claim for the loss of emancipation of any slave; but all such debts, obligations, and claims shall be held illegal and void.

Section 5   The Congress shall have power to enforce, by appropriate legislation, the provisions of this article.

Amendment XV [Adopted 1870]

Section 1   The right of citizens of the United States to vote shall not be denied or abridged by the United States or by any State on account of race, color, or previous conditions of servitude.

Section 2 The Congress shall have power to enforce this article by appropriate legislation.

Amendment XVI [Adopted 1913]

The Congress shall have power to lay and collect taxes on incomes, from whatever source derived, without apportionment among the several States, and without regard to any census or enumeration.

Amendment XVII [Adopted 1913]

Section 1 The Senate of the United States shall be composed of two Senators from each State, elected by the people thereof, for six years; and each Senator shall have one vote. The electors in each Senate shall have the qualifications requisite for electors of the most numerous branch of the State legislatures.

Section 2 When vacancies happen in the representation of any State in the Senate, the executive authority of such State shall issue writs of election to fill such vacancies: Provided, that the Legislature of any State may empower the executive thereof to make temporary appointments until the people fill the vacancies by election as the Legislature may direct.

Section 3 This amendment shall not be so construed as to affect the election or term of any Senator chosen before it becomes valid as part of the Constitution.

Amendment XVIII [Adopted 1919; Repealed 1933]

Section 1 After one year from the ratification of this article the manufacture, sale, or transportation of intoxicating liquors within, the importation thereof into, or the exportation thereof from the United States and all territory subject to the jurisdiction thereof, for beverage purposes, is hereby prohibited.

Section 2 The Congress and the several States shall have concurrent power to enforce this article by appropriate legislation.

Section 3 This article shall be inoperative unless it shall have been ratified as an amendment to the Constitution by the legislatures of the several States, as provided by the Constitution, within seven years from the date of the submission thereof to the States by the Congress.

Amendment XIX [Adopted 1920]

Section 1 The right of citizens of the United States to vote shall not be denied or abridged by the United States or by any State on account of sex.

Section 2 The Congress shall have power to enforce this article by appropriate legislation.

Amendment XX [Adopted 1933]

Section 1 The terms of the President and Vice-President shall end at noon on the 20th day of January, and the terms of Senators and Representatives at noon on the 3d day of January, of the years in which such terms would have ended if this article had not been ratified; and the terms of their successors shall then begin.

Section 2 The Congress shall assemble at least once in every year, and such meeting shall begin at noon on the 3d day of January, unless they shall by law appoint a different day.

Section 3 If, at the time fixed for the beginning of the term of the President, the President-elect shall have died, the Vice-President-elect shall become President. If a President shall not have been chosen before the time fixed for the beginning of his term, or if the President-elect shall have failed to qualify, then the Vice-President-elect shall act as President until a President shall have qualified; and the Congress may by law provide for the case wherein neither a President-elect nor a Vice-President-elect shall have qualified, declaring who shall then act as President, or the manner in which one who is to act shall be selected, and such persons shall act accordingly until a President or Vice-President shall have qualified.

Section 4 The Congress may by law provide for the case of the death of any of the persons from whom the House of Representatives may choose a

President whenever the right of choice shall have devolved upon them, and for the case of the death of any of the persons from whom the Senate may choose a Vice-President whenever the right of choice shall have devolved upon them.

Section 5 Sections 1 and 2 shall take effect on the 15th day of October following the ratification of this article.

Section 6 This article shall be inoperative unless it shall have been ratified as an amendment to the Constitution by the Legislatures of three-fourths of the several States within seven years from the date of its submission.

Amendment XXI [Adopted 1933]

Section 1 The eighteenth article of amendment to the Constitution of the United States is hereby repealed.

Section 2 The transportation or importation into any State, Territory, or Possession of the United States for delivery or use therein of intoxicating liquors, in violation of the laws thereof, is hereby prohibited.

Section 3 This article shall be inoperative unless it shall have been ratified as an amendment to the Constitution by conventions in the several States, as provided in the Constitution, within seven years from the date of submission thereof to the States by the Congress.

Amendment XXII [Adopted 1951]

Section 1 No person shall be elected to the office of President more than twice, and no person who has held the office of President, or acted as President, for more than two years of a term to which some other person was elected President shall be elected to the office of President more than once. But this article shall not apply to any person holding the office of President when this article was proposed by the Congress, and shall not prevent any person who may be holding the office of President, or acting as President, during the term within which this article becomes operative from holding the office of President or acting as President during the remainder of such term.

Section 2 This article shall be inoperative unless it shall have been ratified as an amendment to the Constitution by the legislatures of three-fourths of the several States within seven years from the date of its submission to the States by the Congress.

Amendment XXIII [Adopted 1961]

Section 1 The District constituting the seat of Government of the United States shall appoint in such manner as the Congress may direct:

A number of electors of President and Vice-President equal to the whole number of Senators and Representatives in Congress to which the District would be entitled if it were a State, but in no event more than the least populous State; they shall be in addition to those appointed by the States, but they shall be considered for the purposes of the election of President and Vice-President, to be electors appointed by a State; and they shall meet in the District and perform such duties as provided by the twelfth article of amendment.

Section 2 The Congress shall have the power to enforce this article by appropriate legislation.

Amendment XXIV [Adopted 1964]

Section 1 The right of citizens of the United States to vote in any primary or other election for President or Vice-President, or for Senator or Representative in Congress, shall not be denied or abridged by the United States or any State by reason of failure to pay any poll tax or other tax.

Section 2 The Congress shall have the power to enforce this article by appropriate legislation.

Amendment XXV [Adopted 1967]

Section 1 In case of the removal of the President from office or of his death or resignation, the Vice President shall become President.

Section 2   Whenever there is a vacancy in the office of the Vice President, the President shall nominate a Vice President who shall take office upon confirmation by a majority vote of both Houses of Congress.

Section 3   Whenever the President transmits to the President pro tempore of the Senate and the Speaker of the House of Representatives his written declaration that he is unable to discharge the powers and duties of his office, and until he transmits to them a written declaration to the contrary, such powers and duties shall be discharged by the Vice President as Acting President.

Section 4   Whenever the Vice President and a majority of either the principal officers of the executive departments or of such other body as Congress may by law provide, transmit to the President pro tempore of the Senate and the Speaker of the House of Representatives their written declaration that the President is unable to discharge the powers and duties of his office, the Vice President shall immediately assume the powers and duties of the office as Acting President.

Thereafter, when the President transmits to the President pro tempore of the Senate and the Speaker of the House of Representatives his written declaration that no inability exists, he shall resume the powers and duties of his office unless the Vice President and a majority of either the principal officers of the executive departments or of such other body as Congress may by law provide, transmit within four days to the President pro tempore of the Senate and the Speaker of the House of Representatives their written declaration that the President is unable to discharge the powers and duties of his office. Thereupon Congress shall decide the issue, assembling within forty-eight hours for that purpose if not in session. If the Congress, within twenty-one days after receipt of the latter written declaration, or, if Congress is not in session, within twenty-one days after Congress is required to assemble, determines by two-thirds vote of both Houses that the President is unable to discharge the powers and duties of his office, the Vice President shall continue to discharge the same as Acting President; otherwise, the President shall resume the powers and duties of his office.

Amendment XXVI [Adopted 1971]

Section 1   The right of citizens of the United States, who are eighteen years of age or older, to vote shall not be denied or abridged by the United States or by any State on account of age.

Section 2   The Congress shall have power to enforce this article by appropriate legislation.

Index